THE
SONG
OF THE
AGES

PART II:
THE KISS
OF TWO SEAS

NICK PADOVANI

Contents

Foreword

When Nick Padovani told me he had written his first book on the Song of Solomon, I inwardly grimaced and thought to myself that his was quiet the ambitious project for a first time author. Drawing truths from some of the New Testament epistles is one thing. They're full of obvious application for our contemporary lives but Solomon's Song? I wondered how Nick would tease out enough to entice a reader in the 21st century to go the distance with him on that journey. Then I read the book or, I should say, then the book read me. My heart was thrilled as I identified with the young Shulammite's search for intimacy with her beloved. It's not just that I could understand her journey into union. It was *my* journey too.

With this second edition the reader will encounter the same measure of exhilaration that can only be known by those who have experienced Divine Love. This ancient poem of Solomon's Song will come alive to you as you recognize the voice and the raw beauty of your King as He gently entices your affection to greater heights than you may have known until now. The first book expressed the yearning heart of all us to know and enjoy Him. This second edition bares the Divine Lover's beauty in a way that will enthrall you.

In a way, this book is one of the best I've read that dismantles legalism in a person's life. Legalism is a system of living by which we try to make spiritual progress or gain God's blessings based on what we do. It's an obligatory life driven by rules. In *The Song of the Ages*, Nick Padovani shows the folly of that approach to life by causing the reader to see that, when we know just how much He adores us, we *want* to respond and, not only respond, but respond with passionate love and zeal. I dare you to read this book and walk away saying you aren't compelled to love and live out of the union you share with Jesus Christ.

There may be other good books that speak about the Song of Solomon but the one you hold in your hands does something that many don't do. Like other books on the subject, it will teach you, but beyond that, it will *touch* you in the deep places of your own heart. It will stir up your desire for Him and motivate you to give yourself completely over to the One who wants you more than anything else.

Settle down alone in a quiet place and read. You are about to become aware of a Love that is unlike anything that exists outside of Him. It's a transforming love that not only leaves you breathless but forever changed.

— **Dr. Steve McVey**
Founder, Grace Walk Ministries
Best-selling author of *Grace Walk, Beyond an Angry God*, and others

1

Again, from the Beginning

◆❖◆

The Song of Songs, which is Solomon's.
May he kiss me
With the kisses of his mouth!
For your love is better than wine.
Your oils have a pleasing fragrance,
Your name is like purified oil...
(1:1-3)

How beautiful is your love,
My sister, my bride!
How much better
is your love than wine,
And the fragrance of your oils
Than all kinds of spices!
(4:10)

At the crest of all that is true and good, deep in the heights of God's eternal grace, Solomon's Song has swelled and peaked, rising like a wave over the shores of our hearts. We have begun to tune our ears so as to listen more carefully to its lyrics and sounds, which carry a vast and glorious message. A message of our absolute perfection in Christ and of the ravishing effect we have upon the heart of God. In our listening, a tidal wave of the most brilliant light and the clearest of water began to tower above us. Then, in the middle of the fourth chapter of the Song, this wave of truth finally crashed, bringing with it cleansing and renewal.

Indeed, the shoreline of all humanity is reconfigured and healed through the Song of the Ages—the love Song of Christ to His redeemed creation. Crooked lines are made straight as the truth of this love is revealed.

We now stand soaked as the waves recede and the Song continues its sweet hum, only with new and fresh surfs preparing to come once again to a shore now refashioned and glistening. We are the shore and He is the sea—and in the pages ahead the distinction between the two will become less and less clear.

God continues to sing by bringing us back to the beginning. This is similar to when a music composer wants to begin a composition from its starting notes. They would simply direct the orchestra to the top of their sheet music; hence the phrase "*take it from the top*." That is essentially what is occurring here. The same notes and the same melody continue from where they began in an ebb and flow of musical grace. However, this time around, there is a slight but unmistakable variation to the music...

The Exchange of Reflection

In the beginning of the Song we met the Shulammite. She represents all of us who are on the path to encountering abundant life, freedom, and true intimacy with God. Her search began with an expression of worship and prayer where she acknowledged that the love found within God is greater than all the intoxications of this world. She then began to sing of His fragrant oils, which speak to the perfect beauty of His Spirit, radiating from Him like the rays of the sun.

"Your love is better than wine, your oils have a pleasing fragrance," she said. Now we find ourselves at a new beginning point. This time around the lyrics and tone are very similar, but it is not the words of the Shulammite being sung. Instead, it is the words of her Bridegroom King. Here we will find that He is singing her own words back to her:

8

Again, from the Beginning

How beautiful is your love, my sister, my bride! How much better is your love than wine, and the fragrance of your oils than all kinds of spices!

What a sweet exchange of words between God and the Shulammite—*God and us!* The Shulammite, we discovered, is the maturing *Bride* of Christ who is growing in a mutual exchange of worship and love. This is the inheritance that is available to all, a confident and intimate relationship with God where we see His glory and He pours that glory back upon us. This is something we came across many times in the first half of the Song. We found that worship is not a groveling and shame-based utterance to a distant deity. It is the dance of friends and lovers. Jesus's work on the cross, which is what the whole Song embodies, allows us an effortless entrance into this consummate peace and comfort before God. We can boldly and swiftly enter into the place where we declare the glories of His love. Then, with even greater boldness, we can sit back and listen as He declares wondrous things back to us. The glory of this kind of relationship is far beyond what is communicated throughout many sectors of traditional Christendom.

But there is more to be found in this new beginning of the text. Something even greater is hidden in this passage, which gives us a firm foundation to stand upon as we talk about this kind of intimacy with God. As the Song's melody continues, we find that there is a reflection happening. Not just a reflection of love, but also a reflection of identity. The intoxicating love found within God is realized in us as well. The pleasing fragrance of His Spirit exudes from us in the same way that it exudes from Him!

As Jesus mirrors the Shulammite's own words back to her, we see Him continually referring to her as His *sister and Bride*. Buried under the exchange of these poetic words between the Shulammite and the King is a warm blanket of revelation, which eternally unfolds to reveal more and more of our divine origin and likeness. As we began to discover in our previous study, each of us are His "sister" in a true and familial sense—we bear the same blood and origin as our Brother, Jesus Christ. We are also His Bride in a spiritual and intimate sense: We are equally yoked and united with Jesus. We are heirs to all that He is and all that He has.

God did not beget a foul and miserable creature called humanity. He gave birth by His own seed and what came forth was a sister and Bride for His Son. When we look into the boundless waters of the face of God, we then behold our true face. This reality is the word of Truth and the kiss of Life. It is the constant melody that bounces and crashes along every stanza and verse of the Song.

> *Every good gift and every perfect gift is from above, and comes down from the Father of lights, with whom there is no variation or shadows of turning. Of His own will He brought us forth by the **word of truth**, that we might be a kind of firstfruits of His creatures.*
> *(Jms. 1:17-18 NKJV)*

The beautiful thing is that the truth does not become truer over time.

Truth is truth is truth.

Jesus is the Word who redeems and declares the *truth* that we are His sister and Bride. Again, this is not something that becomes real. It already is. We simply learn to experience more of it and grow in our apprehension and acceptance of it. And that is, of course, the real journey being undertaken as we trek alongside the Shulammite. We are growing in the grace and knowledge of Jesus Christ, extending our roots even deeper into the revelation of our union with Him and the fullness of His redemption and love.

Again, from the Beginning

Long before our present place in the Song, the searching Shulammite was identifying herself as "dark." We wrestled through this false identity in the first chapter of Solomon's poem and then several times after (see Sgs. 1:5). At this point, however, we find that the young maiden from Shulam is starting to see and hear more clearly. Through the redeeming Song of her Beloved, she is realizing that she was created "good" and "perfect" and that she originates from the Father of lights who "brought her forth" (or *birthed*, which is the proper translation of that phrase in James 1:18). Christ has redeemed us from darkness to come boldly back into this truth of our true origin and identity.

As we begin a new study of this Song, we come full circle and find a great summary of all that has been spoken thus far. The Beloved's love is like wine and His oils are fragrant. And yet the Shulammite's own love is like wine and her oils are fragrant as well. As she sings of His love she discovers in His words that the same love and fragrance exists within her. The Shulammite is lost in the worship of His glory and is undone by His love. But somehow, someway, the Lord is undone by her beauty as well—*our beauty*, beloved reader. We ourselves have been drawn into the other-giving love, fellowship, and *identity* of the Trinity.

The idea of the Trinity is a deep bedrock to all true faith and spirituality. It shows us that within the nature and being of God there is a complete oneness and yet there is also a distinction of relationship and love. God is One and yet He is also a relational family. Therefore, as a bride enters into the full rights and identity of her husband's family, we have entered into the family of the Trinity in the same way. Everything They are and everything They enjoy is now ours. As the Trinity celebrates a reflecting likeness and beauty in one another, we can now experience that same celebration of reflection as well. The Gospel itself is the announcement of our redemption back into this circle of life where we mirror God's glory as His children. In the light of this revelation, it is no wonder that this Song outshines everything else.

The Bride has already been kissed and overwhelmed by the wonder of this Word. Now that the Song begins once more, the glory of God is reflecting upon us, glistening like fresh seawater caked over a damp shore. From here, the tide will grow again and the Song will build into a new dimension of revelation and grace. It is only just beginning, again.

When God Sings

Before we move forward and explore the next half of the Song, let's first look at another biblical text that stands as a witness to what we've been experiencing and unpacking. We have to see that this is not some overly poetic interpretation of an ancient love song penned by King Solomon in the days of his earthly romance. Rather, the Song of Songs is the capturing and unfolding of a heavenly Song that is proceeding from the mouth of God over all of us. This Song is real and its notes hang in the air like an invisible mist, felt but not always seen.

Centuries before the coming of Christ, there was a prophet by the name of Zephaniah whom God had commissioned to speak to the people of Israel. This commissioning came at a time when the people were lost in complete rebellion and idolatry, having fallen from their spiritual inheritance and from the true love and worship of God. The people had been warned an untold number of times to turn from the path of deception and darkness, but they had consistently rejected the tearful pleadings of God's prophets. This particular prophet came on the surge of their rebellion. Time had run out and the consequences of the law were reaching their boiling point.

In this context, Zephaniah would have been one of the last people you would expect to declare the mysteries of God's love and the melodic joy bursting from His heart. This was a prophet anointed to bring a message of severe judgment to the people, and his message was in fact one of the worst ever given. Nevertheless, the glorious sounds of heaven hidden within the throat of the Almighty (waiting to be sung out fully with the coming of the Messiah) still managed to make their way into the prophet's words. In the midst of a book filled with some of the sternest passages of Scripture, you will also find one of the most comforting and hope-filled words in all of the Old Testament. These comforting words give us some biblical and prophetic context to what we are experiencing as we tune in to Solomon's Song. Listen carefully to Zephaniah's prophecy as his own words build to a crescendo in the final chapter of his writings...

> *The Lord your God in your midst,*
> *The Mighty One, will save;*
> *He will rejoice over you with gladness,*
> *He will quiet you with His love,*
> *He will rejoice over you with singing.*
> *(Zeph. 3:17 NKJV)*

You might want to read that again.

On the swell of impending destruction, Zephaniah releases a roaring hope that God was still in the midst of His people. This God was coming ultimately not to destroy, but to save. However, Zephaniah does not clearly articulate this salvation (which we now know in hindsight as the work of Jesus the Messiah). Like other Old Covenant prophets, the work of Christ was buried and hidden within his words. So instead of a clear explanation of the Gospel, Zephaniah explained this coming salvation in a different way. Immediately after describing God's intention to save, the prophet declared that God would *sing* over His people. God was coming to

13

release a Song of deliverance; a Song that would outshine every other one.

There are many verses throughout the Bible that talk about the beautiful songs of both men and angels, but through Zephaniah we learn that God Himself was about to release His own melody. We need to pause and consider the weight of this statement. To many people, the idea of God singing might be likened to a wise old grandpa singing a nice tune over his family. Or perhaps an elder with a hoarse voice singing a lovely ditty over his tribe. In these scenarios, we might imagine something cute and special happening, but not exactly a great and wondrous musical experience—nothing that would sell records necessarily. Just a nice attempt by God to jump in the heavenly chorus and then sit back down again so the younger and more talented choirs of angels and saints can continue on with their great hymns. But this unveils a continually jaded and limited understanding of God.

Think about this for a moment. Who is the One who gave the angels a voice to release their heavenly songs? Who crafted the very waves of sound within our universe and built the ear as a perfect platform upon which those waves could crash? Who buried the hidden treasures of wood and string in the earth for mankind to discover and out of which to craft their musical instruments? What then led mankind in this craft, guiding their discoveries to grow and evolve to where one day drum circles, bands, and even symphonies and orchestras could come forth? Who inspired the gifts within the greatest composers, artists, musicians, and lyricists that have arisen across the continents?

Of course, this is the Creator Himself. The One who sourced all music is the same One who came to bring salvation to the earth. In so doing, He was standing up to sing His own personal Song, releasing it from the infinite and vulnerable depths of His own heart. This was no weak attempt at a corny Christian pop song. This was the Originator of all music bringing forth the greatest melody to ever be sung. There is both a haunting and majestic aura to this revelation of God Himself singing. The Maker of all sound and inspiration is now getting into position and readying His voice and instruments. All would make way for this Song to come forth. The One who gifted the earth with the tools of music, who gave humanity their voice and blessed space itself with the essence of sound, is now prophesying the release of His own composition. The journey of the Shulammite has simply been one long encounter with the great Song of Zephaniah's prophecy.

On that note, the wider context of Zephaniah's prophecy is astounding when we see how it connects to the Shulammite's story. Before he mentions God singing, the prophet declared the following:

> *The Lord has taken away your judgments,*
> *He has cast out your enemy.*
> *The King of Israel, the Lord, is in your midst;*
> *You shall see disaster no more.*
> *In that day it shall be said to Jerusalem:*
> *Do not fear; Zion, let not your hands be weak.*
> *(Zeph. 3:15-16 NKJV)*

Zephaniah has subtly revealed the Gospel within his Old Testament prophecy. The pearl of grace hidden behind the hard shell of wrath and destruction is emerging and for a slight moment the people of Judah are catching a glimpse of its beauty. At the cross of Christ, the Lord would take away all judgment. The "lions and leopards" of the law, which we looked at in our last study, would be removed. Our demonic accusers would be cast out and destroyed. Because of this, the Lord would forever be known as

Immanuel—God with us. For the prophet clearly says, "The King of Israel, the Lord, is in your midst." For this reason, we should no longer fear nor let our "hands be weak." Spiritual and emotional paralysis, which flows from fear, is no longer a threat because all doom and gloom is washed away in the coming of God's love.

But let's take an even wider look at the context of Zephaniah's prophecy. Before he speaks of this hopeful deliverance, he first uttered these words as well:

> *Sing, O daughter of Zion!*
> *Shout, O Israel!*
> *Be glad and rejoice with all your heart,*
> *O daughter of Jerusalem!*
> *(Zeph. 3:14 NKJV)*

We are called to participate with God's heavenly Song! To jump into its waters and become one with its joyous truth. This was the pull upon the Shulammite when she began to search for Eden, the place of true life and rest. As she encountered Christ's love and sang of its beauty, she was then led into a deeper understanding that He "took away our judgments." We saw this in the lyrics of the Song when the Beloved declared that the winter was over and the rain was gone (Sgs. 2:11). This corresponds to Zephaniah's word that God's people "shall see disaster no more." They are proclamations of a completely triumphant hope found in the finished work of Christ.

Zephaniah has tuned the antenna of his heart to heaven's eternal melodies and his words thus build up to their own wave of truth. His previous writings spoke of a dark night of prophetic judgment, but now the dawn breaks and the clouds part to reveal the truth of God's heart. His desire and purpose is for us to sing and rejoice! He wants us to shout for joy as we continually encounter the Gospel of peace. Zephaniah subtly articulates this Gospel when he describes an end of judgment and the defeat of our enemy. This then leads to that infamous and beautiful declaration that God would rejoice and sing over us. This progression through the words of Zephaniah is a small picture of the great Song of Songs.

And what a glorious picture it is. The image of God quieting us in His love and singing over us is a stark and vibrant depiction of His fathering heart. In truth, the Father is not standing over humanity with scowling wrath. Instead, He stands as a loving Father who sees the infant of humanity crying in the pain of their deception and His heart's desire is to quiet their cries. As a father picks up his sick child from the crib and tenderly embraces them, God has lifted humanity from a bed of suffering in the resurrection of Christ. Through Christ, all of humanity was embraced and held with tenderness and grace. Now He sings over us in a victorious attempt to quiet our souls. All who are weary, all who are sad, heavy-laden, and sick are welcomed to nestle into His arms and be soothed by the great Song proceeding from His lips—the kiss of His Word that brings life to the soul of man.

Herein lies the priceless value of studying and meditating on the Song of Songs. This is not just a devotional study of poetry that is trying to muster up some encouragement out of the words of a lovesick Solomon. Rather, this is a peak into the great and mysterious prophecy of Zephaniah that declared the coming release of God's personal Song. A Song that would outshine the poetry and sounds of all time and all creation. As we catch the waves of this particular Song, our tears truly cease and our spiritual anxieties begin to subside. We are quieted in His love and we are naturally impelled to rejoice and sing back.

The Song of the Ages: Part II

Already a wave has crashed and as the waters of truth recede we are left to contemplate and soak in the beauty of its message. But the Song is far from over and the water is rising once again. There is much more to encounter in this journey of reflection and grace.

2

Where Eden Dwells

———— • ❖ • ————

Your lips, my bride, drip honey;
Honey and milk are under your tongue,
And the fragrance of your garments
is like the fragrance of Lebanon.
(4:11)

The Lord continues to sing from the overflow of a heart captured by the beauty of the rising church, His sister and bride. In the last part of the Song of the Ages we discussed the meaning of the word "ravished," which is how Jesus described the condition of His heart when He looked into the eyes of His beloved one. It is in this ravished condition—a state of absolute ecstasy and delight—that His words continue to extend toward us. It is hard for us to imagine God being caught up in a state of wonder and ecstasy, but with God all things are possible. God Himself has the ability to create something that could do such a thing to His own heart. And only God Himself has the ability to redeem that *something* if it gets stained and corrupted. In view of that, lets continue listening to the words of a holy and glorious King who is drunk on the beauty of His creation.

"Your lips, my bride, drip honey. Honey and milk are under your tongue," He says.

Even those who are not well versed in the Scriptures can easily interpret the meaning of these symbols. When God came to the enslaved Hebrew people in Egypt and promised them deliverance, He told them that He was going to bring them to a land "flowing with milk and honey" (Ex. 3:8). After their exodus from Egypt, the Hebrews sent twelve spies into Canaan to get a sneak peek at this land and they too used these words for their description of it (Num. 13:27). The milk and honey speak to the idea of the "Promised Land."

But here in the Song we find that this Promised Land is inside of us...

God's Inheritance

Jesus once said, "I came to seek and save that which was lost" (Lk. 19:10). Understanding why God redeemed us and what exactly He was "seeking" is immensely significant. It cannot be sidestepped. Some preachers talk about how God redeemed humanity for the sake of His own glory. This is a paramount truth, but it gets easily corrupted and influenced by hidden Greek mindsets that think in terms of a Zeus-like god who is incredibly egocentric (and this of course goes way further back than the mythologies of Greece).

It is actually very dangerous when some of these preachers begin to emphasize how little His saving initiative had to do with us. One of the ideas that they convey is that if God let us all fall into complete darkness it would stain His reputation. It would lead to the accusation that He was unable to redeem His people, and quotes from Old Testament passages written to the rebellious nation of Israel will often accompany these kinds of messages (see Deut. 9:25-29 & Ez. 36:22). In this point of view, it is all about

His own reputation. God worked out salvation to keep His Name untarnished as the One who created mankind in the first place.

Another major point that some will assert is that His act of salvation (and thus the coming of the Good Shepherd Jesus) was just to showcase His own goodness and mercy. In this case, He saved us to reveal His own saving glory with little connection to who we are, in and of ourselves, as His children. We would be the means to an end. The end was all about His reputation and we were the pawns that could be used toward this goal of magnifying that reputation. But all of this is sadly a poor and watered-down version of the Gospel.

Every false song carries at least a few notes from the Great One. In other words, every weakened Gospel message will often carry a measure of truth within it. There is a lot of "juice" in these messages, but a whole lot of religious and mythological water as well. God's work of redemption does indeed reveal His own glory and it magnifies His reputation. But the motivation behind this redemption needs to be clarified otherwise we can end up with an impersonal and egocentric God. (Of course, in arguing against this egocentric god some preachers will defend the idea by saying that he is holy and perfect and so you must accept everything he does as perfect. But this is often just a pat answer to the genuine seeker or a trump card that theologians throw out to defend their religious positions of a Zeus-like Jehovah.)

There is something much bigger going on in the creation and redemption of humanity. Theological assumptions that focus on certain portions of Scripture written to the nation of Israel cannot give us the full light we need to understand the motives and intentions of God. We have to take the full counsel of the Word, which culminates with the coming of Love Himself, Jesus Christ. We have to remember that God's pursuit of redemption

21

originated in Love—a Love that was entirely focused on something outside of itself. God Himself was in search of a Promised Land. We, His children, *are that glorious Promise!* We are the ones in whom *milk and honey* flows. In the pursuit of this Promised Land, God has also revealed His own glory. His glory and His children go hand in hand.

Like the clockwork of a galaxy, everything works together beautifully in this story of creation and redemption. Some people may choose to focus on certain elements of the story but then miss out on other parts of it. If someone chooses to focus on God bringing about salvation for His own glory, but then miss the other-centric wonder of that glory, they could be in danger of watering down the Gospel's message. They would be stripping the Gospel of its truly good news and leaving us with a selfish mythological god instead of the crucified and risen Christ. There is far more in the star systems of God's Word that we need to see, all of it being held together by the unseen forces of Love. The Gospel is far more beautiful and good than anything we have ever imagined.

Christ came as the Good Shepherd to seek and save that which was lost. We are the ends and not the means of redemption—alongside and in conjunction with God's glory. We were the joy set before Jesus and the inheritance due to Him.

Fixing our eyes on Jesus, the author and perfecter of faith,
*who **for the joy set before Him** endured the cross,*
despising the shame, and has sat down at the right hand of
the throne of God.
(Heb. 12:2)

I pray that the light of God will brighten the eyes of
your innermost being, flooding you with light, until you
experience the full revelation of our great hope of glory...

Where Eden Dwells

And I pray that you explore and experience for yourselves
all the riches of this wealth that has been freely given to all
*His holy ones, **for you are His true inheritance!***
(Eph. 1:18 TPT)

The watering down of the value of humanity is an affront to the Gospel. It denies the value within us, a value that was proven once and for all by the blood of Jesus, which was our ransom price.

Think about that.

The price attached to our ransom was the very blood of God's Son. What does that say about the blood flowing in our own veins? Perhaps we truly are Christ's *sister and Bride?* Perhaps we do originate with glory and the main purpose of redemption was to rescue and recover this valuable pearl? Maybe the man who sold everything to purchase the pearl was *Jesus* (Matt. 13:44-45)? After all, He did sell everything—He gave His entire life away in order to redeem the pearl of His lost sisters and brothers.

Though the research goes beyond the scope of this book, history does show us that Christians with a more egocentric view of God have been very susceptible to selfishness, bigotry, and violence (since we reflect the god we worship). But when we understand mankind's redemption price changes the way we treat and look at others, whether black or white, native or foreigner, believer or unbeliever. Perhaps if God redeemed us with a pile of rocks or an actual sacrificial goat we could turn down the significance of our value by a few cosmic notches. Then maybe we could treat one another like goats and rocks. But our redemption price was the very blood of heaven's pride and joy, Jesus Christ.

Some may legitimately worry that this kind of teaching could de-emphasize the depravity of sin and mankind's ugly and valueless participation with it. However, the blood of Jesus protects us from this other extreme as well. The shedding of Christ's blood shows the weightiness of this issue and the immense perversion of sin. This is not something we are minimizing or avoiding. Sin is insidiously dark and deserves all of the wrath that could be poured out upon it. But this is because it corrupts the original glory of Christ's brethren. The true revelation of our value will only propel us away from sin. When a person finally realizes their eternal worth it awakens a fire within them to walk away from even the slightest corruption of their identity before God. It also propels them to love others in a new and sacred way.

God's Trek Through the Wilderness

It is breathtaking, freeing, and infinitely inspiring when you realize that redemption came about because God was in search of a land flowing with milk and honey—and that this land, the glorious "ends" of redemption, lies within us!

There was a deep desire in the Creator's heart, as deep as the core of our galaxy and infinitely hotter; a desire for children and ultimately for a partner with whom He could share His Kingdom and glory. God Himself had an inheritance and a "portion" that was justly due to Him (see Deut. 32:9). This inheritance was something He loved passionately and longed to rescue. He did not just take pity on us like some giant man standing over a bug trapped in a plastic wrapper, who bends low to fix its humiliating state simply because he's a "good" man who takes pity on ants. (Then all the "ants" honor the giant and bow low before him because of how nice he is.) No. This was a God staring at the glory of His promised inheritance and burning in love for its liberation with an intense wrath toward anything trying to rob or destroy it.

Again, it is in the shedding of Christ's blood that we begin to understand the depths of this love and this God-sized desire for the Promised Land of humanity. So let's really take in this thought in as we meditate on this one particular verse in the Song:

Before the creation of time, God Himself longed for a land flowing with milk and honey...

To put it another way, God's heart was set on a bountiful place of abundant love and multiplication. A place where all the riches of His own glory would be multiplied like fruit on a tree, or like the giant grapes of Canaan (Num. 13:23). This is the true meaning of the Promised Land—a place of bourgeoning love and relationship, which God Himself planted. The yearning for Eden began in Him long before it began in us. And so even though He knows the end from the beginning, the eternal Creator would set out on a trek through the wilderness of time in seeing His beloved Promise manifest.

It is in this trek that God Himself would also go through untold pain within His heart. This is something we don't always appreciate or understand in our knowledge of God. We have no idea about the pain that Christ has endured in the pursuit of His sister and Bride. There is surely an empathy and a recognition within God toward the deepest sorrows of humanity, which He Himself has personally faced. Immanuel, God with us, has endured much in His pursuit of the Promise.

This may be hard to reconcile for people who know of God's perfection and His knowledge of the end from the beginning. How could God feel pain when He knows the triumphant end to all things? Perhaps an analogy might help with this.

Think of a person who has incredibly strong faith, who believes in the finished work of the cross, the resurrection of the dead, and our definite future hope. Yet imagine that they have a child who is violently martyred because of the family's faith. Even in the most perfect trust there is still untold pain in that type of loss. If another person were to counsel that parent and tell them just be happy and have faith, it would rightfully be taken as shallow, religious, and completely insensitive advice.

This analogy can extend to God and His relationship with humanity. God knows the end from the beginning and saw the completed work of His Son even before the universe began. But in the perfect faith of God, there is still pain that comes from seeing His children's pain. In light of this, the person who has actually lost a child has perhaps one of the closest understandings of the suffering of the Trinity throughout this past age. God is not distant or aloof from these feelings. He "mourns with those who mourn" (Rom. 12:15).

There is a day coming when every single person will look into the eyes of Jesus and even the most jaded human being, bitter toward God because of the pain they've endured, will be overcome by what they see in His eyes. There will be a revelation of how much pain God endured with them on their own journey. To the degree of ecstatic love God has felt for His creation—a joyful love that we are encountering in this Song—God has also felt deep degrees of sorrow and suffering. In this light, the cross can also be seen as a monumental moment of exposing the suffering of God with humanity. A full identification with our pain that was already true, but God was now making it public in time and space. God longed for a Promised Land and endured the pain of not having it.

The Glorification of Glory

In discussing these deep yearnings in the heart of God, it is important to note that we are not saying that God was incomplete before mankind came about. In the complete fullness of God's joy and life there was an intense desire for multiplication: *children*—a sister and Bride for the eternal Son of God. The coming of this

Bride would not fill an empty place in God, but rather it would meld into the fullness within Him and further glorify it. This would simply reveal and beautify the depths of perfection already resident within Him. This was a significant part of the "Promised Land" that He was seeking.

To better understand this, think of the color spectrum of light. We know that when sunlight shines through a prism it gets refracted out into a rainbow of color. The prism does not magically create these colors as though light transforms within it and becomes something new. The glass in the prism is only slowing down and separating all the different forms of energy that are already within the light. It is these different forms of energy, or wavelengths, that produce the different colors that come out of the prism. All of the colors are already hidden within the sunlight, but we are not able to see them until they are separated out in unique rays blasting through the glass at different speeds.

This is part of what God had in mind with our creation. Sunlight itself is perfectly complete, illuminating and powerful, but its beauty becomes enhanced and diversified as it goes through a prism. God is perfect light and within Him exist a wide array of beautiful "colors." These colors are the fruits of His Spirit—joy, goodness, peace, beauty, strength, and an infinite array of other elements. All of it is wrapped up in one sunbeam of Love. Like the work of a prism, God has brought forth creation to slow down the different elements of His love as it pours out through each one of us. Our lives are meant to demonstrate the refracting light of God's glory on the earth. We are supposed to manifest His attributes and showcase the depths of His being in a multitude of ways. Creation is a prism and we are the rainbow of God's light!

So we go back to those egocentric perceptions of the Gospel and find a purified version of it here. Yes, God wanted to showcase

His glory through us. But this showcasing was fully connected to an other-giving love. Our refraction of God's light only enhances and magnifies the perfection within Him. We "glorify" His very glory and this all happens in the context of love and relationship. He does not love humanity like an inanimate trophy sitting on a cosmic shelf that makes Him feel better about Himself. Rather, He loves us with the deep and intimate connection that you might compare to the relationship between a mother and her child. That child is a trophy of joy for which she would give her life. But in her other-giving love for the child, her own beauty and identity is more fully revealed as well.

How might a perfect God enhance the infinite perfection within Him? Perhaps even the best scientific or spiritual analogies fall short of giving an answer to this. Some questions will just have to be settled when we finally do look into those holy eyes, when we behold not only the pain Jesus has endured, but the fullness of His joy that came about in our redemption.

The Glory After the Storm

With this in mind, there is one more incredible truth hidden within the reality of sunlight, which also ties in with the text. Obviously, nature does not use manmade prisms to refract the sun's rays. Instead, it reveals a color spectrum in the sky when sunlight goes through raindrops, which act like thousands of little natural prisms hanging in the air. The beauty of this is seen when a colorful rainbow of light appears after a storm has passed and slight drops of rain still hang in the air.

The Gospel is being declared through this element of creation. For even after the storm of sin, rebellion and judgment, God's glory would still come forth—even more majestic and diverse than before. The passion in God for His glory to shine through

His children would win out over the storm. And so in the days of Noah, God set His "bow" in the sky to declare this hope to humanity who would still go through much pain in our deception and darkness. The rainbow declared that one day both we and Him would taste the Promised Land together—in each other.

It is here in the hidden wonders of the Song of Solomon that we can see clearly and explicitly that *we* are the Lord's prized inheritance. We are the ones He pursued through fire and water, through the shedding of blood and tears (Heb. 5:7). We are the ones He longed for and the ones who would magnify His own glory like raindrops after a storm. Within us, and all throughout the world, is a land flowing with milk and honey. In the coming of Christ and our union with Him at the cross, this desire has been fulfilled. From heaven's perspective, this joy is already complete. Jesus has purchased us and is *now* enjoying His Bride as she awakens to the kiss of His light and love. He now calls each of us into this same joy, inviting us to drink of this finished work of redemption.

We are His inheritance and He is ours. *I am My Beloved's and He is mine.* Such is the meaning of this whole Song…and the whole Gospel…and the whole of creation…and redemption. Such is the continual melody rising from the tides of God's love, continuing to build and rise once more.

Tying it Together

Remember that in this portion of the Song the Lord is continuing to *take it from the top*, bringing both the Shulammite and us back to where this whole thing got started. Like the Israelites' trek toward Canaan, the Shulammite began with a journey toward abundance, love and freedom. We found that this journey points to all of us who are searching for Eden, the land of promise that metaphorically flows with milk and honey. For the Shulammite, this search began with a longing for the kiss of God's Spirit and Word. This is where she knew the desired promise of freedom and abundance could be found, just like Adam found it when his created body was touched by the kiss of God's Spirit.

At this point in the Song, we can assume that the literal "kiss" between the maiden and the king has finally come. It does not explicitly say it, but it can be inferred fairly easily. This Song is like the script of an ancient drama. When Solomon wrote the script he did not include all the stage cues and directives to be acted out (at least not in the literature that ended up canonized in the Scriptures). So we don't always know who was speaking when and what all their specific actions are supposed to be. Nonetheless, the dialogue brings out a lot of understanding as to what the "actors" are doing. When the King is overcome by the joy of finding honey and milk under the tongue of the Shulammite, it seems appropriate to say that a kiss has taken place. The Bride has received what she was looking for.

God's Word has indeed met the depths of her heart and it is reaching out to ours as well. This is the great sea of His love kissing the shores of our being. And in this melodic splash of Word and flesh, Spirit and dust, Water and sand, there is a discovery that is made. A surprise has come to the Shulammite. In her desperate search for the Promise of Eden, she learns that the very thing she was seeking, God was seeking as well! This thing for which she sought was actually inside of her. She is the Lord's Eden—His true garden!

As Jesus enjoys the reward of His sacrifice, the promised joy set before Him at the cross, He then goes on to declare something else. He speaks next of the delightful fragrance of her garments, comparing their scent to Lebanon. We looked in the last part of our study at the meaning of Lebanon, particularly its mountains and how they overlooked the Promised Land. The Bride has since caught a clear view of the Promise and it has changed the very atmosphere around her. In her beholding, in her celebrating, and in her believing the realities of divine union, it has begun to change the scent of her garments. She has begun to naturally reflect His beauty and give off His own fragrance.

This is what happens when any of us begin to enjoy the realities of redemption, when we drink in and meditate on the wonders of the finished work of Christ and the eternal love of God. A new fragrance is released in our lives. It is the very scent of God being multiplied through us in a wide array of distinctive color and aroma. In the next portion the Song, the Promised Land within us will be unfolded with more beauty and clarity. We will behold more of the colors of Love that are meant to refract out of us through grace.

So like the spies of Israel who went in to get a good look at the land of milk and honey, let us also go in. Let us get a closer look at what lies within.

3

The Riddle of the Sealed Garden

A garden locked is my sister, my bride,
A rock garden locked, a spring sealed up.
(4:12)

Y ou are probably somewhat familiar with the story of the Trojan horse. It is an old tale about a Greek victory over the impenetrable city of Troy. The story goes that for ten years Greece tried to break through Troy's walls and lay siege to the city, but had failed over and over again. One day, in a stroke of creative genius, the Greeks devised a strategy involving the construction of a large wooden horse with a secret compartment to hide a contingency of soldiers. This giant horse was left on the shores outside of Troy while the Greeks pretended to turn their ships back home and leave the area. After seeing this feigned departure, the Trojans noticed the large horse sitting on the sand and decided to take it into the city as a trophy of their victorious stand against the army. Once safely inside the city, the soldiers within the horse left their hidden chamber and opened up the city gates at night. The Greeks, who had secretly repositioned themselves on the shoreline, were waiting outside and entered through the gates to sack the city. Because of all this, a great victory was accomplished and the city of Troy fell.

The strategy utilized with the Trojan horse is very similar to the way that metaphor and parable operate. There are life-changing truths that want to penetrate our lives and conquer strongholds of deception in our hearts. The city of darkness and deception must fall. Unfortunately, great walls of resistance within our rational and "experienced" minds often block these victorious truths from entering in. Like the Greek army outside of Troy, truth can stand right outside the gates of our minds for years and years without being allowed entrance. Therefore, in order for it to penetrate, the truth sometimes needs to be carried in secretly. Spiritual metaphors, especially the kind that we are reading about in the Song of Songs, carry these truths in a way that bypasses the initial resistance from the mind.

Many times the clear articulation of truth is not enough to reach someone's heart. People grow so hardwired with doubtful arguments in their minds that a plain statement of spiritual reality does not suffice. Over time, walls have been built up in a person's thought processes. They are often created with the heavy bricks of religious baggage and false teaching. Sometimes these bricks are also formed by contradictory life experiences that cast negative judgments against any hopeful truth trying to make its way into us. Beyond this, there are also guards at the gates of our minds—voices from the past or from the enemy of our souls—and they shoot out words like arrows against the reality that is trying to enter in.

Metaphor and parable come like a strange wooden horse to bring the truth through a backdoor in our minds. As it arrives on the shores of our own heart, the truth is hidden deep within it.

The Riddle of the Sealed Garden

The horse may seem completely disconnected from the army of light waiting to conquer our hearts, but that is precisely why it will be allowed entrance. The light is shrouded in the darkness of a riddle. This is why Jesus often spoke in parables to a people who did not have the mental grid to receive the clear explanation of His Kingdom (because of how different it was from the kingdom they were expecting). This is also part of the reason that God loves to speak to us in dreams. Many of our dreams are simply night parables that bypass our waking minds with strange symbols carrying life-changing messages. By night, the soldiers of truth are released even if we consciously resist them during the day.

As we move forward we will start to see more of the bricks that have formed a wall of resistance in the mind of the Shulammite. The kiss of His Word has certainly washed over her, but we will find that its glorious crash has not fully penetrated the city of her being. So do not feel bad if it still seems as though the beauty of these truths have not pierced you in a transformative way either. Jesus is committed to seeing us walk in the light—not just knowing about the light in a factual way, but actually stepping into it and experiencing it.

In this next part of the Song, the Lord is going to release a Trojan horse filled with victorious revelation. He is going to slip a metaphor into this part of the book that will hopefully settle quietly into your mind. As you see this metaphor and unpack the riddle of its meaning, the truth will start to slip out. This truth is something we already covered in our last study of the Song, but now it will come to us in a fresh way. Outward transformation may not seem instantaneous, but a time bomb will be planted in the night, waiting to explode within our city walls. This explosion will effortlessly break down those walls of resistance, showing us that the truth has enough power of its own to bring them down. We need not take on the burden of tearing down the wall by ourselves.

We do not need to analyze and fight off every heavy brick around our heart. Simply drinking in the truth will carry enough power of its own as it brings forth victory from the inside out.

So let's look at this next metaphor. And as we do, let's also remember something very basic about this overall Song... We are reading the Holy Scriptures—writings inspired by the Holy Spirit of God. He has kindled this entire story of the Shulammite and the King. In its spiritual inspiration, the King in the story represents God and the Shulammite represents us.

So this is God Himself talking to *you*. The Shulammite is you.

Take that heart once again as you read the following.

The Sealed Garden

As He enjoys the promise of His Bride, Jesus says that she is a "rock garden locked, a spring sealed up." This is a riddle that can be deciphered and understood by looking at the historical context of the Song.

In ancient times, kings prided themselves in having private gardens that were sealed up and protected, made only for them to enjoy. King Solomon himself had such gardens, which he writes about in one of his other books: "I made gardens and parks for myself and I planted in them all kinds of fruit trees" (Ecc. 2:5). The king had a special garden, which was sealed by his own signet ring, allowing no one entrance but himself. Within this garden was a spring, or fountain, that no outside entity could drink from. It was a gated garden that was shielded from outside influences and impurities.

As Solomon is writing this Song and thinking of poetic ways to describe the Shulammite, the Holy Spirit takes hold of his pen and brings forth a burst of holy inspiration. His mind is drawn to a visual of his own private garden, which has been untouched by the outside world. He then thinks of the centerpiece of this garden: a beautiful flowing fountain that is completely untainted. The Holy Spirit is whispering to us through this ancient writing, communicating deep truth and continuing to slip certain metaphors into our hearts that are packed with explosive power.

Through the Spirit, Christ is using this simple analogy of a sealed garden and fountain to speak more about our identity. This declares an absolute untouched purity that is within us. At the core of who we are lies innocence—an innocence that resembles a fountain protected and flawless. A fountain which no dirtied hands or thieving trespassers would ever have access. This is not just about the general beauty of the garden, but about the absolute cleanliness and purity of it.

Let that imagery of a private spring enter into your heart. Let it bypass the resistance of anything that says otherwise about who you truly are.

Your Soul is Pure

And it must surely bypass a great deal of resistance in our minds, which are often filled with brick after brick of opposing arguments and questions that speak against this truth. Indeed, the church throughout history has strayed very far from the message of this metaphor. Believers all over the world feel that within the depths of their being lies at least *some* defilement or wickedness. We may acknowledge that the Holy Spirit is within us and we may even carry the vague idea of having a pure spirit of our own. However, we then go on to feel that the majority of our inner waters, springs, and gardens have surely been touched, tainted, and defiled.

Stop for a moment and take something into consideration. The image and concept of the "garden" in the Song of Songs represents the entire being of the Shulammite—not just some elusive inner spirit that is separate from her soul. This is something countless commentators and translators agree with. The garden represents all the dynamics of her soul (or her heart, or mind, or whatever other term you want to use, since the Scriptures are very loose and interchangeable with these concepts). It is simply referring to *her*. The different fruits and spices in this garden speak to her emotional life as well as elements of her physical will, desires, and intellect.

This might be a revolutionary concept to some, but the Song is declaring that our entire garden—both our spirit and soul—is completely sanctified. We are pure through and through.

Now if you disagree with this, I'd encourage you to look at the epistle of Peter and take up your argument with him:

> *Since you have (past tense) in obedience to the truth*
> ***purified your souls*** *for a sincere love of the brethren,*
> *fervently love one another from the heart.*
> *1 Pet. 1:22 (parenthesis mine)*

Here is one more Scripture to emphasize the purity of the soul…

> *And the very God of peace sanctify you wholly; and (I*
> *pray God) your whole spirit and soul and body be preserved*
> *blameless unto the coming of our Lord Jesus Christ.*
> *(1 Thes. 5:23 KJV)*

There is a parenthesis around the words "I pray God" because they were added in by the English translators. If you read the Greek, the words are not there. So Paul isn't making a request here. He's actually proclaiming something. The whole verse is an apostolic proclamation. And what exactly is he proclaiming?

That God will "preserve" our spirit, soul, and body as blameless.

To preserve something means to keep it the way it is. So think about that. Paul is talking about God preserving us as blameless *until* the coming of the Lord. In other words, we are already blameless by the work of Jesus. God is simply going to *preserve* us in our current blameless state until the coming of Christ.

Most people will agree that we are blameless in Christ (because they cannot deny other Scriptures that say it), but they have a hard time believing their entire being is "without fault," which is the meaning of the word *blameless*. It's easier to say that their inner spirit is blameless, but that they have a dirty soul that needs to be cleaned up—which will usually take their whole life to do. However, this idea is quite silly when thought through a little bit. What if a Christian dies one year after they find the Lord? Does she enter heaven with a less sanctified soul than someone who had a fifty year go at it? Obviously, this is ridiculous. And its silliness is further exposed by the fact that the New Testament already declares us blameless and complete (see Col. 1:22).

What About My Sin?

So at this point I know the bricks in the Trojan wall are beginning to rumble and the guards at the gate are making a commotion. They are resisting the preceding words by asking about the emotional, spiritual, and physical struggles people face. How does our everyday experience *fit in* with the fact that our entire being is perfect and blameless?

First of all, we've already covered the fact that the realities of faith need to trump our earthly experiences. God's Word needs to hold more precedence than our temporal struggles. This is why outward sanctification comes by faith. In other words, by trusting that we're already sanctified, we will live and act sanctified!

But none of this is meant to dismiss the fact that our souls can get beaten up and thrown down in this world. Things can affect our minds and lead us into negative directions, which may need the counsel and prayer of others. But we can never forget that our soul—our unique personal make-up—is actually pure in its essence. The soul *has been* purified. Our true self is totally clean. Just because a person falls in the mud, it does not make them a mud-human. They are completely human, even if a little mud gets on them. Even if *a lot* of mud gets on them.

The soul can certainly get affected by outside influences and genetic deficiencies from our bloodline, but those things do not redefine the soul's true nature of holiness and purity. When someone awakens to the salvation of Christ, there is a redefining of the self that occurs. This redefining is not just a theological fact but a sure and solid reality empowered by the Spirit of God. And the truth that the Spirit brings has the power to break off any outside influences that are affecting our everyday lives. The revelation of our innocence can truly overcome anything that says otherwise, whether it's a negative family trait in your life or an oppressing voice of demonic condemnation.

There is a place to deal with some outside influences that have impacted our purified soul over the years. But we must be careful here, because many who pursue the "healing" of their souls are operating from a lie that says that impurity is still resident within. This may seem like an issue of semantics, but it is far more than that. This is a foundational issue of identity, which defines how we deal with the darkness around us.

The Lie of Inner Darkness

Believing in some dark "flesh-nature" leads people on a never-ending witch-hunt to remove poisons and impurities from their well. In this case, the pursuit of holiness becomes something that is outside of them. Something they must attain, which for many people involves years and years of inner healing, counseling, and suffering in order to "clean out the well." But all of this reveals a self-perception as follows:

> *I am not a rock garden sealed. I am garden defiled and ransacked. My well is filled with vile creatures and ugly motives. There are curses in the water and demons under the rocks.*

But all of that is a lie from the pit of hell.

There's lots of terminology that gets thrown around in the church that highlights the apparent inner darkness of our being. People will talk about demonic strongholds, generational curses, emotional scars, and all other kinds of poisonous infections and intrusions in the garden of our being. But, surprisingly, this is not how the Lord addresses His Bride. He sings over her and His Song has little to do (in fact, nothing to do) with poisons and problems and curses and cobwebs. He does not sing over His bride about how she is beautiful and perfect, and then proceed to belt out a few notes about the many problems that need cleansing and purification. Unlike many preachers, there is no double-mindedness with the Lord. He sees the full truth of incorruptibility at our core. All the elements of darkness have been thoroughly washed in His blood. And, as we've seen, His blood is the focal point of the entire Song.

Many Christians treat the blood of Jesus like some special cleaning agent that can be used while *we* do the majority of the scrubbing and washing. But this is not the truth. The blood of Jesus is not a little tool we wield in the left hand to find healing, while with the right we muster up all sorts of spells and prayers and actions and sacrifices to clean ourselves up. In that case, the

41

blood of Christ does not ultimately do the work—it only helps. We are then left with the task to wash our own clothes as well as that of others. But this kind of thinking, even if it is subtle and unconscious, carries the ever-appealing residue of self-righteousness.

The reality that we have died with Christ speaks to a once-and-for-all bath where we were washed through and through. He did the scrubbing, the cleaning, *and* the drying off. In other words, there is no "work" involved in becoming righteous (which is what the metaphor of a pure inner garden is all about). We are sparkling clean and untouched right here and right now. This part of the Song reveals that if you really want to get introspective and search far and wide through the deepest core of who you are (the wounds of the past, the effects of a sin-cursed world, or a sin-cursed bloodline)—if you really want to throw a hook into the ponds of your soul and fish out the darkness of impure motives and inner greed as well as the roots of selfishness and dishonesty, well then, you will be sorely disappointed. For the words of Jesus declare something entirely different about who you really are. And His words do not lie, nor do they shift and turn like a shadow.

How a Blameless Soul Sins

Another question that comes up with this teaching is "how can a pure and blameless soul sin?" Our last study in the Song already addressed this by talking about how Adam and Eve were blameless in the Garden and *without* sin and yet they still committed a sinful act. This time around we'll approach this question from a different vantage point, using lust as a specific example.

As the waters of our innermost being mingle with the world they can become misguided, and that is when sin manifests in the life of a pure and holy believer. Lust is only a misdirection of a pure and holy desire at the core of who we are. A desire that is actually good and holy. There is an intense desire placed in us that mirrors the passionate desires of God, which includes the yearning for a Bride and the pursuit of absolute beauty and union. We were also made for pleasure, which is the very meaning of the Hebrew word "Eden". Lust comes from this pure desire, but it is the result of that desire going in a wrong direction as it reaches out and interacts with the world around us.

So imagine a river of pure water constantly flowing in a good and godly direction. The water itself is clean and holy and good. Such are the waters of life within you and the very essence of who you are. This is how God always sees you. The water of your being is ever-flowing in the direction of godly desire and passion. Yet as it flows through this world it may come across little tributaries on the sides of its riverbanks that go into dirty and fruitless side paths.

Lust happens when the pure stream of our godly desires trickle down a dirty path that is seeking after intimacy and pleasure. It comes from a good place, but it was tricked to turn toward a ditch (pornography, adultery, etc.) as it looked for fulfillment. Being tricked does not change the truth of the water, it only misguides a very small portion of it. However, at any moment, a person can come to their senses and trust that the river within them is pure and that little side-stream does not define them nor does it empty the full river within them. The water within you is eternal, made in the image of an eternal God. No matter how much your waters spill into unhealthy places, it never changes the truth of the overall river.

This is so important to see in the Shulammite's journey—and remember, this is *our* journey. Jesus never acknowledges our sinful detours as an identification of who we are. In His eyes, we are completely holy and the well of our being holds complete innocence and righteousness. This is why we can approach the Father at any time without a guilty conscience, because we are truly pure in His sight. This is a *reality*, not a wishy-washy theological statement. Even the person whose inner waters have gone out into the deepest of mud is still a pure child in the sight of the Father. Their water is being emptied into a fruitless place, but the person remains God's holy child. They are simply deceived and wasting the precious waters of their life. But God looks at His child and His vision is set on the source of their waters, not the misguided directions they take.

So here's the problem. When many believers see lust in their lives, they begin to feel this deep and foreboding sense of guilt. This turns into a strong identification with that lust. In other words, something is inherently "wrong" with them. They begin to define themselves by the little side-stream instead coming back and resting in the larger, more glorious river of truth within them. Because they are focusing on the side-stream, it ends up getting magnified in their vision and they start to believe it's this giant amount of rushing water that needs to be conquered. This then makes them feel like they have this overwhelming task to clean themselves up. Many ministries are built upon this false foundation of identity. That's why this issue is bigger than words and semantics.

This approach to sin leads to failure after failure (usually depending on the level of willpower within a person). Sadly, after a good amount of failure, people finally adjust their theology to fit in with their experience. They take certain Scriptures and twist them to believe they are still dark and sinful. And then they settle for a frail hope that when they die and get to heaven they will finally be clean (or when some great end-time harvest comes, then they will be fully free. But not now. Now it's clean-up time). Sin becomes a part of who they are and something they must fight off their whole lives and get tons of healing and ministry for. And again, this is the wrong foundation for ministry and healing.

When someone gets a revelation of the finished work of Christ and beholds the utter purity within them (and even the specific purity behind their issues, such as lust), it breaks the power of that sin. They don't live with this sense of guilt and shame at how "bad" they are. Instead, they discover that they are pure and free. Then they start to realize they can naturally live this way! In the confidence of their purity they can more easily stand up against these misdirected and perverted desires that hit them. Instead of trying to clean up dirty ditches through years of self-introspection and guilty confession, they just return to the truth that they are pure and holy and deeply loved by God. This brings greater victory than all their previous efforts.

And this is true repentance, beloved one. It is agreeing with God that we are already forgiven and sanctified. Completely. You can go ahead and ask God for forgiveness about something in order to feel an inner release in your own mind, but please know that you were forgiven and restored before you even uttered the prayer. Before you even wanted to utter the prayer. If anything, that prayer was for you, not for God.

Counseling and Healing

We've already addressed this, but it bears some further thought. There are times when the ditches of misguided desire have grown deep and ingrained, and in these instances there may be a place for outside interventions and stronger accountability. But these are only temporary tools to keep people from utterly destroying their temporal lives. All the while, their inner eternal life remains intact. However, extra assistance is sometimes needed as an immature believer learns how to stand firm in their identity. True deliverance ministry is meant to counsel someone's heart back to where they were already delivered *2000 years ago*. This may involve some prayer and verbal release, but never think that the prayers and words are accomplishing something in and of themselves. The work is already accomplished. These things are only tools to help us come into a place of faith.

The fear underlying most people is the deep and dark worry that something evil or "bad" dwells within. This is the knowledge of good and evil that has corrupted man from the beginning, turning us from seeing our perfection in God to a place of self-judgment and darkened identity. True counseling, deliverance and personal ministry should always point people to the finished work of Jesus Christ, which is the Tree of Life. It is meant to support someone in their journey of discovering the truth. It is not to be the source of our salvation. Salvation has already come. We are already free. We are already new. True ministry should renew the mind and help break agreements with deception.

It is unfortunate that many ministries (some that even use the phrase "break agreements") end up focusing more on demons and inner darkness and put all the attention there. The sad fact of the matter is that this idea sells. It makes you reliant on the minister or the author or the spiritual guru to help you defeat this ugly beast. Prayerful lip service will be given to the blood of Jesus. Again, the magical "additive" of Christ will be thrown into the pot (but only after you follow their recipe for freedom—and come back when you need a new batch).

There are far too many ministries, and even worship songs and sermons that affirm a false identity of imperfection. This often comes from a genuine desire for humility and holiness, but all of it is an affront to the finished work of Christ. We've already covered this many times, but it's important to say it again. The belief that we have a sinful nature that will always be within us is the very reason that sin is so strong in the church! You become what you believe about yourself.

This is a dead horse we absolutely have to beat, so let's explain this even more...

The Boogey Monster

Boogey monsters have a way of coming to life the more we feed them with fear. Shadows in the closet grow and morph into monstrous entities the more we look upon them with dread. They especially grow if you refuse to turn on the light of truth, leaving the shadows to rise and dance at the whim of your imagination.

It is the same with our "inner demons." Some people are so introspective and focused on darkness, so worried about the depths of their impure motives and the potential monsters that might lurk there, that they empower the lie of this darkness. The light of the pure Gospel is never turned on in them—only a watered down Gospel that declares they are somewhat forgiven, but not completely sanctified. They then stay focused on shadows, which appear to take on powerful shapes when they encounter misguided desires in their lives.

You can especially see this when Christians make statements like this: "*Look at David. Even a man after God's own heart sinned. We are all susceptible to sin, because, after all, we have a sinful nature!*"

Or this: "*Look at Paul. Even he said he was the chief of sinners*" (even though Paul in 1 Timothy 1:15 was clearly talking about his life as a murderous Pharisee, not His present life in Christ).

Or they read the words of Jeremiah and affirm that "*the heart is deceitfully wicked*" and thus they cannot trust their own heart (Jer. 17:9). Within the heart lurks a monster that they must fight off their whole lives and it will only really be defeated when they die. But just imagine the day when the church gets out of the Old Covenant (the period in which Jeremiah was writing) and actually starts believing the new one; the covenant of grace that declares our hearts are totally new. The announcement that our deceitful wickedness was crucified with the Body of Christ! That will be a day of great freedom throughout the church.

Thankfully, that sound of freedom is already growing. But there is still a lot of work to be done. Too many believers are still exalting the inner demons of lust, envy, selfishness, greed, depression, and anxiety. They then trace their generational origins and give them names and write whole books about them (going into way more detail on these things than the apostles ever did). Then, the more they abide in the darkness of these false identities, the more their shadows grow and the more they seem to take shape. Before long, the lie takes hold and we begin to act in accordance with them. The boogey monster becomes "real" in our hearts and we are paralyzed by sin and fear. Like the ten spies in the Promised Land, these issues become undefeatable giants. Yet all along, God has given us full victory over the land of our hearts (see Num. 13).

Remember that we are made for reflection. We mirror what we look at. When your heart is focused on the idea of an evil entity of sin, you end up mirroring the lie and reflecting its dark glory. But when you look at Jesus and realize that you are in Him and He is in you, the lie of sin loses its luster. When you stop fearing sin and its power over you, the boogey monster suddenly loses its grip. The lights come on. What happens in that moment is that you start to *grow up*. Like a developing child, you realize that the boogey monster does not even exist!

And so it is with the maturing believer. The Christian goes from a babe to a mature man or woman when they grow up and realize that sin is dead. The old man is crucified. The boogeyman is gone. Now we are just as pure and clean as King's Solomon private garden.

> *For though by this time you ought to be teachers, you*
> *have need again for someone to teach you the elementary*
> *principles of the oracles of God, and you have come to*
> *need milk and not solid food. For everyone who partakes*
> *only of milk **is not accustomed to the word of***
> ***righteousness**, for he is an infant.*
> *(Heb. 5:12-13)*

The problem of immaturity in the letter to the Hebrews had to do with the fact that people were not accustomed to the word of their righteousness—the word that declares that they are garden sealed and locked.

So, once again, let's make this word extremely clear: You are a well of perfect purity and complete righteousness! In the deepest core of who you are lies innocence and love, and that is what God constantly sees and even feels when He looks at you and interacts with you.

And when He sings His Song of love over you, it's *all* He talks about.

Lord, Impart Revelation...

I have no doubt that as this chapter went on and a clearer articulation of the truth was given that some readers' minds put up a fight of resistance. If that's the case for you—if the joy of this revelation is not stirring up—then go back to that strange wooden horse that Jesus planted at the shore of your heart. Look more closely at the metaphor of a private garden filled with crystal-clear water. Look at that water and see the untouched wonder of Eden all around it. Ask the Lord to help you understand how that image speaks to your *entire* soul.

Allow the image to settle into your mind and trust the Holy Spirit to bring its truth into the core of your heart, shining its light on that supposed dark closet of sin in your life, over which you have spent so much time fearing and worrying. You will eventually find that there is nothing in the closet. You are God's child and you have been delivered from that thing.

Let the light reveal the truth.

The boogey monster is gone.

Amen.

4

The Wrong Prayer

———— • ❖ • ————

Your shoots are an orchard of pomegranates
With choice fruits, henna with nard plants,
Nard and saffron, calamus and cinnamon,
With all the trees of frankincense,
Myrrh and aloes, along with all the finest spices.
You are a garden spring,
A well of fresh water,
And streams flowing from Lebanon.
(4:13-15)

The King goes on. His Song builds and its melody overshadows the glory of His Bride like a massive eagle ascending over her head. This eagle's wings cast a shadow over her that is unlike any other. This shadow does not darken. Rather, it enlightens, and in its illuminating shade we behold even more of the Promise within. Here we will be reminded once more of the glory of Eden.

The Garden of our origin was described as a place of fruit-bearing trees, which were pleasing to the eye and sweet to the taste. We've discovered that, all along, Eden was only a picture of the true Promised Land to come. A land that God Himself desired and that Christ redeemed. *We are* the Promised Land. We are the ones overflowing with delicious and captivating fruit. We have become the metaphoric trees of Scripture that are planted by streams of water and bear a variety of spices and fruits (see Ps. 1). These tastes and aromas captivate the heart of God and satisfy His eternal purposes.

But what are all these metaphors really describing? What does this true Garden of Eden look like? What exactly is the "fruit" in which God so delights? If the fruit is the cream of the crop and the ultimate purpose for which something is planted (whether it's bananas or grain or spice-laden buds), then what fertile purposes are behind God's work of creation and redemption?

The Fruits of Creation

We will look at a famous passage from the epistle to the Galatians to help us better understand all of this:

> *But the fruit of the Spirit is love, joy, peace, patience,*
> *kindness, goodness, faithfulness, gentleness, self-control;*
> *against such things there is no law.*
> *(Gal. 5:22-23)*

This is the fruit that God has always longed to see fill His creation. When the seed of the universe was planted, exploding and sprouting into order and complexity, the "cream of the crop" of the cosmos was supposed to be the fruit of Galatians 5. Creation was to be a paradise not only of starlight and organic life, but one of love and faithfulness.

The heart of God had surged with a desire to see people made in His image walking love, joy and peace. God longs to see each and every one of us experiencing and manifesting these fruits. All of these qualities carry an Edenic glory as they radiate from the branches of our lives. These qualities sum up true paradise. Shared in relationship with God, they are the end purposes of creation. And they are much more than emotions, even though our emotional lives are often the stems whereby these fruits can come to the surface and blossom.

Now did you notice how many different types of "fruit" are mentioned in Galatians? In the Passion Translation of the Song of Songs, Dr. Brian Simmons highlights the amount of "fruit" that are in Solomon's account of the Bride's inner garden. The number is the same:

Your inward life is now sprouting, bringing forth fruit.
What a beautiful paradise unfolds within you. When
I'm near you, I smell aromas of the finest spice, for many
clusters of my exquisite fruit now grow within your inner
garden. Here are nine:

Pomegranates of passion, henna from heaven, spikenard
so sweet, saffron shining, fragrant calamus from the cross,
sacred cinnamon, branches of scented woods, myrrh, like
tears from a tree, and aloe as eagles ascending.
(Sgs. 4:13-14 TPT)

There are nine fruit in Galatians and nine different types of "fruit" in the Song of Songs. This is not a coincidence. All Scripture connects in a powerful way as you unpack and study it through the lens of Christ's redemption. In the Song of Songs, the King is clearly expressing His delight in the same things that Paul describes as the "fruit of the Spirit." When He speaks of things like henna and nard, He is relating their sweetness to the joy and peace that is resident within His church.

As we have already discussed, God intended for the goodness of His glory to be reflected on the earth. When we walk in patience and self-control, the smoke of God's own glory rises back to heaven like a sweet-smelling sacrifice. Our lives manifesting kindness and goodness are like the soothing smells of frankincense and cinnamon ascending from our hearts. This is why many of the Hebrew prophets declared that God never actually desired animal sacrifices. The real "sacrifices" would be the offering up of thanksgiving, mercy, and love (see Hos. 6:6). The budding and blossoming of these attributes are sweet and savory to the Lord and they are also the very things for which mankind has been searching. In all our pursuits and imaginings of paradise, it is here that we find the clearest picture of it. This is the image of true fertility and beauty in the earth.

The Wells Within

The King also mentions a "well of fresh water," which is yet another Scriptural connection between the Song and the New Testament. Hopefully by now you can see the deep associations between this poetic story and the New Testament revelations of Christ and His church. We are not talking about earthly love poems and agriculture. We are talking about the underlying reasons as to why we were created.

This Scriptural connection relates to the book of John. It is there that Jesus says a well of living water would spring up inside of us, which refers to the presence of the Holy Spirit within (see Jn. 4:14 & 7:38). In Solomon's Song, this is what the King is describing when He closes up His fruitful analogies with the declaration that the Shulammite is "a garden spring, a well of fresh water." These spices of love and peace are the results of her garden—the entirety of her life and soul—being watered by the Spirit of God within her.

The Wrong Prayer

In this portion of the Song, Solomon goes on to write that our "streams flow from Lebanon." This is a connection to the Lebanese summit of Amana, the mountain peak we looked at in our previous study which spoke of the place of absolute truth and heavenly perspective. The statement that our "streams flow from Lebanon" reveals the headwaters of the Spirit's activity in our lives. It all comes from that high place of truth where we beheld our complete union with Christ and the reality of His unfailing love for us. We are called to abide in this truth and then watch as its streams awaken and ignite all the glorious fruits and spices that are *already* within the garden of our hearts.

Having heard the Lord's declarations of these inner fruits and fountains, the Shulammite will now speak for the first time in a while. She will explode with a desperate prayer of response. This prayer will sound holy and noble at first, but we will soon find that a religious sleep is still trying to dull her mind to what Christ has been saying...

> *Wake Up, O God!*
> *Awake, O north wind,*
> *And come, wind of the south;*
> *Make my garden breathe out fragrance,*
> *Let its spices be wafted abroad.*
> *May my beloved come into his garden*
> *And eat its choice fruits!*
> *(4:16)*

Like the imagery of the well and fountain, the "winds" also speak of the Holy Spirit. In the book of John, Jesus compares the Spirit not only to a well of living water, but also to blowing winds (see Jn. 3:8). In the book of Acts, when the Spirit was released upon the early church, He came with the sound of a "violent rushing wind" (Acts 2:2). The wind of the Spirit comes to bring new birth in the world. He is the breath of God that was released into Adam, and He is the same One who releases the life of Christ out of the hearts of Adam's children.

In asking that her garden would "breath out" its fragrance, the Shulammite is expressing her continual desire for the life and glory of God to come out of the garden of her soul. And so, once again, she is asking for the breath of God to kiss her soul in order to awaken those inward promises of fruitfulness. It is the same prayer she prayed in the beginning but now in different words. Here she is calling on the winds of the Spirit to come from every direction (and however necessary) to fill her life so that the glory of God within her can manifest its fragrance.

As right and wonderful that this prayer appears to be, there is a strong contradiction in her words when you compare them to the beautiful Song that the Lord has been singing over her. In describing that well of living water and His current delight in the Shulammite's garden, Jesus has clearly communicated that this "wind" is already inside her. She is looking for something (or Someone) that she already has. And so there is an enduring lie that plays out in her dialogue with the Lord. This lie has to do with a continued sense of separation and delay. The following is one way to paraphrase what is being spoken here:

> *God, You say that I am Your garden of glory, but I do not see it. I do not see the fragrance of Your life bursting forth. I do not see this land of milk and honey that you have described. So God, wake up! Holy Spirit, be roused from your sleep and fill my life that these promises might come forth! I want you to be pleased with me. So come and "eat of my fruit"—come and find pleasure with the garden of my life!*

The Wrong Prayer

On the surface this sounds like a godly prayer. And there is no doubt as to its sincerity and that it arises from a pure desire to please the Lord and experience His promises. But it is apparent that the Bride still hasn't taken in the full impact of her King's words. This desperation still conveys that sense of separation with which she has wrestled since the beginning of the Song. It will thus become clearer than ever that the melody of the Song has not completely penetrated the walls standing on the shores of her heart. She has seen progress, but there is much more for her to experience in the grace and knowledge of Christ.

Desperation for God can be sweet and wonderful when it drives a person to realize the work of Christ and the fullness of His presence already within us—when it breaks our continual dependency upon self and our religious systems, carrying us joyfully into the arms of divine grace. But desperation is not the end of the story and it is certainly not the goal. Any wilderness of perceived lack is not the main plotline, even though many Christians make "desert seasons" to be the end-all-be-all of this present life. In actuality, we are not called to a lifestyle of desperate longing with only short water breaks of refreshment throughout a parched and weary land. As believers, we are called and invited to be fully satisfied in the abiding life of Christ. We are called to a continual feast—to *eat, drink, and imbibe*, as the Song will later say. Eating must start with hunger, but it does not end with a constant wilderness wandering—a continual desperation for a land of milk and honey that is outside of our reach.

The deception in the Shulammite's prayer is like an abrasive undercurrent in the water of her words. It involves a feeling of distance from God—and not only distance from God's living presence, but distance from His character and glory as well. The desperate desire for oneness still involves a lack of heart-knowledge that she has been made one with the *living* presence of Jesus and all that He is. So it is here that we find these deceptive feelings continuing to undergird the Shulammite's words. In this portion of the Song, the young maiden is asking again for union with God. After requesting that the winds awaken and come into her garden, she then makes it even clearer as to what she is really trying to say:

"May my beloved come into his garden!"

She is asking for the Lord Himself to come in and fill her. But the Lord does not respond by sending wind. Instead, He declares once more that they are already one:

"I have come into my garden, my sister, my bride!"

He is dropping some of the metaphor here and speaking very clearly:

*I am already within you! Did you hear me sing about a
well of living water inside of you?
Guess what? That's Me!*

The Shulammite has not believed this. Instead, she feels that the lack of outward fruit must mean that God's Word is not fully true (or perhaps she feels that she is misinterpreting his poetry). So therefore, in her mind, the wind and water of God must be sleeping and needs to be awakened by prayer.

A Move in the Prayer Movement

Millions of believers today are praying in the same vein as the Shulammite in this part of the Song (which is not a surprise, considering the Shulammite's journey is the journey of the corporate church throughout history). The church is praying desperately for the Holy Spirit to "come" in such a way that denotes He is not here. People hear Scriptural and prophetic promises from heaven, but when they see a disconnect between the promise and reality, they enter into what they believe will change it—countless hours of crying out to God. A hidden motivation behind this is that God might "wake up." We want Him to get off His throne, *rend the heavens*, and come down to turn those promises into reality. But we will find soon enough that there is a fatal flaw in this kind of thinking and it pervades much of the "prayer movement" that is happening today.

While much of this movement is a Holy Spirit inspired blessing to bring refreshment and heavenward focus to the church, there is a shift happening where God is calling us to go from a prayer movement to a new Jesus movement. This is much like the transition between John the Baptist and Christ. John the Baptist did a lot in preparing the way for the Messiah, but a time came when John's emphasis and style needed to be exchanged with something completely new. The desert-dwelling, locust-eating, judgment-oriented message needed to be a replaced with a message and a Messenger who ate and drank with sinners, who released healings and miracles, and who gave a word of present hope and abundant life. It was a move from the desert to fulfillment. Wilderness to Promise.

Obviously, this is not saying that John the Baptist was wrong. We are simply acknowledging that his time was only for a season. It served a specific preparatory purpose. It is the same with much of the prayer movement today. As long as there is relationship with God, there will always be prayer. Prayer should be a part of everyday life. But a shift is occurring in the message and expression of the prayer movement—a transition from mournful fasting and desperate "crying out" to feasting and rejoicing on the glories of Christ's victory and His all-present incarnation. The Lord is moving the church more into prayers of thanksgiving and heavenly awareness instead of begging and pleading.

But the seeking Bride is still not there in this part of her journey. So she uses the word "awake" when she calls upon the Holy Spirit to come—as though He is the one sleeping and not her.

The Answer to Our Desperation

This exchange between the Shulammite and the Lord is not contained to just this part of the Bible. If you think that this has been one isolated interpretation of a single Bible verse, then take a look at the book of Isaiah. There you will find more Scriptures where this same type of exchange between God and His people takes place. Chapters 51 and 52 specifically deal with this. They begin with a message of hope and promise from the Lord (much like Jesus's previous words to the Shulammite). Isaiah then gives voice to the prayers and thoughts of the people of Israel as they respond to those promises. Here is their response to God's glorious Word:

> *Awake, awake, put on strength, O arm of the Lord;*
> *Awake as in the days of old, the generations of long ago.*
> *Was it not You who cut Rahab in pieces, who pierced the dragon?*
> *Was it not You who dried up the sea, the waters of the great deep;*
> *Who made the depths of the sea a pathway for the redeemed to*
> *cross over?*
>
> *So the ransomed of the LORD will return... They will obtain*
> *gladness and joy, and sorrow and sighing will flee away.*
> *(Isa. 51:9-11)*

The Israelites hear amazing promises from the Lord, but they respond by asking God to wake up and bring those realities about. They tell Him to arm Himself with strength so that the ransomed of the Lord can return once more to their full inheritance at Zion, which is their own term for the "Promised Land" of milk and honey. (Remember that God has been speaking to the Shulammite about the Promised Land of His glory within her and now she is telling the wind of the Spirit to wake up and bring those promises into outward reality.)

The Israelites expand on this prayer by reminding God that He has brought deliverance before. The reference to Rahab was a reminder of God destroying Egypt and redeeming His people from slavery when He first brought them to the land of their inheritance. Now they are asking God to do it again. And it is the same thing proceeding from the lips of the Shulammite. In essence, she is saying to her Beloved:

> *The kiss of Your Spirit has brought life before. Come and bring life again! Come and bring redemption!*

And so it is with much of the church today. Many are saying to their Beloved:

> *Your Spirit has brought life before (as in the days of Pentecost). Come and bring that life again! Come like a violent rushing wind and bring life to our garden once more. Come and bring out true fruitfulness in the church again!*

But the Lord does not respond to these prayers for revival in the way that the Shulammite, the Israelites, or the church today might expect. Let's look a little bit more deeply into this, because this will help solidify what the Holy Spirit is trying to teach us in the Song of Solomon...

In Isaiah 51, God first responds to His people's desperate pleading by addressing the issue of fear. He says, "Who are you that you are afraid of man who dies" (Isa. 51:12). He points out that even with their noble prayers for God to send His reviving winds, they are actually stuck on a bed of fear and unbelief. They do not understand the fullness of what He already accomplished for them as well as the fullness of their identity in Him (and thus the meaninglessness of fear).

The same goes for the Shulammite. And the same goes for us today. The answer to this prayer is not found in some outside wind to blow again. The answer is the call for the people to move beyond their fear and deception and to wake up to what God has already done.

Look at the next way God responds to their prayer...

> *Awake, awake! Rise up, Jerusalem,*
> *you who have drunk from the hand of the Lord,*
> *the cup of his wrath,*
> *you who have drained to its dregs,*
> *the goblet that makes people stagger...*
>
> *Therefore hear this, you afflicted one,*
> *made drunk, but not with wine.*
> *This is what your Sovereign Lord says,*
> *your God, who defends his people:*
> *See, I have taken out of your hand*
> *the cup that made you stagger;*
> *from that cup, the goblet of my wrath,*
> *you will never drink again.*
> *(Isa. 51:17, 21-22 NIV)*

God tells them that they are the ones who need to wake up!

He goes on to acknowledge that they have experienced judgment and loss in the last season. He compassionately recognizes the roots of their fear by talking about the defeat they have suffered and the experience of an apparent separation between then and Him. But He quickly tells them that the cup of wrath has been taken out of their hands (Isa. 51:22). This is an allusion to the work of Christ who took away our judgments and broke the power of separation. He drank the cup for us! This is similar to what Jesus said earlier in the Song when He told the fearful Shulammite that "the winter and the rain is over and gone." All of these things tie together beautifully.

The Father is saying there is nothing to fear anymore. Redemption is complete and they are able to now walk into a new life of Promise. The perceived separation has been completely removed when Jesus drank the cup of judgment on our behalf. And so God continues His words through the prophet Isaiah in the next chapter by continuing to call them to wake up to this reality:

*Awake, awake, Zion, **clothe yourself** with strength!*
Put on your garments of splendor, Jerusalem, the holy city.
The uncircumcised and defiled will not enter you again.
*Shake off your dust; **rise up, sit enthroned, Jerusalem.***
Free yourself from the chains on your neck, Daughter Zion,
now a captive.

For this is what the Lord says:
"You were sold for nothing, and without money you will be
redeemed."
(Isa. 52:1-3 NIV)

Earlier they had asked God to awake and clothe Himself with strength. But He responds by telling them that they are the ones who need to clothe themselves. They need to "rise up" into the redemption they already have through the work of Christ (when

He redeemed us not with "money" but with His own precious blood).

Let's be clear about something here. This is not God calling us to work and strive for victory and fruitfulness. This is the Lord telling His people to believe in what is already true. We, like the Shulammite, are to rise up and "sit enthroned." In other words, we are to realize that we are already seated with Christ. It is the call to set our hearts on things above by seeing ourselves raised with Christ, completely accepted before the Father and given full authority and victory (see Col. 3:1).

In all the exchanges between the Shulammite and the Beloved, we see how Jesus has been trying to get her to wake up and move past her own fears and unbelief. In the second chapter of the Song He told her the rain of judgment was gone and that there was no need to hide behind the wall of a perceived separation from God. This included the call to walk away from a sinful and guilty conscience. As we move into the fifth chapter, He is continuing to address her in the same way. The waves of truth are building once again.

An Exodus from Separation

One final note here. This type of exchange with the Lord is not only found in the words of the Shulammite, the people in Isaiah's day, and in today's church. This same dialogue goes all the way back to Moses in one of the first images of redemption that the Bible gives us. This is the scene where much of our understanding of deliverance finds its beginning—the crossing of the Red Sea.

At the Red Sea, God's people appeared to be stranded on the shoreline. They were told of God's promise of deliverance, and had even experienced a measure of it. Yet in the natural they only saw defeat. The Egyptians were behind them (which speaks of the slave-masters of sin from our past still coming and attacking us) and the sea was in front of them (which speaks of a blocked pathway to the Promised Land of fruitfulness in the Holy Spirit). So, in similar fashion to the Shulammite and Isaiah's contemporaries, the people began crying out to both Moses and God in anguish over their present state.

Look at what God says to all of this:

> Then the Lord said to Moses, "**Why are you crying out to me?** Tell the Israelites to **move on**. Raise your staff and stretch out your hand over the sea to divide the water so that the Israelites can go through the sea on dry ground.
> (Ex. 14:15-16)

Think about that response.

"Why are you crying out to Me?" God shouts from heaven. "Tell the Israelites to *move on.*"

It is time for the prayer movement and many of God's children today to "move on." We need to stop crying out for a "wind" to come and believe that the wind *is already within us* by the grace of God. There is nothing to fear for the way has been completely opened. The blood of Christ has been shed and the sea of separation has been parted. There is only divine love and eternal hope bursting forth like flowers in the spring.

For the winter and the rain are over and gone. He has *already* come into our garden…

5

Invited to the Trinity's Bliss

———•—◆—•———

I have come into my garden, my sister, my bride;
I have gathered my myrrh along with my balsam.
I have eaten my honeycomb and my honey;
I have drunk my wine and my milk.

Eat, friends;
Drink and imbibe deeply, O lovers.
(5:1)

The eternal melodies and lyrics of this Song have come in like a fresh tide. Though the shores of the Shulammite's heart had already been washed over with revelations of union and grace, we are now seeing that there are still walls erected across the sand; walls that seem to bar the entrance of the full joy of her salvation. The message of the Beloved is still looking to penetrate. To that end, the tide grows and a new billow forms on the horizon. At first, this seems to be the same type of exchange between the Shulammite and the King that we saw earlier in the Song. But this time the wave will rise even higher and its crash will be even stronger.

But that's getting ahead of ourselves.

Let's first go back and recap some of the earlier lyrics to understand what is happening here—again. Previously, in the second chapter of the Song, the Shulammite encountered great refreshment and revelation under the apple tree and in the house of wine. This came about when she sat at the table of the Lamb, which was her first encounter with the realities of the cross (Sgs. 1:12-2:4). Because of this experience, she became overwhelmed by the revelation of grace and was looking for something to sustain and maintain this experience. She then asked for a permanent and unchanging union between her and the singing Shepherd (Sgs. 2:5-7).

When we studied this further, we discovered the same problem that we're still seeing play out in the Shulammite's thinking. She ultimately saw Jesus on the "mountains of Bether," which is a Hebrew word that denotes separation (Sgs. 2:17). She saw herself separate from Him in all of His life and glory, which was a contradiction to the truths being revealed under the shade of the cross. As a result of this sense of estrangement, the Shulammite felt unable to victoriously climb the mountains of difficulty and opposition with her Beloved. She walked away from this adventurous call because of fear and deception, feeling unready and inadequate. This led to the imagery of her lying on a "bed" of spiritual sleep, seeking after her Beloved in different religious ways but never truly arriving at the place of sustained intimacy (Sgs. 3:1-5). Soon we will see her once again on a bed of slumber. But that's also getting ahead of ourselves.

In the previous exchange of spiritual sleep and searching, Jesus ended up responding to His beloved in a similar way that He is doing now. He had told her that He was not on a mountain of separation, but that His feet were planted on the mountain of myrrh and frankincense. This was the mountain of Zion, the place of His death and resurrection. It is the mountain that declares a finished work of divine union (see Sgs. 4:6). We were united to Him in the myrrh of His death and in His fragrant intercession we were raised to everlasting life.

So let's look further at the current exchange between Jesus and His desperate and prayerful church. He tells her that He has already come into His garden, which speaks of her entire soul and being. After declaring this, He once again brings up myrrh and other fragrant spices. He is explaining the same thing once again, bringing a new wave of truth to her questioning heart. It is such a wonderful joy to know that Jesus is relentless in His pursuit of us. He is unyielding in the face of our deepest doubts and fears. His love is an ocean spanning light-years of space while the walls of our fears are only a few inches thick. Eventually they will wear down into dust.

The Suffering Servant

"I have gathered my myrrh along with my balsam," He says.

Once again, myrrh is a symbol of death because in biblical times it was often used for embalming dead bodies. It was also used as a spice to anoint the dead in preparation for burial. In the Song of Songs, it is a symbol of Jesus's death on the cross. The Song says here that He has already gathered this myrrh. The death is already accomplished, and so its results are already active. As we've said over and over again, our entire being was completely united with Him on the cross and our sins and curses died with Him. While many "Shulammites" might believe that His death only released a heavenly wink of forgiveness with a promise of victory far out in the future, Christ's death brought about far more than this. It was a complete destruction of everything that separates us from the life of God.

Balsam is the next word Jesus uses. In the Hebrew, it is often translated as "spice" because the word can refer to a number of different spices. Regardless of their exact plant genus, these spices are fragrant and aromatic. Like frankincense, they speak of the fruitful resurrection of Christ. Just as some people underestimate the cross, the same goes with the resurrection. Many "Shulammites" believe that the resurrection was only about Jesus revealing His divinity or strictly showing us His power over death. But that is only a part of the Gospel. The resurrection is also where we rose to new life with Him. Because of this, we now share His name and identity as a beloved Son, heirs to the Father's Kingdom and favor.

Therefore we have been buried with Him through baptism into death, so that as Christ was raised from the dead through the glory of the Father, so we too might walk in newness of life. ***For if we have become united with Him in the likeness of His death, certainly we shall also be in the likeness of His resurrection.***
(Rom. 6:4-5)

In calling the Shulammite's attention to His death and resurrection, the Lord is continuing to do the same thing that He did to the Israelites in the book of Isaiah. In the last chapter we compared the Shulammite's dialogue with the Lord to a similar exchange between God and His people in Isaiah's writings. They were calling for Him to awake and arise, while God was saying that they were the ones who needed to wake up. Then, just as the Beloved brings up His death and resurrection in the Song, the Lord also brings up His future death and resurrection to the Israelites through Isaiah.

Isaiah chapters 51 and 52 pave the way for one of the most important chapters in the whole Bible. The 53rd chapter of Isaiah hangs like a centerpiece in the biblical canon and gives us one of the clearest prophecies of Jesus's work on the cross. After telling the people that they were in fact the ones who need to wake up, the Lord explains the reason *why* they should wake up. He shifts from calling them to wake up to suddenly telling them to "behold" something...

> *Behold, My servant will prosper,*
> *He will be high and lifted up and greatly exalted.*
> *(Isa. 52:13)*

All of their ability to rise up and sit enthroned in a victorious identity hinges on what He tells them to behold and focus on. This begins the famous prophecy of the Messiah who came as a suffering Servant to ransom us from slavery. It leads us right into Isaiah 53, which begins with a question:

> *Who has believed our message?*
> *And to whom has the arm of the Lord been revealed?*
> *(Isa. 53:1)*

Remember that earlier the Israelites were praying for the "arm" of the Lord to come and deliver them (Isa. 51:9). It is the same thing the Shulammite prayed for in asking for the Holy Spirit's wind to come into her garden. It is the same thing the church prays for today in asking for His power to come and fill us. But God responds to these desperate pleas by asking a question:

Does anyone understand where true power flows from (and how it has already been released)? *To whom has the arm of the Lord been revealed*, He says. With that question in mind, the prophet goes on to explain the finished work of the Messiah.

The Song of the Ages: Part II

Surely our griefs He Himself bore,
And our sorrows He carried;
Yet we ourselves esteemed Him stricken,
Smitten of God, and afflicted.
But He was pierced through for our transgressions,
He was crushed for our iniquities;
The chastening for our well-being fell upon Him,
And by His scourging we are healed.
(Isa. 53:4-5)

These words describe what happened when the Messiah endured the suffering of the cross. It is here that we discover why God calls us to wake up instead of Him. When we feel defeated and ask Him to clothe His arm with strength and deliver us, we are often missing something vitally important. God has already extended His arm for us. In fact, His arm of power was stretched out once and for all on the wooden beams of Calvary's tree. There He was pierced and wounded on our behalf. In that astonishing moment, something happened that affected all time and space. The Messiah of God took on all our powerful enemies with one sacrificial shot. Our sins, our fears, our sorrows, our pains, our isolation—even our literal sicknesses and diseases. He gathered *all* of it to Himself and bore it on His servant body. When He died, He took it all away as a free and glorious gift.

And when He rose, a new life opened up. A springtime of everlasting union, and a life of victory over sin, sorrow, and disease.

A New Fragrance Rising

The next part of Isaiah—chapter 54—is then the celebration and outflow of this wondrous work. Read that chapter carefully. It is the "balsam" that He also gathered, which calls His people to a life of fragrant joy and multiplication (see Isa. 54:1-3). He tells the people to let go of their shame and fear and to embrace the unfailing covenant of peace that has been established (Isa. 54:4-5, 10). He then tells them to trust in this new realm of victory, knowing that no weapon formed against them will prosper. The fear of sin, sickness, or demonic attack is made void in the truth of our union with Christ.

Already Pleased with Us

Right on the heels of His words about myrrh and balsam, the Beloved continues. "I have eaten my honeycomb and my honey. I have drunk my wine and my milk." Let this seep down into the soil of your heart: Jesus is affirming once more that *He is already satisfied and pleased with us.*

Apart from our works, apart from the fruits of our inner life "breathing out," this is the response to His praying Bride. Jesus takes great joy and pleasure in His church, and it is all because of the work that He has accomplished. Every hindrance to intimacy and friendship was removed at the cross. Whether we currently feel it or not, Jesus delights in us—presently and fully—and in this delight we can find a renewed source of strength.

There is an amazing revelation found in Jesus's reference to "*My* honey," "*My* wine," and "*My* milk." The Lord is showing us even more explicitly that the Promised Land is currently and fully His. He has truly purchased us back to Himself. We are now invited to discover the wonder of this conclusive redemption. As we've already explained, we are the Lord's inheritance. The Promised Land was sold into slavery, but He bought it back (redeemed it) by His own blood (by uniting us with Him in death). We ourselves may still be on a temporal journey of waking up and embracing the joy of this truth, but He remains fully satisfied in His work. Standing outside of time, He sees and enjoys the finished product of His death and resurrection. We are fully His and our destinies are filled with nothing but glory and eternal friendship with God.

The Ecstasy of the Trinity

In light of these amazing words, the Song issues a call for "friends" and "lovers" to come and "eat...drink and imbibe deeply." The King James Version translates this verse more accurately:

> *Eat, O **friends**; drink, yea, drink abundantly, O **beloved**.*
> *(Sgs. 5:1b KJV)*

The plural "friends" and the singular "beloved" is a hidden reference to the entire Trinity—for the Friends and the Beloved are one and the same. The Song is calling out to Christ our Beloved, but we know that in Him lies the intimate friendship of the complete Godhead. Thus, this is a call for the Trinity to drink and feast on the redeemed garden of the Shulammite. It is a picture of the celebration of the Father, Son, and Holy Spirit as they take delight in us. God, in all His fullness, is taking actual pleasure in the redemption that was accomplished through Christ.

Heaven is already celebrating and partying over the finished work of the cross. That is why the apostle John, when he was taken up to the throne room, finds the "slain Lamb" in the center of everything (see Rev. 5:6-13) Heaven is literally gathering and reveling over the work of Him who has "overcome" the curse. When John starts weeping, a heavenly elder tells him to restrain his tears and enter into the revelation of victory (Rev. 5:4). In this present age, we do not see the full manifestation of this and so we often fall into tearful pleadings, sorrow, and desperation. But the Psalms declare that He who sits on the throne of heaven *laughs* in the face of all His enemies (Ps. 2:4). Why is this? Because the sacrificed Lamb at the center of the throne has already overcome all powers of darkness. He has defeated every ounce of authority behind the voices of pain, sorrow, and separation.

To reiterate something that has been said previously in our study of the Song—this is not saying that God dismisses our sorrows or is far removed from the temporal pain we experience. Jesus stands secure in heaven, but He is also with us in temporal time. He feels our struggle and He often weeps with us. This is why you will not see the least bit of condemnation towards the Shulammite's insecurities and doubts. He is walking with her through the questions and contradictions. *Yet He is also relentless in reminding her of the truth.* Even though Jesus weeps with us, do not think for a second that Jesus falls to a place of doubt and questioning. With one arm He holds us near and collects our tears, but with the other arm He lifts our heads up high so that we will learn to focus on heavenly reality. He calls us to behold His glorious work and to gaze upon His arm of power extended on the cross.

The Trinity sits at an eternal banqueting table and feasts on the pleasures of divine love and redeemed humanity. This feast goes far beyond a little bite of honey or a small sip of wine and milk. The Song adds the word "imbibe" to signify over-the-top feasting and drinking. It is a word typically connected with getting heavily intoxicated. It is the same Hebrew word used when Noah got drunk and uncovered himself in his tent (Gen. 9:21). It is also the word used when David tried to get the soldier Uriah so inebriated that he would do something against his conscience (2 Sam. 11:13). Furthermore, it is the Hebrew word used in Isaiah 51 when God acknowledges that the Israelites were "drunk" on the overwhelming wine of wrath during the devastating invasion of Babylon.

Now each of these instances are very negative references to drunkenness. This is obviously appropriate considering the devastation that drunkenness brings to people's lives. But there is a pure and heavenly "intoxication." Drunkenness is simply the state of being affected by something to the point that it overpowers your thoughts, actions, and emotions. Mankind has pursued intoxication in all the wrong places and yet they do this because they are made in the image of a Triune God who parties and *imbibes* on a regular basis. The key is *imbibing* on the right things.

God is so full on love and joy that His actions, thoughts and emotions all reflect this overwhelming love. While this might sound crass or demeaning, this is a holy "drunkenness." Some may feel there are better terms to use, but the point is that God feasts and drinks on His love for us and on the victory of His Son. There has always been a continual bliss and ecstasy in the heart of Trinity, and Their celebration of the Lamb only magnifies this divine inebriation. Make no mistake about it—heaven is having a party and the Song of the Ages is playing on the cosmic sound system.

Our Invitation to the Party

It is no wonder that many of Jesus's parables involve invitations to a wedding party. This is not an accident, but rather a vivid metaphor that describes the whole meaning of the Gospel! Jesus calls us to heavenly bliss and intoxicating love! We are invited to the table of grace to drink of our redemption and be filled with the same bliss that the Trinity is currently enjoying.

There is a famous worship song that invites the singer to turn their ear to heaven. Let's go ahead and do that right now. Forget about the facts of where you're physically located and put aside any heavy circumstances of your life (circumstances that will so quickly pass you by). Go ahead and put it all aside and consider something...

While you are reading the very words on this page, right at this very moment, God Himself is happily rejoicing. See that in your heart of hearts. God—in all of His glory and majesty and wonder—is laughing. He is incredibly over-the-top happy. The fullness of joy itself is beaming from His heart (yes, that's what Psalm 16 really says—the *fullness* of joy). The Trinity is at peace and is celebrating right at this very moment. A hefty portion of this celebration is because They are so happily in love with us—*with you*. They have already forgiven you for every sin you have committed and will ever commit. They have completely embraced you and now They see you united with the Son of God. You are as holy as He is, joined together in His death and resurrection. There is a divine family that will live happily ever after and They are celebrating this *right now*.

This is really, really good news!

Because of Christ's work, heaven looks down at the earth and repeats something that was said in the beginning of creation, before sin entered the world. They look at the earth and say *it is very good!* You may not believe this. It may sound preposterous, especially because of our current state of affairs. But Jesus came to take away the sin of the world, and He was successful. When heaven looks at earth, the angels repeat one of their favorite choruses which is a tune right out of the Song of the Ages. They shout:

> *Holy, holy, holy is the Lord of hosts,*
> *The **whole earth** is full of His glory!*
> *(Isa. 6:3)*

Heaven declares the earth is filled with God's glory! This is why we are called to enter into the Sabbath rest of Christ (see Heb. 4).

When Christ said, "it is finished," a new seventh day of rest began, because God looked again at the earth and said it was *very good*. This is how real our unification with Christ is. This is how much power and love was in the death and resurrection of Jesus. This is the food on the heavenly table. It is *real* and delicious and strong.

And so once again we are back at the Table of the Lamb. This is where the Bride found herself in the beginning of her journey and she has now come full circle. There is no maturing beyond the revelation of the cross. Do not let anyone fool you with any such thought. Jesus is the Alpha and the Omega, the Beginning and the End. A deep enjoyment of His finished work will forever be the greatest maturity a person can experience. In all of her sleepy wanderings, the Shulammite has been hearing this same call from her Beloved. It is the call to discover how firm and tangible, how *true* and *finished* His work really is.

The Lord Himself is already drunk on the wine of the New Covenant. The entire Trinity has long been imbibing on the milk of the eternal Word—the Person of Christ and the Word of our union with Him. Even though we are often asleep to this and we cry out for deliverance and help, God calls us to look at His outstretched arms and join the celebratory party. He calls us to see that the mountain of *Bether*—the separation between God's glory and us—is gone. We are invited to see the glory of God in *all* the earth, in every situation and in every person, including ourselves. *This* is what waking up is really all about.

Learning to Receive Abundance

As we come to the end of this portion of the Song, there is one more amazing parallel between the Song's dialogue and the words of Isaiah. We will see even more how these two passages tie together. But first, let's first give another quick recap:

Invited to the Trinity's Bliss

In Isaiah 51, the people cry out to God in desperate intercession for Him to wake up and bring about His strength and power. God responds by exposing their fear and in Isaiah 52 He tells them to wake up to His deliverance and then to rise up and "sit enthroned." He explains the reason for this in Isaiah 53, detailing the work of His Son that has removed every obstacle to His glory. He continues in Isaiah 54 to declare the promise of new life, calling the people to completely move on from their shame and fear and embrace the full joy of redemption.

All of this lays the groundwork for Isaiah 55, which is a prophetic invitation to the wedding party of heaven. It follows all the preceding words like a blasting trumpet in the ears of God's people. A call is issued in this chapter that succinctly lines up with the portion of Solomon's Song that we have been studying. Let's take some time to read through it:

> *Ho! Every one who thirsts, come to the waters;*
> *And you who have no money come, buy and eat.*
> *Come, buy **wine and milk** without money and without cost.*
> *Why do you spend money for what is not bread,*
> *And your wages for what does not satisfy?*
>
> *Listen carefully to Me, and eat what is good,*
> *and **delight yourself in abundance**.*
> *Incline your ear and come to Me. Listen, that you may live;*
> *And I will make **an everlasting covenant** with you,*
> *According to the faithful mercies shown to David.*
> *(Isa. 55:1-3)*

Hear the call, beloved reader. We are to *incline our ear* and listen to the Song of all songs, the Song ringing throughout all ages and all eternity. We are to feast on the covenant that has been made between God and His Son. We freely and effortlessly benefit from this covenant because we are fully included in Christ. This really is over-the-top good news. This is not a Gospel that gives an occasional smile to your face or a slight feeling of relief here and there. When understood in its fullness (when we *delight ourselves in abundance*), this Gospel brings a heavenly intoxication to all who partake of it. Such was the call to Isaiah's listeners and it is the call to God's seeking church today.

6

An Outlawed Celebration

I was asleep but my heart was awake.
A voice! My beloved was knocking:

Open to me, my sister, my darling,
My dove, my perfect one!
For my head is drenched with dew,
My locks with the damp of the night.
(5:2)

We have noted before how the great stories and fairy tales of the world communicate different elements of the Gospel's truth. They weave themselves around the lips, pens and movie screens of humanity and whisper of a greater reality around us. Their origin lies beyond the imagination of the storyteller. A true artist is simply someone with a strong and unique antenna that can pick up its frequency and express it through different mediums of story and art. But regardless of the medium, each of these stories arise from different aspects of the Song of the Ages as it plays its tune throughout creation.

The Song of the Ages: Part II

Moving forward in the Song, I want to call your attention to one particular story that typically involves a great prince or king standing over his promised bride who is fast asleep. Sleeping Beauty is the main story that aligns with this, although it has been told in many other ways before and after. In the many variations of this story, the prince is relentless in his pursuit of this woman who has fallen asleep due to a deceptive spell that has been cast over her. Upon finding her, he is told that her awakening must come out of true love. It is not something that can be forced. The life of the bride is only awakened when the prince's love is poured out over her in a kiss. This is what breaks the witch's spell.

Such is the case with the Bride in the Song of the Ages. The King of creation and the Prince of Peace, Jesus Christ, repeatedly says, "Do not awaken my love until she pleases." While other people might try to shout in the Bride's ear or violently shake her out of sleep, the King understands this must be a work of love. And so this is why He sings over her, whispering to the depths of her heart, releasing a spiritual kiss that calls her to arise.

At this point in the story we are not yet at the full breaking point. A kiss has certainly been poured over her, but there is still some resistance keeping her to a bed of sleep. It is in this scene that we will receive a clearer understanding of this. In fact, we will enter right into the dream world of the sleeping Shulammite. We will see things from her hypnotic perspective, even as the King continues to stand over her sleeping body and sings His words of love.

"I was asleep, but my heart was awake," she begins.

This phrase about being asleep with an awake heart is describing the experience of having a dream or vision. The person is actually asleep, but they are seeing things while in that state. Jeremiah uses the same word for the heart when he talks about "visions of the heart" that people can have (see Jer. 14:14 & 23:16). In this state of sleeping and dreaming, the Shulammite acknowledges that she is hearing a voice. Somewhere, somehow, her Beloved is speaking to her, calling her from another realm—a truer realm. She does not completely understand this yet, but she can hear His voice and it sounds like someone knocking on a door calling her to wake up and come out.

"A voice! My beloved was knocking."

The Journey So Far

This scene in the fifth chapter comes as a deep and climactic confrontation of all that has occurred up until this point. If you have read carefully, you would see that there has been one sweeping theme in all of the lyrics and melodies that have preceded this moment. In order to wisely approach this scene, it might be good then to quickly rewind the tape and recapture the overarching themes of the Song. Let's give one more look at the full breadth of the Song before we listen to what happens next.

At the start, a young woman from Shulam went looking for righteousness, rest, and love. While others around her may have settled for bodily death to bring these realities, the Bride believed in hope against hope that Jesus had already brought these things to earth. And so she cried out for it and the Beloved came to meet this desire in her heart. Strangely, His response came by first addressing the Shulammite's self-perception, which was filled with a conflict over loveliness and darkness (or a sinful nature). He spoke to the complete purity and righteousness already inside her and brought her to the first stop on her journey which would settle this issue once and for all—the Table of the Lamb. There He showed her His work on the cross, and how her union with Him in His death and resurrection brought about the release of all that she was seeking. She began to taste of the wonders of divine mercy as she ate the fruit of His cross and dined in a house filled with the wine of the New Covenant. He called her to believe and trust in these wonderful truths—to abide continually in the kiss of His grace.

But that trust came with difficulty. Soon she became overwhelmed by everything and looked for something to sustain her in this place of intimate acceptance. She fell back into old patterns of thinking and we discovered that a wall of fear and judgment had been erected over her eyelids. Although there was no separation between her and Jesus, an imaginary veil stood over her heart keeping her from seeing and trusting in His words. This veil prevented her from experiencing the fruitfulness that flows from His grace. And so Jesus called out for her to come away from this wall and enter into a life of victorious freedom.

Yet she remained on a bed of spiritual sleep, unawake to the full glory of His work on the cross. The Shulammite ended up going into the "city" of religion and to its watchmen leaders to help her find Christ, but this was often to no avail. Though there were passing encounters with His presence during this time, the full manifestation of His promises seemed distant and elusive.

In the fourth chapter of the Song, the Lord picked it up a notch. Still relentless in His pursuit, Jesus began to shout out the words of His gospel with more intensity and depth. He declared seven facets of her identity, speaking to the absolute perfection He has always seen within her. To this end, the Lord called her "altogether beautiful" and connected this statement once more with the cross—the mountain of myrrh and frankincense. From here, He continued to call her away from the wall of sleep-inducing fear, this time comparing it to the lions and leopards of demonic condemnation and judgment.

An Outlawed Celebration

All of this built up to the Almighty Creator of heaven and earth opening up the most vulnerable places of His heart to the sleeping Bride. Up until that portion of the Song, this was the highest and greatest crash of His rising waves of truth. This was the very Summit of Truth. He vehemently declared just how much her beauty impacts Him. God is completely affected—ravished and undone—by the splendor of His Bride. If there was any doubt that she was deeply loved, rescued, and holy, this should have certainly settled the matter. Any possible fear of a future life without God's favor and presence should have been quenched with these surging expressions of eternal love.

But in His extravagant grace, God did not stop there. Jesus's voice continued to call out to the Shulammite who was still hiding behind her veil. He went on to say that she is *His Promised Land*, flowing with milk and honey, bringing absolute pleasure to His heart. The Lord assured her once again that she is no longer dark as He compared her to a sealed rock garden with a flowing fountain right in the middle. He made it perfectly clear that the fullness of the Spirit (and all the Spirit's fruit) is present within her, waiting to burst forth.

Now as we listened to this glorious melody of identity and redemption, we may have missed the fact that the Bride has still not woken up from her spiritual sleep. Here, we come to the portion of the Song where we find her lying on her bed once more. While there have been moments that her eyelids stretched and opened, a full awakening has not yet come. Slumber still pulls her back onto the bed. The witch's religious spell still tugs at her heart.

This became clear when we saw the Bride's first response to all of the preceding words of awakening, which were some of the most transcendent and life-changing truths a human being could hear. She responds to all of this by asking God to wake up! She called on the wind—a symbol of the Holy Spirit—to awaken and bring forth the glory of His Word. Part of this prayer arises from a pure place within her that longs to taste everything He's described. But like so many in the church, and even more out in the world, this prayer still comes down to the fact that she sees God as far and distant. To this end, the faith of the Shulammite has not reached maturity.

In response to her pleading, God gave the Shulammite the same answer that He gave the praying Israelites in Isaiah's day when they also asked Him to wake up and deliver them from captivity. In essence, He told the Shulammite to set her gaze upon the suffering Servant and to celebrate His atoning work. It is there that we discovered the ecstatic joy of the Trinity as They revel and feast upon the completed work of Christ. The Bride is simply being called to wake up to eternity's perspective. All along, this has been the kiss of the Word, which the Lord has been pouring out over His sleeping beauty. It turns out that receiving this kiss is the only pathway to true maturity.

And so now we arrive at the climactic scene of chapter five as the voice of truth comes once more to the Shulammite like a gentle knocking on her heart—like a new wave beginning to crash as it approaches the shores of her soul and challenges the veil that is still peeled over her eyelids...

The Knock of the Gospel

With one statement, Jesus the Beloved reinforces everything that has been said thus far:

"Open to me, my sister, my darling, my dove, my perfect one!"

Do you think the Lord could make it any clearer?

An Outlawed Celebration

Sister, darling, dove, perfect one.

It is as though with each identifying title there is another knock upon the ears of her heart with the fullness of the message He has been trying to convey. He speaks these words of identity once more and then He continues His sentence with the word "for." He says next, *"For* my head is drenched with dew, my locks with the damp of the night."

Right here Jesus is explaining *why* she can open to Him and fully trust in this Word—the kiss of the Spirit, the crash of heaven. Instead of *for,* you might substitute the word *because.* He is saying, "Open to me, *because* my head is drenched with dew, my locks with the damp of the night."

Why can she open the door and fully receive His message of grace? It is the same answer as the one that has come to her from the beginning of the Song. The *damp of the night* speaks of the suffering He endured in the night season of His crucifixion. Jesus is saying to open to Him because He has already suffered and thus already united the two of them together. The barriers and separations have been removed. Love and union is restored. His hair is damp from being outside in a night of suffering. This message is the pummeling wave that has risen, receded, and returned over and over again.

Once more, Jesus is calling the Shulammite to "rise up" and "come away," *because* He is still standing on "the mountain of myrrh" (Sgs. 4:6). Basically, He is continuing to say, "Open up and believe! Trust in this reality. *I have already gathered my myrrh…* I have already suffered and joined us together as one. *Do you see this yet?"*

This is not meant to sound redundant or go overkill on this one particular point. We are simply revealing more and more that this is truly *the Song of the Lamb.* The chords always draw us back

87

to the work of the cross. A full revelation of the cross will be both the cornerstone and the capstone of the Shulammite's journey, and thus all of church history. Jesus will continue to bring us back here until we understand the cross correctly and joyfully.

Forbidden Feasts

In order to get a stronger grasp on this verse, let's look at another passage of Scripture that parallels this one with incredible precision.

> *"Behold, I stand at the door and knock; if anyone hears
> My voice and opens the door, I will come in to him and will
> dine with him, and he with Me."*
> *(Rev. 3:20)*

In this passage, Jesus is pictured as standing outside the door of the church of Laodicea, an ancient city located in the Roman province of Asia. Through the apostle John's letter, Jesus speaks a word of correction to the church in this city, reprimanding them for being "lukewarm." He clarifies this frustration by explaining how the church thinks that they have it all together, but that they are actually poor, blind, and naked (see Rev. 3:17). He then calls for them to buy three items from Him: gold, eye salve, and white garments—each of which will truly enrich them, remove their blindness, and clothe their nakedness. All of this is then followed up with a reminder that He loves them (Rev. 3:19). This leads to the preceding words of Him standing at the door and knocking, waiting to come in and dine with them.

There are a few things to understand in order to appreciate the context and meaning of this tough passage. First, we need to remember that the early Christians did not gather in big buildings and cathedrals, but in individual homes. A typical "service" consisted in having a meal together, which always involved communion, and then times of prayer, worship, and ministry to one another. These gatherings were called "love feasts" (see Jude 1:12 & 2 Pet. 2:13) and were a continuation of the model Jesus set at the last supper. Communion was shared in the midst of fellowship, prayer, and mutual encouragement. In the early church, everything was centered around this ongoing celebration of the work of Christ through communion. This was the fuel and life of the church, causing it to prosper and multiply throughout the entire world.

So when Jesus says to the Laodiceans that *if they hear His voice and open the door to Him, He will come into them and dine with them*—He is not speaking to individuals. He already dwells within individuals. He is speaking to the entire church community. They were doing their love feasts, but it was without a true recognition of Christ. They were gathering and "dining," but the focus wasn't on Jesus.

What most likely occurred is that the Laodiceans had lost track of the meaning of the feast. Perhaps it had become ritualistic and routine and the supernatural life of the Spirit had faded. Or perhaps it was similar to what happened in the city of Corinth when Paul gave a strong rebuke regarding their own love feasts. The Corinthians were only coming to the love feasts to fill their bellies or to hang out in their different factions and groups (see 1 Cor. 11:17-22). They too had lost sight of the meaning and power of communion. Like the Shulammite, both Corinth and Laodicea were spiritually asleep to the work of the cross.

Some people think that the Laodicean call to buy "gold" means that they needed to endure some heavy amount of labor, spiritual discipline, and suffering. But the gold Jesus mentions is not the gold of our religious works. It is the gold of the Gospel and Jesus's suffering on our behalf. Furthermore, the "garments" are the garments of righteousness in Christ that remove our shame (the naked shame that began all the way in the Garden). The eye salve is what finally breaks the spell of religion and opens our eyes to the glory of God's love and our true reflection in Him.

When Jesus says to "buy" these things from Him, He's issuing the same call of Isaiah 55 that says, "Come, buy wine and meat without money and *without cost*" (Isa. 55:2b). Some people will teach that you need to pay a dear cost for the gold, garments, and salve of Revelation 3. But Jesus is the One who paid the price for these things. People who over-emphasize our personal works unfortunately have the same heavy veil of religion over their eyes as the Shulammite. In Revelation, Jesus is simply calling the Laodiceans back into the simplicity of grace—to rid themselves of barrenness and shame through their acceptance in Christ and the enrichment of His love.

Losing sight of Christ's blood (which is the entire revelation of identity and redemption that has been unfolding throughout the Song of Songs) leads to lukewarm Christianity. There may be religious rituals and routines happening with much sweat and zeal, but they will lack the manifested presence of God and the Eden-like fruits of the Spirit. The ultimate issue with the church at Laodicea was not apathy toward the things of God. Apathy is what we normally think of as "lukewarm" living and many preachers have used this passage to rail against spiritual laziness as a result. However, apathy is really just a fruit of something much deeper. The real issue with Laodicea was that they were encumbered by religious rituals and earthly distractions and were lacking a living heart-encounter with the Song of the Gospel. They were lukewarm with their celebration of the ecstatic Good News of heaven! They were no longer rejoicing in the meaning and power of Jesus's body and blood. That was their core problem.

An Outlawed Celebration

This has been the issue throughout all of church history and it extended way beyond Corinth and Laodicea. There has always been a war against the saints celebrating the feast of the Lamb. This culminated into church councils where religious officials eventually prevented Christians from taking communion in their own homes. The life-giving love feasts of the early church were officially outlawed not long after the faith became highly politicized in the fourth century. Rules were set in place that only approved clergy could administer communion in sanctioned settings, and this was often done in a somber and graceless manner.

And here is a sad, but amazing fact for you: The "outlawing" of love feasts in the home happened in a religious council that took place in the city of Laodicea! The official outlawing of love feasts occurred in the *Council of Laodicea* in 363-364 A.D.

The Real Sleeping Beauty

Religion always wants to "outlaw" the feast of grace. It wants to put obstacles in our way, which includes heavy burdens of manmade rules, religious discipline, striving, and condemnation. It ultimately wants to complicate the meaning of true faith and put the focus back on us (and our systems) instead of Jesus Christ and His finished work.

And so, unfortunately, it appears Laodicea did not open the door to the Lord's voice. If they did, the door did not stay open for long. This region of the early church did not embrace the eye salve of the Gospel, but stayed on a bed of religion, which led to a fruitless life. Like the Shulammite, the early church fell asleep. That sleep of religion led to the formation of some man-centered councils that were devoid of God's transformative grace. The church had once again gone into the "city" of religion and to its

91

"official" watchmen, which defiled the life of the church and left multitudes in spiritual poverty and shame.

Right now, we are discussing the literal bewitching spell that was cast over the church throughout history. A spell that has worked hard to keep the Bride fast asleep. Please don't think that we are just giving flowery explanations of the church's lack of power through fairy tale analogies and poetry. Don't think that Sleeping Beauty is just a nice devotional metaphor. All of this is rooted in verifiable history, where you can track the rot and decay permeating throughout corporate Christianity. The Bride has literally fallen asleep from the feast of the cross (the house of wine, the table of the Lamb, the wine, milk, and honey). False watchmen set over the Body outlawed love feasts and kept the Bride away from the full meaning of redemption and our true identity in Christ.

But Jesus continues to call to His Bride, as He always has. Just like He did in the book of Revelation, Jesus is knocking on the door of the Shulammite church. He calls her to heed His voice, which continues to pour out the kiss of the eternal Gospel. "If anyone hears My voice," He says. He calls us to open up the door of faith and receive the message of the cross. He is calling His Bride to a feast—to dine with Him in the richness of the Gospel; the milk and wine of His New Covenant of grace. This same call to "dine" in Revelation 3 is the same call in Isaiah 55 and Song of Solomon 5:1. Again, all Scripture is interwoven and tied together by the scarlet thread of the Lamb.

The Timeless Call

One practical take-away from this is that the Lord is calling the church to return to the true love feast. To come back to a living celebration of communion that engages with the full meaning of the finished work of the cross. This is the real power that brings awakening to the church. This awakening has already begun, but it is building momentum in the days that we currently live. As we've noted in our previous study of the Song, the church has figuratively been in the ground for two days in God's calendar (nearly 2000 years). But it is now the third day, and a resurrection of the Shulammite is upon us. This is a resurrection that will center on a people fully *opening the door* to the Gospel of grace.

And so let us turn our ears again to the call of the King as He stands over His sleeping Bride and sings His Song of truth. "Open to Me," He says.

The billowing wave that has been rising anew has become a giant tidal wave, even greater than the last crescendo in the Song. Everything Jesus has already spoken in the entirety of the Bride's journey is encapsulated in this one simple plea to the Shulammite.

Open to Me...

...My sister. You who are one substance with Me, who share the same Father as I, and thus the same essence and likeness. Knock!

...My darling. You whom I cherish and tenderly care for. Knock!

...My dove. You who carry the very purity of My Spirit and the eyes of My Father. Knock!

...My perfect one. You who have been perfectly redeemed, and are now perfect in My sight. Knock!

> *Open to Me, for I am drenched in the dew of the night.*
> *I bear the marks of suffering that brought you into this*
> *place of divine union and grace. Open to the beauty of*
> *My Gospel and experience the fellowship of My Presence.*
> *Experience the joy of the Father, Son, and Holy Spirit,*
> *abiding and celebrating all around you.*

The Song of the Ages: Part II

Throughout the ages, from the days of the exodus, to the people of Isaiah's time, to a Roman province in Asia, to today's global church, Jesus makes this call loud and clear.

7

The Rising

———— •─◆─• ————

I have taken off my dress,
How can I put it on again?
I have washed my feet,
How can I dirty them again?

My beloved extended his hand through the opening,
And my feelings were aroused for him.

I arose to open to my beloved;
And my hands dripped with myrrh,
And my fingers with liquid myrrh,
On the handles of the bolt.
(5:3-5)

God has taken His hand, the hand that fashioned all creation and now holds and sustains every star and cell, and with it He has knocked upon the door of the Shulammite's heart. This of course is the door to all of our hearts, the entranceway into the depths of our being. His knock carries a reverberation that fills the room of our souls like sunlight pouring into a valley and we are suddenly stirred by the strength of its echo. While still sleeping upon her bed, the Shulammite's eyelids begin to flutter and her legs and arms extend into a stretch. Though a full awakening does not come just yet, the fogginess and grogginess begins to subside and a new clarity dawns.

We can see this fresh clarity by the way that the Shulammite responds to His knock. Here she makes an interesting statement about her dress and her feet. Many people have interpreted this passage as though the Bride is hesitating and resisting the call to come away, because they assume she is saying that she doesn't want to put her dress back on or get her feet dirty. In the self-deprecating arenas of Christianity, which taints our biblical hermeneutic and forever points out everything that is wrong with us, this is the natural interpretation that arises. And while there may be a measure of truth in that interpretation (since we know the global church has very often hesitated to respond wholeheartedly to the call of grace), this is certainly not the main thrust of the verse.

In keeping with the overall theme and musical quality of the Song, we do not want even the slightest deviation from its original tone and harmony. While there may be certain allowances for variations and remixes of the Song, which can speak other messages to the listener, we want to examine the purest version of Solomon's ballad. For in the Song's original purity, we will discover that the Bride's response is actually a very good thing. It speaks to the awakening that is occurring within her. This fluttering of the eyelids and the stretching of the limbs parallels what has been happening within the church for many centuries now, which continues to grow and build to this day. This part of the Song marks the beginning stages of a full awakening. Let's look more closely at her words.

"I have taken off my dress, how can I put it on again?" she asks. "I have washed my feet, how can I dirty them again?"

While it may appear like she is hesitating to come outside because she doesn't want to get dirty, the Shulammite is actually asking a rhetorical question here. A rhetorical question is a figure of speech that uses a question to make an obvious point. The Bible is replete with such questions. Think about this one: "If God is for us, who can be against us?" (Rom. 8:31 NIV). The apostle Paul posed this question in his letter to the Romans. He was not posing it in order to find out which of our enemies might actually be able to stand against us. Rather, he was plainly stating an obvious truth: "If God be for us, *no one* can stand against us!"

So it is with the Shulammite: *I have taken off my dress, I cannot put it on again.* As we continue to unravel the poetic symbolism of the text, this interpretation of her rhetorical question will become blatantly clear. We will see that she is starting to confess how complete and how final the work of Christ truly is. She is coming to terms with the fact that her redemption is accomplished.

The Fundamental Elements of the Word

Numerous commentators have highlighted an important connection between this verse and the New Testament. Different scholars and teachers of the Word recognize that the removal of a garment is often an Old Testament picture of our "old man" (or "sinful nature") being "put off." Paul is the one who primarily develops this Old Testament picture by comparing the putting off of sin to the removal of old clothing. There are many instances where he uses the Greek word for "unclothe" when he declares that our sins were "put off" through our death with Christ. One of the main instances is from the book of Colossians:

> *Do not lie to one another, since you have **put off the old man** with his deeds.*
> *(Col. 3:9)*

97

So the Shulammite is making this same connection, but in poetic Old Testament language. She is rhetorically saying how it is impossible for her to ever put on the old garment of sinfulness again. She has taken off her "dress" (which in the Hebrew can also be translated as "garment"). She *cannot* put it back on. In other words, she has been washed completely clean. She has heard the knock and its call to partake of the Lamb's sacrifice and she is once more embracing it in her heart.

As we have seen, the Word of God is laced with layer upon layer of interlocking connections. We need to remember that the same hand that engineered the universe, sustaining stars and knocking on hearts, is also the hand that engineered the creation of the Bible. So you will find similar handiwork in both the cosmos and the Scriptures. For instance, when you study the solar system you find many interlocking patterns and connections amongst its different elements. From a large-scale perspective, the orbits of planets around the sun very much resemble the smaller scale realities of subatomic particles circling around the nucleus of an atom. In the same way, when you study the handiwork of God in the Scriptures you will find interlocking patterns between the large-scale picture of the Bible and the small details that make it up. These connective patterns are all over the place, whether in creation or Scripture.

Scientists need to use tools such as microscopes and telescopes to discover many of the beautiful patterns within creation. Students of the Word have their own focusing tools, one of which is a lexicon. Greek and Hebrew lexicons help modern readers discover the meaning of the original languages of the Bible. They will also help you find where certain Hebrew or Greek words show up in other parts of the Scriptures. This helps reveal some of the interlocking connections within the Word. So, for example, when you study the Hebrew word for "dress" you can find other places that this Hebrew word shows up and start to discover some underlying patterns.

The Rising

One way that people utilize a lexicon in this regard is by looking at the first place a particular word shows up in the Bible. This is sometimes known as the *law of firsts*. When you find the first place that a word shows up, you can look at the context of that word and gain deeper insight into its meaning when you study it in later parts of the Scriptures. At the risk of going overboard with scientific analogies, this is similar to studying the elements of the periodic table. These basic elements are the primary molecules God created. When they come together, they form all the large-scale structures that we see around us, whether rocks, people, or planets. Studying these fundamental molecules gives you deeper insight into those larger structures.

In the same way, when you study a word's original placement and meaning in the Bible, you can sometimes get a deeper understanding of the word's fundamental spiritual meaning. Then you will have greater insight when that word shows up again and pairs up with other words to form the large-scale structures of verses and chapters.

The Garments of Adam

So let's simplify all this and actually look at the Hebrew word for "dress," which the Shulammite declares she has "taken off." When you open a lexicon and find the Hebrew word for dress, you will find that it simply means "garments." Then, when you go to the first place this word shows up, you'll see that it appears in the third chapter of Genesis. This is when Adam and Eve partake of the Tree of Knowledge and God clothes them with "garments" of animal skin in order to cover their nakedness.

> *The Lord God made **garments** of skin for Adam and*
> *his wife, and clothed them.*
> *(Gen. 3:21)*

The Song of the Ages: Part II

Here you are finding a fundamental "element" that makes up the word "garment" when it shows up in other parts of the Scriptures, such as the verse at hand in the Song of Solomon. The clothing of Adam and Eve with garments made from an animal sacrifice is a direct picture of the work of Christ. Through Jesus's sacrifice on our behalf, Christ took away all of our false garments of shame and covered us with His own clothing of righteousness and peace.

Interestingly enough, this same Hebrew word also shows up in the book of Exodus where it describes the beautiful garments to be made for the High Priest (Ex. 28:4). The High Priest was also a symbol of the coming Christ who would clothe humanity with His righteous identity. In the book of Numbers, Aaron the High Priest is told that when he dies his sons are to be clothed with these garments (see Num. 20:26). This is also a picture of Christ's death and the ensuing transfer of righteous clothing. Later in the biblical account, another high priest arises who is metaphorically shown as wearing dirty clothes which then get taken off so that he can be re-clothed with clean and festive garments (Zech. 3:3-4).

The most beautiful connection and fulfillment of this word shows up in the New Testament, right in the heart of the Gospel story during Christ's crucifixion. When Jesus was crucified for our sins, his robe was stripped and divided between the four Roman soldiers who were crucifying him. This is an amazing picture of Christ giving away His righteousness to the four corners of the earth—even to all of humanity, for we all bear the same bloodguilt as the Roman soldiers. What's even more amazing however, is that the Bible goes into further detail and mentions a specific undergarment or "tunic" that Christ had been wearing (Jn. 19:23). This was a seamless garment for which the Roman soldiers cast lots to see who would take it home. The Greek word for this tunic comes from the same Hebrew word in Song of Songs 5 and

Genesis 3! All of these words tie together. Like the cosmos, the beauty and synchronicity of the Word is breathtaking.

Jesus Christ united us to Himself and took on our shame and sinfulness. When He died, this shame was unclothed and discarded for all eternity. When He rose, we were still united with Him and thus took on the new garment of resurrected holiness and peace. The Shulammite is identifying with this, seeing herself truly crucified with Christ. She is seeing that the death of her sin is as real and true as the death of Jesus of Nazareth. She is beginning to feel this in her heart of hearts. This is happening to such an extent that she rhetorically makes the statement that she has taken off her own garment and *cannot* put it back on again. The meaning of this word is now completely clear. The old identity is buried—forever.

Now the washing of her feet speaks to the same thing. It reminds us of another connection in the Gospel of John where Jesus washed the disciple's feet. This happened right before He went to the cross where He would re-clothe us with purity. The foot washing was not only a picture of His servant heart, but also of the entire purpose of His servanthood. We have all walked through a corrupted world, and the Messiah has come as Isaiah's suffering servant to wash our feet from the cursed soil of this earth.

So let's make it very clear that the Shulammite is not hesitating to come outside. She is simply realizing what Jesus has been trying to show her all along. She is making a true confession of her righteousness. She is demonstrating what the book of Hebrews says will happen when we truly accept Jesus's final sacrifice on our behalf—we will have no more "consciousness of sins" (see Heb. 9:26-10:2). Our old garments can never be put back on. Our dirtiness and guilt are fully wiped away. We are new, through and through.

Rightly Dividing the Verse

Someone may argue with this rhetorical interpretation and say that Jesus wants the Shulammite to come outside, and so that would signify that the Bride is hesitating by not wanting to put on her dress again or dirty her feet. The reasoning for this interpretation might be based on the fact that earlier in the Song Jesus asked her to leave her wall and "come away" with Him. At that point, she did not want to come outside, but told Him to turn away. Therefore, some would say that the Shulammite is doing the same thing again. However, Jesus is not asking her to come outside this time. This time He actually wants to come in. It's a different picture of Jesus's same desire for His church to grow in intimacy and freedom.

We saw earlier how Jesus wants to dine with His sleeping Bride. As He stood outside the door, He spoke of His hair being saturated with the dew of the night, which revealed His work of suffering on her behalf. Jesus knocked on the Shulammite's door much like He knocked on the door of the Laodicean church. There He wanted to *come in* and dine with them so that they could feast on His grace. If you remember correctly, Jesus was not only looking to dine with the Laodiceans, but was also calling them to buy white *garments* from Him. In the context of the Gospel, this simply means that He was calling the church to believe that their old man was crucified and that they are now eternally clothed with His very identity. Therefore, they didn't need to look to their own works and rituals to find spiritual riches.

The Shulammite is finally receiving the message of her true garments. As a result, her eyes are being anointing with salve and the gold of Christ's sacrifice is being deposited into the account of her heart. She is not saying, *I don't want to go outside because I'll get dirty again.* No, she is responding to His word and realizing that she is truly clean. She is dining with Christ and seeing that there is nothing to fear anymore.

The boogeyman has been killed once and for all.

An Opening in the Heart

As she begins to embrace the love feast and confesses this long-coming revelation, an opening is formed in her heart. In the realization of how finished His work really is, the Shulammite says, "My beloved extended his hand through the opening." The extension of the Lord's hand is a picture of His strength and presence manifesting in her life. The Shulammite is beginning to wake up and the Lord's hand is becoming more evident within her. This shows us that having a fearless heart, confident in grace, enables the hand of the Lord to move more freely in our lives.

Let's call to mind something else from the wider context of the Song. Remember that in the book of Isaiah the Hebrew people were trying to wake up a God who they assumed was sleeping. They were interceding and asking that God would awaken and extend His arm of power into their midst (Isa. 51:9). But then God responded and said that they were the ones who needed to wake up. They had to come out of their fear and awaken to His work of redemption. Out of this, His hand of power and strength would flow. In the Song of Songs, we are discovering the evidence for this. As the Shulammite awakens to the redemption in Christ, the "hand" of power that she has been seeking all along finally starts to appear.

And this is what it all boils down to…

We are not waiting on God.

God is waiting on us to believe; to let go of fear, of a false identity, of an affair with guilt and law—and to rest in His love.

The Shulammite has come into a new awareness of God's hand in her life—the same hand that formed every molecule in the cosmos and fashioned every verse in the Scriptures; the hand that molds and sustains every human being and knocks on their hearts with everlasting words of love.

As this hand becomes more evident (even though it was always there, reaching out to her fearful heart), the Shulammite next declares that her "feelings were aroused."

A Stirring Within

We will once again utilize the tool of a lexicon and look more closely at these words. First, the Shulammite mentions her "feelings." This is a word that is often translated as "bowels" and it simply describes the deepest places within a person. The next word is "aroused," which means to be stirred up, such as when the waves of the sea are stirred up and begin to roar (see Jer. 31:35). So here we are seeing that the deepest places within the Shulammite are being stirred up and awakened. In other words, her inner garden is finally being released, causing the inner fragrance of Jesus to be displayed. Everything she has been desperately searching for (as well as sometimes questioning and doubting) begins to effortlessly manifest as she embraces the truth of the cross!

The law of firsts proves to be powerful here as well. The first time the word for "feelings" or "bowels" shows up in the Bible is in Genesis 15. There, God tells Abraham that from His *bowels* will come forth a seed—a promised son (Gen. 15:4). In its historical context, this verse is referring to Abraham's promised son Isaac. However, we know that the ultimate seed of Abraham was Christ (see Gal. 3:16). So God was saying to Abraham, *out of your bowels, your innermost being, the Christ will come forth.*

The Rising

So it is with us. As we believe in the Gospel of peace and dine upon His Word, Christ within us is stirred up and ignited. Eden begins to blossom and the seed of the Word germinates. This is what the Shulammite is experiencing. As a result, she is finally shaking off her spiritual slumber. She is beginning to *feel* the cleanness of her soul and the substance of her freedom. She now sees the Lord's hand moving in her life, which releases the sweet and fruitful nature of Christ within her. In this celebratory experience of grace, the Shulammite finally starts to rise from her bed.

And she goes to open up the door...

The clearest indicator that the Shulammite is waking up to the Gospel comes at this last part of the text. The Song says that as she goes to open the door, her hands and fingers "dripped with myrrh." This of course is a picture of her embrace of all that we have been discussing. We have made it profusely clear that the myrrh is a symbol of death and it speaks to our union with Christ in His crucifixion. So the Shulammite has taken her own hands—small and fragile in comparison to the mighty hand of God—and she has done something that releases more power than anything else. She has answered His knock by taking hold of the cup of wine and the bread of grace. She is truly partaking of His sacrifice. She is confessing her righteousness with a believing heart and is receiving the overwhelming love of God. She is finally feasting and dining on the reality of His death and all that it entails. Accordingly, the door of her heart is opening and her spirit is brimming over with life.

This is a wonderful moment in the Shulammite's journey. And yet we will see that it is linked with an incredible crisis, unlike anything she has experienced before. Thankfully, like any other crisis, this will also come with an unbelievable opportunity.

Fourth Selah

— ◆ —

Before moving forward, it is important that we continue to pause and reflect. The attention span of every new generation seems to shrink with the advent of new technology and stimuli—but do not think that the spirit within any person shrinks, no matter what generation they are from. There is a deep well within all of us that we can sink into regardless of the mind's agitations. Within that well, there is peace untold. The words of Christ are firmly planted there. And all of us have access to that place of peace.

With that in mind, let's briefly return to the shores of Troy. Earlier, we discussed how Jesus goes about unlocking the truth in people's hearts. He sometimes sneaks a Trojan horse of metaphor into us, which can often take years to fully explode. This is because it can take a while for us to *get it*. There is a process. Even though we are unfolding the meaning of these things in plain language, Jesus is speaking in parables, because He knows there is a journey of growth as we embrace these truths. He plants the seed of His Word, hiding it in the soil of parables, which will then lead to a process of sprouting and blossoming.

A lot has been said in the poetry of the Song with its many symbols declaring our righteousness in Christ. Yet as we speak so plainly about the theological and spiritual meanings of the text, there is a word of caution here. Sometimes we are not at the point in time where these truths are ready to manifest. And so I want to encourage the hearts of those who are still journeying in this message of grace. Having patience with yourself is like pouring water onto those planted seeds. And remembering God's warm patience towards you is like the sunlight that will quicken them even further.

And another important note for those who want to bring this message of grace and union to the world: Sometimes things need to come through the backdoor of people's hearts and this can happen through mediums like music and the arts. Not everyone will get the message of grace through a direct explanation of it. As a result, God is raising up writers and artists with a new kind of poetry that will carry the heavenly wisdom of Solomon. Such people will send forth their own Trojan horses of revelation into the hearts of this generation, and in time the multitudes will wake up from the lies as well.

Again, these truths may not even be settling down into your own heart just yet. But that's okay! We can take serious comfort here, because even the Shulammite is not ready to receive it all, which we'll see in the next part.

8

The Wall Beyond the Jordan

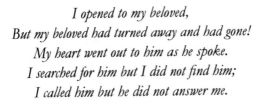

I opened to my beloved,
But my beloved had turned away and had gone!
My heart went out to him as he spoke.
I searched for him but I did not find him;
I called him but he did not answer me.

The watchmen who make the rounds in the city found me,
They struck me and wounded me;
The guardsmen of the walls took away my shawl from me.

I adjure you, O daughters of Jerusalem
If you find my beloved,
as to what you will tell him:
For I am lovesick.
(5:6-8)

nd so the door iinally opened. The Shulammite is learning
to harmoniously join in her Beloved's intimate Song. In a
new position of trust and acceptance, we find that she is
leaving the bed of lies and stepping out onto the waters of divine
union. But as she does this, something unexpected takes place.

Something that appears both contradictory and tragic. Something that will tempt her to doubt everything she has just confessed and sung forth.

The Shulammite opens the door and God is not there.

He is gone.

Through an apparently empty doorframe, the night season of the world stands before her with all its tribulation and difficulty—cold, dark, and empty.

It might seem as though the melody stops at this moment and the Song's beauty fades into the gray fog beyond the door. The volume is abruptly diminished and there appears to be only silence and mist. The Shulammite stands there facing the cold as it whispers to her heart and calls her back onto the bed of a comfortably deceptive sleep.

If we were to place ourselves in her shoes at this point, we might imagine a surge of conflicting emotions rushing to our hearts. Though she has chosen to move beyond the lies of rejection, separation, and a sinful identity, it is quite possible that the force of these old emotions and thought patterns are seeking to come right back into the Shulammite's lap. In the realization of her union with Christ, she has seen the end of all of these things. Yet they now appear to be calling out her name in an attempt to bring sorrow and sleep back to her heart.

Now in this scene it is important to remember that we are still seeing things from the Bride's perspective. Although she has begun to wake up to the full truth of the Gospel, we will find that there is still some haziness in her eyes that keeps her from taking in the full light of Christ's words. We can see this because of the next statement that comes out of her mouth. Even though the Shulammite has just confessed the realities of her union with the

Lord (which includes His promise to never leave her nor forsake her), she now speaks something entirely different. It is like one eye is shut to the gospel while the other eye is open.

"My beloved had turned away and had gone!"

The Shulammite goes back to focusing on her outward experience instead of the underlying truths of the Song. And so her journey progresses in what appears to be two steps forward and one step back. But this is where we can take great encouragement, especially in view of our own fears and setbacks. Though it often appears that we take debilitating steps back in our own journey of grace (steps that sometimes feel like we've completely lost the path), God uses those backward steps only to position our feet into a stronger stance. Because of this, we are poised to leap forward and move further and higher than we have ever gone before. Every step back only builds momentum for the next phase of the journey.

We will find that the Lord is at work and He is bringing forth something that will ultimately launch the Shulammite (and us) into a deeper experience of what had been confessed when myrrh dripped from her hand and the old garments were declared as gone.

Immersed in the Jordan

To grasp the fullness of what is taking place here, let's look once again at a story in the Old Testament that parallels the Song. This time we will explore the story of the Israelites in the book of Joshua when they crossed the Jordan River and entered Canaan.

In Solomon's Song, the Shulammite has been learning to trust the Father's word and is now entering by faith into the Promised Land of a victorious union with Christ. The Israelites parallel this journey in their entrance of the literal Promised Land of Canaan.

Like the Shulammite, they had first wandered in a wilderness of doubt and fear. Even though they had been completely ransomed and delivered from slavery, they believed the Promised Land was too good to be true and stayed in a nomadic cycle of unbelief. They remained slaves in their minds even though reality dictated something else. As a result, they made their bed in the wilderness of Sinai, asleep to the redemption that had been accomplished for them.

But the time emerged for them to finally believe and cross over into the land of their inheritance. This was the moment of "opening the door." They too had been called to feast and dine on the milk, honey, and wine of the Promised Land (see Ex. 3:17). The knock of God through the voices of Moses, Joshua, and Caleb had reached a peak and they finally came into agreement with His truth. Like the Bride in the Song, the Israelites began to get out of bed. In the book of Joshua, the people rise up and approach the Jordan River, which was a natural boundary line separating Canaan from other territories.

This river was in fact the bridging point between the wilderness and the Promise, and so as the people crossed the Jordan you might say that their hands "dripped with myrrh." This is because the crossing of the Jordan is a powerful symbol of our death in Christ. All along, this crossing was a foreshadowing of the church rising out of the wilderness of fear (or the bed of deception) in order to fully embrace the resurrection life of Christ. This is made exquisitely clear in a few small details from the story.

In the third chapter of Joshua, we find that the Israelites first receive very specific instructions from God on how to proceed through the river. The Lord tells the people to wait until the Ark of the Covenant has gone before them. The Ark of the Covenant was the most important item in Israel, representing the very presence of God. It was essentially a throne set upon a wooden chest that was covered in gold and held items of immense importance such as Aaron's budding rod and the Ten Commandments. The Ark was to be carried by twelve priests who would take it into the Jordan River and plant their feet into the water. Once this happened, God said that He would cause the river to stop flowing so that a path would be formed and the people could cross over into Canaan. The story also notes that the Jordan River was overflowing at its banks because they arrived there at the time of year when the floodwaters were at their highest. As the Israelites follow these instructions, the waters of the Jordan stop flowing and a path is formed for the people to walk upon.

So let's unpack the meaning of this story. The Ark of the Covenant represents Christ, the One in whom God's presence is fully manifested and enthroned. The twelve priests exemplify the twelve tribes of Israel, for it is from the womb of Israel that the Messiah was carried into the world. The overflowing floodwaters then speak to us of death and judgment. (This negative element of floodwaters was unpacked in the first study of the Song of the Ages; although it will become even more clear in a moment.) Therefore, the Ark of the Covenant entering into the Jordan represents Jesus the Messiah planting His feet in the grave and entering into death on our behalf. Having gone before us, He made a way for everyone to cross over into a new realm of life and promise. Through His death, the floodwaters of judgment and destruction have been stopped.

Now a very interesting detail is given regarding how and where the waters of the Jordan were stopped. Look at it closely:

> *The water from upstream stopped flowing. It piled up in a heap a great distance away, at **a town called Adam** in the vicinity of **Zarethan**, while the water flowing down to the **Sea of the Arabah** (that is, the Dead Sea) was*

The Song of the Ages: Part II

completely cut off. So the people crossed over...
(Josh. 3:16 NIV)

The meanings of names are very important in the Scriptures, including the names of geographical regions. The water was cut off at a place called "Adam." This is probably the easiest symbol to understand. It speaks to us of our first father Adam. From the place of "Adam," the floodwaters of death and judgment came coursing through humanity, keeping us all from the promise of eternal life and inner freedom. Yet Jesus the Messiah stepped into the waters of death on our behalf. *In so doing, the Lord "cut off" the flow of the curse from Adam.* The entirety of the Adamic nature and its overflowing curse was crucified and judged at the cross.

It is also important to note that the town of Adam was located in the vicinity, or region, of "Zarethan." This word is translated as "their distress." Distress can be defined as extreme anxiety or pain and can also signify wear, tear, and aging. Such is the state (or general "vicinity") in which mankind finds themselves due to Adam's sin. But this power of distress was also cut off through the work of Christ!

Furthermore, the text goes on to say that the waters were stopped between the town of Adam and the "Sea of the Arabah." The word Arabah brings an even greater color and depth into this Old Testament portrait of the work of Christ. The meaning of this word is simply "wilderness." This shows us how the flood of the curse that is sourced from Adam's sin leads only to a *wilderness* of unbelief and separation. Nevertheless, a way has been made to cross through these two places (sin and its consequences) in order to enter into a fruitful and vigorous life. Both Adam and the wilderness have been destroyed at the cross of Jesus. We are now called to a life free from "distress." Though we are often perplexed, we are no longer slaves to sin and despair. Though we may be afflicted, we cannot be crushed or destroyed (see 2 Cor. 4:8-9).

So the crossing of the Jordan is a picture of our immersion into the death of Christ and all of its benefits on our behalf. It is our confession that the old garments of Adam have been washed away in Christ's death! The wilderness is over and the Promised Land is ours for the taking! This is what the Shulammite has been embracing in the previous portion of the Song. She was exiting the bed of the wilderness and walking through the waters of Christ's death, opening the door in order to feast on the resurrection life of Christ—the land flowing with milk and honey!

Jericho's Lies

But then, when she finally did open the door, the Shulammite found darkness. And what happens next to the Israelites after they cross the Jordan reveals a similar thing. We find that the people cross the Jordan but are immediately confronted by a wall—literally. The walls of the city of Jericho stand in their way. After their victorious march through the Jordan, the Israelites "open the door" and find the cold stone walls of Jericho staring in their faces. It looked here as though the way into Canaan's fruitful territory was completely blocked. Even though they were officially in the Promised Land at this point, they were not able to experience its fruits.

You can imagine the legitimate fear and worry that might have hit the hearts of the people at this point. This is where those lies and temptations to go back into the wilderness try to take root in the mind. They are the same doubts that hit the Shulammite when she was confronted with the empty doorframe. They are in fact the same lies that tower over all of humanity, and when a person rises up into the full truth of the Gospel, these lies try to increase the volume of their voice.

The Song of the Ages: Part II

The walls of Jericho basically declare that full access into the Promised Land is an impossibility. When you step out and begin to trust in the love of God and the reality of your union with Christ, the "wall" comes as a follow-up voice that says that this is something you can't fully experience. It says, *even though Jesus paid the price, you can't really receive all the benefits of the cross right now. It may be all right to believe in His sacrifice, but it is another thing to expect to taste the full fruits of that sacrificial work.*

Unfortunately, the coldness and darkness of this present age seems to back up the voice of these lies when we find ourselves in apparently distressing or curse-infused situations. When we see things like sickness and death or a particular stronghold of sin, we start to accept the doubts that scream against Christ's finished work. And when these things persist, an even viler lie begins to fester. We begin to think that God has abandoned us. He has *turned away and gone*. He has left us as orphans to fend for ourselves. We may say that He left us with forgiveness and some small token of His presence here and there, but we don't expect a full and victorious life in His Spirit. We might as well accept the "distress" of an Adamic identity and the resulting curse, limiting the salvation of God to an extended stay in the wilderness with those occasional water breaks.

Of course, we have already covered this dynamic of the Shulammite's journey in many ways. But this lie is now reaching its boiling point and the Shulammite is confronting it head on. Her pursuit of Eden and her awakening to the Gospel of union is now facing its deepest test. We know that God has not abandoned the Shulammite anymore than He abandoned the Israelites. Instead, He is having her face her greatest fear in order to discover once and for all that what was promised in the Jordan (what the Shulammite spoke as she awoke from bed) is more solid and firm than anything else in all of creation. God is building a conquering faith in His loved one that will soon manifest in unstoppable freedom and joy. We will see that God turns these contradicting situations and fears into a rich gasoline that is poured upon the fires of our budding faith.

This momentum-building confrontation is the key part of this portion of the Song. We have described it through two parallel images in the Bible. One is the Israelites standing on the banks of the Jordan and staring at Jericho's wall. The other is the Shulammite standing at the edge of her door and looking into the cold night. Let's go on then and see where this confrontation leads.

The Idolatry of Religion

The Shulammite has indeed started to wake up, but her words about the Beloved turning away have revealed that she is still yielding to a sense of abandonment and separation. She has not yet learned to fully adjust her opened eyes. Though awakening has come, it sometimes takes a while to see clearly after you emerge from a lifelong slumber. And so we find that the Shulammite starts to move about in a state of darkened vision. She begins to turn back to some of what is familiar and comfortable. She starts "searching" again. As in earlier parts of the Song, she is still looking to outward things to confirm and bring about the truths of her Beloved's Song. Her heart is still in the right place, but her initial efforts will be unfruitful.

In her searching, the Bride decides to go back into the city to find her Beloved, which is where she searched earlier in the third chapter of the Song. To give a quick recap of our previous study of this, the city basically represents man's corporate religion, including the organized church. The watchmen are then the leaders of these religious systems. We discussed how there are indeed many good things out in the "city" of the corporate church, but there is also a

117

deep disconnect from the Gospel throughout much of its history and present state.

The problem here, like in Song of Songs 3, is that the Bride continues to look to the system and its leaders to quench her thirst for God's presence. When she looked in the city the last time she did not truly find Him. It wasn't until she moved past the leaders that she found Jesus at the outskirts of the city (see Sgs. 3:4). As said before, this interpretation of the Song is not an attempt to discard the importance of leadership. Rather it is to signify the inestimable value of leaders pointing away from themselves in order to guide a person into true intimacy with Christ.

When the Bride goes searching through the city this time around, the Lord is going to allow her to learn the lesson that she did not learn the first time. We will find that God is exposing her subtle idolatry of the city and its leaders. He will do this by allowing those idols to painfully crumble and break all around her.

Now idolatry is a strong word. It can conjure up images of people bowing in front of golden reptile statues or someone staring mindlessly into a television set day in and day out. But these images do not necessarily reveal the essence of idolatry. For starters, idols are not things you necessarily bow down before and fixate upon. Biblically, they are things that you look to in order to find salvation and deliverance. The idols of Israel were almost always fashioned for this purpose.

Idolatry involves putting your trust in something other than the Lord to find *shalom*—the experience of wholeness and restoration. Consequently, an idol can be something you look to in order to find God. Therefore, religious leaders and good works are prime candidates for idols and many young Shulammites turn to them for that purpose. Now because their hearts are genuinely seeking His Kingdom, Jesus will shed an abundance of grace upon their idol-filled journey. He will even bless them while in the midst of this confused and half-asleep state. (This is what happens to many churches who are walking in God's blessing and miracles but still engage in a deep idolatry of religious systems and leaders.) Nonetheless, the true pursuit of freedom will always lead to an eventual exposure and destruction of these idols, as we will see with the Shulammite in this part of the Song.

Religion's True Colors

It is now apparent that she did not really come to understand the level of darkness behind this idolatry after her previous encounters in the city. Otherwise, she would not return to the city in search of Jesus, the One who is our *shalom*. Of course, religion had certainly shown itself to be burdensome and ineffective, but its true ugliness has not been revealed. But here, when she ends up getting violently wounded by the "guardsmen of the walls," we find this ugliness coming out in full blast.

This picture of the Shulammite getting wounded by the guardsmen of religion can look like many different things in our lives. One of the major ways of getting wounded by religion is through direct persecution. Other ways that religion ends up wounding us is through things like church splits or authoritative abuse, control, and manipulation. Many people think that church splits and religiously abusive situations are the works of the devil. While demonic lies and strongholds are certainly involved, these things are often just the fruit of religion being exposed for what it is. The foundation was not set upon grace, and so the church or the unhealthy relationship eventually crumbled. The abuse, the splits, and the backbiting were inevitable because people were feeding off a false identity of sinfulness all along. They were not secure in the love and grace of God. The finished work of the cross was not at the center of the city.

And so eventually the Lord will allow the systems and its leadership to fall apart. Experiencing the fallout of this can seem like punishment or a demonic attack, but it is often just the healing hand of our Father bringing us into a deeper place of freedom and rest. Since religion only provides a false sense of comfort and safety (which often leads to more burdens and more fear), the destruction of these things will only bring greater liberty—even though it is often disruptive and intense. Once the air clears, joy and rest is the lasting result. As long as one doesn't let bitterness or unforgiveness fester in their hearts during the fallout, the result will always be greater joy and deeper peace (see James 1:2-4 & Heb. 12:11).

Let's reiterate that this is not an attack on any religious structure or on the general idea of leadership. This deals with the pervasive lack of intimacy and grace within a particular structure or leader. That's important to note because there are people who are anti-structure and anti-leadership who have thrown the proverbially baby out with the bathwater in their attempt to find freedom. But what they often find is just a new system of isolation with grand philosophical ideas.

Persecution

The ugliness of religion will manifest itself most clearly through intense persecution. This is also what the Shulammite is experiencing. Earlier in the Song, she was not ready to leave the full boundaries of the system and so there was not as much of a need for the guardsmen of the walls to fight against her. But now that she is serious about leaving those walls, the leaders of the system will up their ante and strengthen their intimidation of her. Indeed, leaders who preside over structures that reinforce the wall of distance and separation will always persecute those who are awakening to the message of grace and union. This is something history affirms over and over again, but it was probably demonstrated most clearly in the life of Jesus.

Jesus was obviously someone walking in a great deal of freedom and grace. This level of freedom directly confronted the religious system that the leaders of Israel were propping up. Christ was seen as a threat to the temple system itself. He offered a way into God's presence that circumvented the Holy of Holies and thus discarded the need for an intermediary priestly system. Both the livelihood and the personal identity of the priests were at stake—a livelihood and identity rooted in centuries of tradition and certain biblical interpretations. (While not approving of their actions, we can at least understand why this was so tough for them.) Furthermore, the religious leaders were also concerned that Rome would come and take away their "city" if this Jesus figure continued in the direction He was going (see Jn. 11:48). This is a good reminder that those who walk in the true grace of God will always challenge and upset those who are comfortable to camp out and stay in a safe and controlled operation.

One of the main types of religious leaders who came against Jesus were the Pharisees. The word Pharisee means "separatist" and thus the person holding this position would often pride themselves in being elevated and *separate* from the "unholy" or "unbelieving" world. The Pharisees were seen as holy and godly people, and many of them indeed were. But when Jesus came around, their true colors came out in full force and the separatist spirit manifested itself in intense violence and hatred. The spirit behind the pride and idolatry of their system was fully exposed.

Do not think that intense persecution will always come from some anti-Christian movement. Some of the most insidious persecution comes right from within the camp of "God's people." There is indeed an intense and violent hatred within Pharisaical

Christianity that is covered up in nice religious language. You can catch a small glimmer of it at times in heated debates on social media or in scathing articles written against those who are promoting grace and freedom in the Spirit of God. Now, of course, the Pharisaical spirit will not let itself be totally revealed. Rather it will say that it speaks harsh words out of the need to balance out grace with "truth." They will say that they are using "tough love" to protect the sheep.

But for those with eyes to see, the same spirit behind these verbal religious attacks is the same one behind the religious persecutions of the past, which often led to the murder of other people groups in the name of Christ. That might sound extreme, but Jesus is the One who said that if you despise someone in your heart then you have already committed murder. That ugly seed of murder lies in the words of many graceless Christians who speak in the name of so-called "truth." Were their own true colors exposed, we might find them in the future shouting at the awakened Bride: "Crucify her!"

Unfortunately, facing this type of persecution is a part of the "awakening" process. This is the path that the Bride is called to walk upon. Paul promised his disciple Timothy that anyone wanting to live godly in Christ (meaning, someone awakened to their union *in Christ* and thus manifesting *godliness*) will face persecution (see 2 Tim. 3:12).

Now the watchmen not only wound the Shulammite, but they also remove her "shawl." The shawl was an outer garment that covered her body. This scene could then represent the religious system removing its spiritual "covering" over the Shulammite. Covering is a word that can often be understood as spiritual oversight and relationship. So the religious system can no longer "cover" or stay in alignment with the Shulammite's journey. She is too far out of the boat. It is not that she has separated herself from fellowship and relationship with the Body of Christ. Rather, she has been rejected by those who are propping up the system and not embracing the true Spirit of grace. These persecutors may be true disciples of Jesus, but like young James and John they do not know what spirit they are speaking from (see Lk. 9:51-55).

Fellowship in His Sufferings

As we have seen over and over again, the tale of the Shulammite is the tale of the church throughout history. There have been innumerable times where a certain faction within the Bride of Christ receives a fresh and restorative revelation from the Holy Spirit and the wider group of which they are a part begins to persecute and shun them. This scene is thus demonstrating church history and how the corporate system has treated those who have been awakening to the message of freedom. Nonetheless, this persecution and shunning has always been a key part of forward progression in the Body of Christ. God has turned around all our crazy religiosity and used it to propel His Bride toward full maturity in Christ.

It is also important to understand here that there is a fine line between those who are forced out of their "covering" in the name of freedom, and those who leave out of a spirit of rebellion and bitterness. Some leave the covering of religious institutions not because they seek true intimacy and connection with Jesus, but for other motives that are hidden behind super-spiritual and elitist language. Many times they have just been wounded and have deep issues with authority and cannot stomach being in an environment that breeds even the slightest level of control. If this is the case, such people may develop a martyr complex in the name of "freedom from religion." But really they have little understanding about true grace and intimacy. (Remember that Jesus stretched out

His arms and died for the Pharisees just as much as He gave His life for the orphan and the widow. Let's not speak a word against a "Pharisee" until we can do the same.)

So let's wrap up this discussion and move forward with the Shulammite's story. We have seen that she is encountering several things that all resemble the imagery of the walls of Jericho. The voices of doubt and fear continue to bellow at her while at the same time she is being confronted by those who "guard" those walls. Just as Christ was rejected and His literal clothing was removed, so His Bride is encountering the same thing in her journey out of religion. This is part of what it means to have fellowship with Jesus in His sufferings. You are sharing and participating in rejection from the religious system while also having the voice of darkness attack your identity (as Satan did to Christ in the wilderness). Darkness comes and whispers that God is not present, that He has forsaken you, and that His promises are not truly accessible. Ultimately, it makes you question if you are truly a son and daughter of the King.

Not Giving Up

Thankfully, a seed of glory resides in the Shulammite just as it does in each one of our hearts. It is this that prevents her from giving up. The same spirit in Christ that raised Him from the dead dwells within her and causes her to rise from this place of shame, doubt, and wounding. Even in this state of persecution and fear, she continues to seek after the Lord.

She turns next to the daughters of Jerusalem and asks them for help in finding the presence of Jesus. Remember that the daughters of Jerusalem can represent all who are from the womb of Israel, whether spiritually or naturally. In the Song it often speaks of other people who are not yet awakened to the Gospel of grace. And so we see that while her covering is removed from religious systems, she has not removed herself from fellowship within the Body of Christ. She is in relationship with other believers, even those who are not as spiritually mature or understanding as she. She turns to them and gives a desperate request.

I adjure you, O daughters of Jerusalem. If you find my
Beloved, tell Him that I am lovesick!

The Shulammite is basically asking them to pray for her. Her request is that if they encounter the presence of Jesus that they ask Him to come to her again. She is of course asking for something she already has. She is *still* adjusting her eyes. Her heart is in a frantic state and she is looking for the peace and presence of Jesus to bring His Word of truth to her once again.

The Heavenly Axe

We will look at their response in the next chapter. For now, we will return once more to the Jordan River. This time we will look at something that happened there over 1500 years after the Israelites crossed over between the town of Adam and the Sea of the Arabah. A millennia and a half later, this river continued to be the key setting in which the music of God's great Song unfolded. There in that same river stood a man named John who came to prepare the spiritual instruments and dust off the seats so that the musicians of God's orchestra could come and release the Song of the Ages in full blast.

John the Baptist stood in the Jordan River right before the ministry of Christ kicked off and he declared an end to the old system of fear and religion. He spoke to the Pharisees, the guardsmen of the walls, and he prophesied: "The axe is already laid at the root of the trees; therefore every tree that does not bear good fruit is cut down and thrown into the fire" (Matt. 3:10). John was prophesying the literal destruction of the walls of the temple in 70 A.D. as well the spiritual destruction of the religious system that these watchmen were guarding and supporting. He promised that a Messiah would come and take the fire out of the Holy of Holies and put it into the hearts of everyday people.

What will begin to unfold in the remainder of chapter five is the axing deathblow to Jericho's walls—walls that have long stood in front of the Shulammite's own heart. This is similar to the axe mentioned in John's words, which would cut at the deepest roots of religion's lies and intimidation. This axe has struck her own heart in the coming of the Gospel and the knocking of Christ's hand. We will now start to see the final adjustment of her eyes as she continues to wake up and rise into her complete and shining stature.

And it will all begin with a simple question from the daughters of Jerusalem.

9

Who is He?

————•◆•————

What kind of beloved is your beloved,
O most beautiful of women?
What kind of beloved is your beloved,
that thus you adjure us?

My beloved is dazzling and ruddy,
outstanding among ten thousand.
His head is like gold, pure gold;
His locks are like clusters of dates
and black as the raven.
His eyes are like doves besides streams of water,
bathed in milk, and reposed in their setting.
(5:9-12)

Sometimes it takes a simple question to open up the eyes and stir up a sleeping heart. A good question has a way of illuminating our present way of thinking and can thus open a pathway into a new direction. Such questions have a way of letting the responder discover the truth for themselves, as opposed to just being told the answer. This is something every skilled teacher and counselor recognizes at the fundamental level of their work.

Once Jesus asked a good, simple question to His disciples as the time approached for His death upon Calvary, when everything would change and the disciples would have to walk in a new dimension of faith and love (see Matt. 16:13-16.). This was a question that resembled the one that we are seeing the daughters of Jerusalem ask the Shulammite. Jesus began this question by first asking an anteceding one.

"Who do people say that I am?"

The disciples spoke up and gave their Lord a wide array of responses regarding the current opinions of the masses. Some said He was a prophet, others said He was Elijah, others John the Baptist resurrected. Jesus listened to their responses but then moved to the heart of the matter.

"Who do you say that I am?"

In one sentence, Jesus got at the crux of why they were even following Him and what this relationship and journey was all about. The timing of such a question was appropriate because the road was becoming quite dangerous, filled with many shadows of doubt and persecution. Multitudes of people were beginning to question the validity and outcome of Christ's ministry. Even John the Baptist had doubts about Christ in the days before his execution. Moreover, the religious leadership was mounting a strong opposition to Jesus and anyone who dared to follow Him.

After soaking in the question, Peter eventually spoke up on behalf of the other disciples and gave an answer that would bring immense joy to Jesus (though He would also acknowledge that it was the very grace of God that allowed Peter to come up with such an answer).

"You are the Christ. The Son of the living God," Peter said.

In a moment of divine inspiration, Peter declared the full identity of Christ, noting His divinity as the Son of God as well as His sacrificial and kingly calling as the Christ or, in the Hebrew, *the Messiah*—the Anointed One. Everything about Jesus is wrapped up in this response and it also gives the very reason why the disciples are on this road and why it was worth continuing to walk down.

The Bride is confronted with a similar question from the daughters of Jerusalem upon her request to help her find the Beloved Shepherd. "What *kind* of beloved is your beloved," they ask.

At this point, they are blown away by the Bride's persistence and love. They ask her what it is about Jesus that gives her this resolve; that regardless of the persecution or her travels through dark clouds of doubt, she continues to fix her attention upon Him. *Who is He, really?* they wonder. *This person seems like more than just another shepherd or good friend.*

The Bride is forced to answer this pivotal question, and in answering it, we will see that the last walls of any remaining sleep start to crumble around her. Her eyes will widen with each response until a full vision of His glory begins to dawn. We will find that each response she gives to the question is a different aspect of the same answer. It is like seven different blows of a trumpet announcing the same glorious message…

The Fall of Jericho

The image of a trumpet brings us back to the Israelite's confrontation at Jericho. Thankfully, their story did not end in front of the wall just as the story of the Shulammite does not end in front of an empty doorframe. After the Israelites stared up at the large and ominous walls of Jericho, having borne the weight of whatever emotions and thoughts came rushing to their minds, they began to move forward with the next set of instructions they received from the Lord—instructions that continue to paint an Old Testament portrait of the work of Christ.

They are told to march around the city for seven days with seven priests carrying seven trumpets right in the midst of the people. On the seventh day, the people were to march seven more times. After the final march, they were commanded to sound the trumpets. At this, the people were then to release a shout to the Lord, which would bring down the walls of the city. They would then be able to take hold of the full fruit of the Promised Land, which they had already entered after crossing the Jordan. Upon following these directives, all of this happened exactly as God said it would (see Josh. 6).

It is obvious here that God wanted the Israelites (as well as all the readers of His Word) to focus on the number seven. As another reminder from our previous study in the Song of Songs, the number seven is a symbol of perfection and completion. It is why the seventh day of the week is a day of rest, for it celebrates God's completed work of creation. Coinciding with this, the number seven is a symbolic reference to the finished work of Christ and His perfect redemption of humanity. The work of the cross released an eternal Sabbath rest, because it is there that God completed His work of the new creation (see Heb. 4:9). We looked into all of this when we tuned our ears to the Beloved's words, when He sang about seven different facets of the Bride's beauty (see Sgs. 4:1-5). Each facet declared a different dimension of her perfection, showcasing the fact that she is indeed the mirror image of her Beloved because of His work on the cross.

Who is He?

The seven blows of the trumpets also represent a victorious proclamation of the finished work of Christ. The symbolic march around Jericho and the concurring trumpet-blasting was not giving us a picture of some religious work we need to copy in order to break down the enemy's walls. The complete peculiarity of this sevenfold act should actually point us away from our performance and abilities. Instead, it should lift our eyes unto something of much higher significance—something that would not become clear until the full light of the Gospel shone forth. The marching and the blowing of the trumpets came right on the heels of other strange things that occurred as the people left slavery and entered into Canaan. Each one of these events are also like different facets of the same diamond, all pointing to one reality.

Whether it was the Lamb's blood on the people's doorposts, the splitting of the Red Sea, the march through parted water in between Adam and Arabah, or the entire army being circumcised, all of these events tie together into one message. It is like wave after wave of the same ocean water coming to knock down the walls of darkness and separation. These incidents do not give some strange war strategy that we need to embody in order to overcome the enemy. Instead, all these stories show us that the war is already won! Each of them speak of the great Warrior, Jesus, who defeated all darkness at the cross.

The idea of an impenetrable city being defeated through marching and trumpeting is so utterly ridiculous and counter-intuitive that it shows us that victory does not lie in our hands. Victory lies in the work of the Lamb. His is the blood on the doorposts while the people were still in Egypt. His body is the true entity that was pierced and split as seen in the image of Moses piercing the Red Sea with his staff. He is the Ark of the Covenant that sank into the waters of death so that we might be freed from the curse of Adam. Furthermore, the circumcision of the whole camp by one man named Joshua is a picture of our spiritual circumcision (the removal of our corrupted self) by the one Man Jesus (see Josh. 5:3). And finally, the seven blasts of the trumpets show the people advancing through a position of Sabbath rest— celebrating and resting in the complete redemption of Christ.

These trumpets that the Israelites used were ram's horns, or *shofars*, which comes from the same Hebrew word as "Jubilee." In fact, the words *shofar* and *Jubilee* are really one and the same. Jubilee speaks of redemption, which is obviously what Christ's work is all about. He has defeated the powers of darkness and removed our sinfulness—the old garments of Adam. He has redeemed us back into our original identity as the sons and daughters of God. There is truly no wall that can stop us from experiencing the abundant life and fruitfulness of His Kingdom within. The only "wall" that hinders us is the bewitching veil over the eyes that keeps us from seeing and accepting the extravagant goodness of Jesus. (Hence the need for God to reinforce this message all over His Word as He sends wave after wave of the same truth to remind us of it.)

The culmination of the people's marching led to a great and final shout. This is a picture of the release of faith. The week-long marching and trumpeting is like a period of time where faith and truth is built up and reinforced in the heart until it finally overflows in a confident and triumphant confession (see Rom. 10:10). They were in full agreement with God's Word and their shout was the sound of that agreement. It was this expression of inner faith that led to the complete shattering of Jericho's walls. It was the final wave crashing upon the shores of deception.

A Radiant Red Diamond

Let's come back to the Shulammite. We've seen that she faces a wall of fear and persecution, which demands that she let go of her trust in God. As a result, she's taken another step back into some continued blurriness of vision and faith. As she gropes in the dark, the young Bride requests help from the daughters of Jerusalem, who respond to her request with a question that completely refocuses her heart. She turns her attention away from this perceived darkness and shifts it back onto the Person of Jesus. In so doing, the Shulammite will begin to blast the trumpet sounds of grace and freedom (which will lead to a final shout of agreement in the sixth chapter of the Song). In verse ten, she responds to the daughters of Jerusalem by first summarizing everything to come. To continue with the analogy of a jewel, the Shulammite's response is like one diamond, which she will turn this way and that, exposing different facets of its glory.

She starts by giving the other women an overview of the whole diamond, declaring that her beloved is "dazzling and ruddy, outstanding among ten thousand." The word "dazzling" speaks of sunlight and radiance. This attribute reveals Jesus as the One who is the express image and radiance of the living God. He is the very light of heaven who fully reveals the glory of the Father. This divine description is then followed by a more human word—*ruddy*. This word is *adom* in the Hebrew, which is very closely related to the Hebrew word for Adam. These two words put together show that she is stating the overall identity of Jesus as both the Son of God and the Son of Man. He is a perfect and breathtaking human, but He is also the radiance of God's glory, the Creator's eternal Son.

The word *adom* holds another important element. It can also refer to something that is stained red. "Ruddy" is a word used to describe someone with redness of face, which was a sign of health and vibrancy. This is yet another clear reference to the atoning work of Christ as our High Priest. As perfect Man and true God, Jesus allowed His body to be stained with His own blood to redeem us back to the Father. With this one statement, the Shulammite is giving a visual picture of how the book of Hebrews describes the Messiah, Jesus of Nazareth:

> *And He is the **radiance of His glory** and the exact representation of His nature, and upholds all things by the word of His power. When He had made **purification of sins,** He sat down at the right hand of the Majesty on high.*
> *(Heb. 1:3)*

The glory of the Beloved is wrapped up in two words— *dazzling and ruddy*—because His glory is manifested through His divine nature as well as His atoning sacrifice. As a result, He stands out "among ten thousand," for He alone embodies these glorious qualities. In a massive sea of people, He would be easy to spot. In saying that He stands out like this, the Bride is declaring that Jesus is more than what the crowds might say. He is more than a prophet, more than a good man, and more than a great teacher. Jesus, the Beloved, is the One who upholds all of creation. He is God in the flesh, the Anointed One who carries our sins and brings us into union with the Father. The Bride is giving the same answer to the daughters of Jerusalem that Peter gave to Jesus.

Who is the Beloved?

He is the Christ, the Son of the living God!

It is from this opening response that she will now proceed to describe seven different facets of His glory, all of which declare this same overall identity. To return to the rainbow analogy, all these qualities are like seven different colors that come together in the white light of His glory as the Son of God and the Son of Man. In the pages ahead, we will look at each shade of His being and allow these colorful descriptions to soak into our own being. Let your heart be ready then, fully expectant and poised for the radiance of His glory to wash over you as you listen to the great trumpet blasts bursting from the Shulammite's lips…

1: A Head of Gold and Black

The Shulammite starts with the most standout and crowning feature of a person—the head.

"His head is like gold, pure gold," she says.

Throughout the Scriptures, gold is a symbol of divinity. In comparing His head to gold, the Bride is then deepening her affirmation of Christ's divinity. The Shulammite begins these trumpet blasts by specifying the exact reason why Jesus stands out among ten thousand, which again parallels the response of Peter. Jesus Christ is actually God Himself. And He is not just special and divine gold. She emphatically adds the phrase *pure gold*. In other words, He is not some special divine entity among many others, or another separate deity underneath Yahweh. Jesus is God Himself, through and through, without any deviation or corruption. As you can see, the divinity of Christ is absolutely foundational as we grow in our knowledge of Him.

But the Shulammite does not stop with this description of pure and perfect divinity. The head, she says, is crowned with waves of hair that are "black as the raven." While the head of gold speaks of His divinity, the raven black hair points out His sin-bearing work. Besides a few positive scenes, ravens are rarely pictured as good symbols in the Bible. They are often paired up with vultures and speak of death and decay. Furthermore, the word "black" is the same word the Shulammite used to describe herself in the beginning of the Song when she compared herself to the cracked tents of Kedar. This had spoken of her identification with a sinful nature. And so in this poetic imagery of gold and black, Jesus is seen as the One who has taken our death-dealing sinfulness upon

His beautiful and perfect being. And He will forever be known as the One who did this. Even in His resurrected glory, Jesus's hands still bear the holes from His sacrifice (see Jn. 20:27).

All of this brings us back to her opening statement of Jesus being dazzling and ruddy. The Song is a melody that continues to provide repeated and varied poetry declaring this very simple concept. But simple as it is, this reality is infinitely deep and can be described and celebrated through a multitude of different lyrics and sounds. The absolute beauty of Jesus is wrapped up in His work on the cross. Sometimes you can't see the true beauty of a person until you see them in action. This is exactly what the cross accomplished. It exposed the infinite and precious love within God. It brought it into our vision like a light shining into a dark chest to expose the most precious treasure in all creation.

The Apostle John explained this with utter clarity: "This is how God showed his love among us: He sent his one and only Son into the world that we might live through him" (1 Jn. 4:9 NIV). The word "showed" is the Greek word *phaneroo*, which has to do with *illumination*. The work of Christ is the light that shines upon the beautiful love in God's heart. You cannot see the completeness of His glory without looking at the cross of Jesus. The golden glory of His head (His divine glory) is covered in the beauty of His death (the raven-black hair).

This is the truest response to the question, *what kind of Beloved is your beloved...*

He is the God who laid down His life for us.

2: Dove's Eyes

Next, she turns her attention to His eyes and gives a similar description that Jesus gave of her own eyes in the fourth chapter of the Song.

Who is He?

"His eyes are like doves beside streams of water, bathed in milk, and reposed in their setting."

Once again, this image relates to the Spirit of God who came in the form of a dove at Jesus's baptism in the Jordan. By extending the description of the doves to their placement and setting ("beside streams of water"), the Shulammite is making this connection to the Jordan River. Christ's vision—pure, holy, and united with the Spirit of God—finds its resting place in the waters of grace. As we've seen before, the Jordan River embodies the baptism of Christ, where He took away our guilt-ridden garments. By saying that His vision is situated by streams of water, the Shulammite is showing us that Jesus has only one frame of reference when He looks at us: *we are righteous and redeemed.* When He sees us, His eyes are filled with a peaceful delight, for they only behold innocence and perfection.

And not only are these doves situated by streams of water, but they are also "bathed in milk." The reference to baptism continues here since it is a form of spiritual bathing or cleansing. We also know that milk represents the "word of righteousness" (see Heb. 5:13). This is the message of our righteousness in Jesus. By saying that His eyes have been bathed in milk, the Bride is still saying that His vision is completely inundated with righteousness. Standing "beside streams of water" and being "bathed in milk" are two sides of the same coin. Christ's eyes have been washed in the milk of the Word and in the baptism of the Jordan River. They now see us and everything else through a filtering lens of holiness.

This revelation should bring us an immense peace, especially when we think of other biblical images of Christ, such as His eyes of blazing fire (see Rev. 1:14). Theologians and preachers sometimes interpret this imagery to denote a fire of fearful judgment. But this is not the case when we incorporate the whole counsel of the Word and the revelation of Solomon's Song. His eyes certainly contain a fire of judgment—*but this fire judges us as holy and beloved.* It is a fire of intense and unquenchable love. The only things that burn away in the light of these flames are our false identities and the heavy burden of shame that comes with them. Thus, when the apostle John encounters these eyes of fire and falls to the ground before Him, the first thing Jesus tells him is to not be afraid! There is nothing to fear even in the fierce fires of His gaze (see Rev. 1:17). Those eyes of fire in Revelation are the same ones we're seeing in the Song of the Lamb which rest beside streams of grace.

The Shulammite's heart is once again brought into deep comfort as she remembers the way Jesus sees her. His eyes are not darting out with accusation; rather, they are "reposed in their setting." In other words, His vision is still and calm. He is not taken aback by anything He sees. He looks at us and sees our full potential and true nature. And there is nothing that can sway Him from this perspective.

10

Emotions, Rivers, and Thrones

———— • ❖ • ————

His cheeks are like a bed of balsam,
Banks of sweet-scented herbs;
His lips are lilies dripping with liquid myrrh.
His hands are rods of gold set with beryl;
His abdomen is carved ivory inlaid with sapphires.
His legs are pillars of alabaster set on pedestals of pure gold
(5:13-15a)

Y ou can imagine that a new strength is beginning to return
to the Shulammite as she continues to release these trumpet
blasts of the Gospel. The wall in front of her is beginning to
shake and something is starting to change. Though we do not yet see
the full destruction of this wall, we can feel its approach. Like seeing
a sharp flash of lightning and knowing that thunder is imminent, we
can be confident that great change is about to occur as we behold these
words. The Shulammite continues to turn her attention away from
herself and gazes upon the glory of Jesus.

Soon she will see with eyes wide open that His glory is her very own.

3: A Fragrant Disposition

The Bride moves next to a description of the Lord's "cheeks." In comparing this part of His face to a "bed of balsam" and "banks of sweet-scented herbs," we are immediately given a picture of the sweet joy and warmth within the temperament of Christ. A person's cheeks are where their emotional expressions are made visible. The word for cheeks can also be translated as the jawbone, which is the area of the face where one's smile is expanded and chiseled out. This paints a lively image of Jesus, one that is brimming over with smiles and merriment. Overall, the resemblance of Jesus's cheeks to flowerbeds and herbs gives us a warm impression of His goodness.

A flowerbed of balsam and a hill of sweet-scented herbs are delightful places to be. The imagery exudes a sense of absolute comfort and invitation. There are no thorns or foul smells to keep you back nor is there any threat lurking in the shadows. Such is the inviting nature of God's personality. For all of His thundering and majestic depictions in the Bible (a testament to His power and strength), there is an equally strong depiction of warmth and comfort within His presence.

This shouldn't surprise us, because the "fruit" of God's Holy Spirit—His very Presence—is marked by qualities like gentleness, kindness, and joy! For some reason, however, it's been hard for some in the church to pick up on this. Unfortunately, there is an ingrained tendency within many people to think of the Lord as cold and stoic. They visualize Him with statue-like qualities and a fierce and stone-like expression. We see hints of this in many cinematic depictions of Jesus as well as medieval images of Him and His

140

Father. Such images arise from a deeply flawed conception of God, which is rooted more in mythology than Scripture. Imagining God laughing or walking around with an infectious smile does not come natural to the human mind. Man's corporate thinking has been hypnotized by lies about the Father, branded and broadcasted by the walls of fear and religion, which carry false paintings and etchings of God's face upon their bouldering scaffold. It is before these images that the Shulammite blasts the trumpet of her poetry.

People will agree theologically that Jesus loves us with a passionate love, but there is often a deep disconnect in the actual personality and drive behind that passion. Devoid of warmth, joy, and friendliness, the passion of this love becomes a stony religious idea and not a real revelation in the heart that promotes intimacy and safety in God's presence. Some might say that such statements exalt emotion over truth in the understanding of God's love, but that is a pointless assumption. Though many good books have been written about the significance of truth, commitment and action within our understanding of love, we can run the danger of completely throwing out the value of emotion. Some forget that God designed our emotions when He made us *in His image*. He is an emotional God—in the healthiest and liveliest kind of way! Greek and stoic influences might tempt us to minimize passionate emotion, but we must resist this at all costs. God's love holds all of these elements together, whether commitment, action, or emotion.

The implications of seeing God without a warm and friendly disposition are bigger than you can imagine. Let's do a simple thought experiment to demonstrate this. Imagine that you are approaching a stranger to converse in a potentially intimate subject. Depending on your level of comfort in social situations this could be a relatively difficult task in and of itself. But then imagine approaching two different kinds of strangers. One has a stoic and even harsh look on their face. The other has a warm and inviting smile with an overall disposition of joy and kindness. With whom would you be more likely to engage? Who would you approach with less of a guarded tightness in your chest?

Most people would obviously be quicker to engage the friendly and smiling individual while maintaining some physical (and emotional) distance from the other stranger. This little experiment has tremendous consequences for our relationship with God. Engaging in conversation, particularly the intimate and close kind, is one of the main ways that the fires of relationship are forged. So as we see the cheerful and friendly disposition of God, and as that image is rooted in our consciousness, it will produce a deeper level of confidence in us. It will build the fires of an intimate dialogue with the Lord. We will be less guarded around Jesus and will thus allow more of His truth and presence to permeate our hearts. This is why the revelations of Christ in the Song of Songs are so paramount. Inner transformation is inevitable when you realize the true disposition of the Trinity.

All of this takes the theological truths of the Shulammite's opening answer to the daughters of Jerusalem (His divinity and sacrifice) and brings them into a deeply human context—one that you can reach out and touch. The declaration of Jesus as "the Christ, the Son of the Living God"—the One who is the radiance of God's glory and the perfect Man—these are not just philosophical concepts describing some ethereal entity in the sky who promises to be with us on our journey in a mysterious and vague way. This is all describing a very real personality, a Person who actually does walk with us and invites us to rest under the sweet rays of His smile. This invitation comes from a place of incredible friendliness and joy. This is the truth of who Christ is. The person who knows this deep in their hearts can enjoy an intimacy with God that is unparalleled.

Emotions, Rivers, and Thrones

4: *Lips of Lilies and Myrrh*

From the fragrant description of His warm and inviting nature, the Shulammite then announces that Jesus's lips are "lilies dripping with liquid myrrh." Just like the earlier descriptions of the Shulammite's own lips, this feature speaks to the words that come from Christ's mouth. Even more than that, it describes the *essence* and *theme* of His words.

So once you approach this wonderfully fragrant and inviting Man (whose smile would light up the darkest night), you are next confronted by the contents of His speech. Now just as you can gain a sense of the overall state of a person's heart by the disposition of their face, you can also learn the detailed contents of their heart by listening to what comes out of their mouth. When a person consistently talks about a certain subject, you are given a clear window into their soul and the thoughts of their mind. Therefore, if a person is passionate about something, you could draw a similar analogy as the Shulammite by comparing their lips to the thing they are passionate about. For instance, if a person is obsessed about healthy eating and exercise, you might say that their lips are "like a gym dripping with dietary wisdom."

When the Shulammite says that Jesus's lips are like lilies dripping with myrrh, you have to remember what both of these symbols represent, for that reveals the contents of His speech. First recall that we are indeed the lily of the valley (see Sgs. 2:1). God compares His children to lilies others times throughout the Scriptures as well (see Hos. 14:5). Therefore, when Jesus's lips are likened to lilies, this shows us that *we are* the focus of His speech and thus the content of His heart. Solomon gives a clear vision of what his father David wrote about in the Psalms:

How precious are your thoughts about me, O God.
They cannot be numbered!

143

The Song of the Ages: Part II

I can't even count them; they outnumber the grains of sand!
(Ps. 139:17-18a NLT)

The Song of Solomon should hopefully be confronting every doubt you might have concerning Jesus's passionate love toward you. If you think we're going overboard with some of these descriptions and becoming too *us-centric*, then you only have a small idea of the heart behind Jesus when He went to the cross. Such a thought betrays a lack of understanding behind the motivation of that event. If that is you, however, please don't feel bad about this. A vast amount of people have no idea as to the true nature of Jesus's passion. Many are content to believe that Jesus died for us out of some divine obligation to God's holiness and this dry theology satisfies their understanding of salvation. There is obviously some truth to that, but many people drastically miss the *heart* of it all.

Jesus is obsessed with us!

When we fell away from our glory in Him and moved toward a false identity of shame, Jesus had already purposed to do whatever it took to gain us back, even if that meant going to the cross. This was not some obligatory action, but was rather a passionate act motivated by the joy in His heart. And so you can see this joy within Him when you look at the content of His lips—*us*.

We are the lilies of the valley who are dripping with the myrrh of His sacrifice. That simply means that we are beautiful lilies who are covered in the blood of Jesus. We now drip with His righteousness. No matter where we go or what we do, we are surrounded by the truth of His death: our old nature has died and we are now innocent, redeemed, and pure! When God thinks those innumerable thoughts toward us—thoughts that "outnumber the grains of sand"—it is always in the context of this reality!

5: *Majestic Hands*

Next, she moves her attention to the Lord's hands. There's a lot that can be communicated through the imagery of a person's hands. Besides being a symbol of work and labor, a person's hands also offer strength and help to others. With our hands we serve and touch the people around us. Hands are how we connect with other people at the fundamental level of a handshake or the deeper embrace of a hug as the hands extend around another person and draw them in.

The Shulammite says Jesus's hands are "rods of gold set with beryl." Once again, the gold speaks to the divine glory laden in Christ. When Jesus touches us, it is with the very hand of God. The same hand that established all of creation is the same hand that establishes us and offers us help and service. A true understanding of this is central to living a life of peace and confidence. This deserves a pausing *selah* in and of itself.

Other translations of this verse state that the Bride is comparing the Beloved's hands to *rings of gold*, which is a more accurate reflection of the Hebrew. The image this conveys is of the fingers being curled, such as when they are wrapped around a scepter or around another person's hand. In this position, they resemble a large ring of gold and the fingernails are like precious stones of beryl set within it. These gemstones reveal an ever more subtle message hidden in the Shulammite's poetry. In the Bible, precious stones often represent God's people. The imagery shows us then that God will extend His helping hand through the medium of His people. We are the gemstones within His hands and feet and thus a physical source of God's support to the world.

Remember that at this point the Shulammite has moved from describing different features of the "head" and is now focusing on the body. In many ways, this is her beginning to not only describe

145

Jesus in and of Himself, but also the church, *which is His body*. She is starting to describe the beauty of His nature manifested through His people. The divine hand of God longs to establish, strengthen and uphold the world, and He has chosen to do this through the precious stones of His saints.

The image of precious stones also speaks to the work of apostles and prophets, which are the "foundation stones" of the church (compare Eph. 2:20 and Rev. 21:14 for further clarity on this). This opens up a deeper discussion of how God has chosen to build up and strengthen His body. This work involves what people often refer to as the "five-fold ministry." Paul writes about five gifts of grace that God has given to His church in order to strengthen her and build her up.

> *But to each one of us grace was given according to the measure of Christ's gift...*

> *And He gave some as apostles, and some as prophets, and some as evangelists, and some as pastors and teachers, for the equipping of the saints for the work of service, to the building up of the body of Christ.*
> *(Eph. 4:7, 11-12)*

This vividly connects back to the five fingernails being set like precious beryl within the hand of God. Paul's words reveal that the hand of the Lord will strengthen and establish His church through these five different gifts. The analogy of a "ring of gold" then speaks of the divine authority behind these gifts (an authority marked by grace, servanthood, and example—not hierarchy and control). Now of course the Lord uses all of the gemstones of His saints to offer a helping hand to the suffering world. In fact, gifts such as the apostle or teacher are only meant to help others shine with the precious light of Christ that is already within them. "Equipping" is primarily about awakening people to their identity in Christ and to the gifts already bursting inside of them.

This connection to the apostolic and prophetic dimension of the Lord's work is an important dynamic to see. Part of this scene involves the Bride coming into a deeper revelation of these ministries and their proper functioning in the light of the finished work of Christ. This is part of her own journey of awakening and it is certainly the case with the Shulammite's collective journey in modern history. In the past few decades, there has been a growing renewal of understanding regarding these five ministries in the church, especially the gifts of the apostle and prophet. While there have been many abuses and misunderstandings of these gifts, this is only because the complete Gospel of grace has often been a missing part of the journey. But the full message of our union with Christ will set the five-fold ministry in its proper place. As a result, maturity amongst the Bride will accelerate like never before.

Though a whole intensive study can be done on this, we will leave it at that for now and move to the next part of the Bride's response to the daughters of Jerusalem.

6: *The Innermost Being*

The next feature she describes is the Lord's "abdomen." Once again, a better translation can be found in other versions of the text, such as the King James, which uses the word "bowels." The concept of a person's bowels comes from a Hebrew word that symbolizes somebody's innermost being. It speaks to the spiritual depths within a man or woman. This is what the Shulammite is beginning to describe in this part of the text. She is talking about Jesus's innermost being. With this in mind, we will look at the two descriptive features given to this part of His make-up. The

Shulammite first compares it to "carved ivory" and then says that it is "inlaid with sapphires"—blue gemstones of great worth.

Remember that Solomon is writing though the inspiration of the Holy Spirit and is drawing upon personal images as he pens the text. When he writes about carved ivory there is one particular thing that we might assume he's thinking about. Solomon had a personal throne that he most likely sat upon every day (and may have even sat upon it when thinking about the lyrics of this Song). This throne was specifically made of *carved ivory* (see 1 Kgs. 10:18).

Now this becomes very interesting when you study the imagery of sapphires as well. When you survey the entire Bible, you find that different prophets had visions of the throne that God sits upon. Several of them compared it to the *sapphire* gemstone (see Ez. 1:26 & Ex. 24:10). Therefore, the Scriptures compare the heavenly throne of God to sapphire while also stating that the earthly throne of Solomon was made of ivory. The connection between these two symbols, which are paired together in this verse, is not an accident. Both descriptions converge into one image of Jesus's authority, which is obviously what a throne represents.

Jesus is the Son of Man who reigns over the earth (represented by Solomon's ivory throne) and is also the Son of God who reigns over the heavens (represented by God's sapphire throne). Solomon simply melds these two images into one: *the sapphire is laid within the ivory*. We see here that heaven and earth are joined together through the kingship of Jesus Christ. In a moment, we will see how this also reveals God's plan for His heavenly authority to be embedded and released through our earthly lives. But in order to get there, we need to first answer a certain question:

Why is this picture of the heavenly and earthly throne centered around Jesus's abdomen—His "innermost being"?

Emotions, Rivers, and Thrones

To answer this, we have to look at a few more Scriptures, which will weave together and form a beautiful tapestry of revelation. We'll start in the New Testament. In John 7, Jesus Himself talks about a person's bowels, or the innermost being. The King James uses the word "belly," which is referring to the same feature of the body that the Shulammite is describing in the Song. Jesus said that our innermost being is the host of God's Holy Spirit. From the place of our "belly," the rivers of the Spirit spring forth:

> *He who believes in Me, as the Scripture said, 'From his innermost being will flow rivers of living water.'" But this He spoke of the Spirit, whom those who believed in Him were to receive; for the Spirit was not yet given, because Jesus was not yet glorified.*
> *(Jn. 7:38-39)*

So the Spirit of God flows from a person's innermost being. But how does this all connect to the imagery of thrones? This will become clearer when we look at the books of Revelation and Daniel. Here are two relevant verses from each book:

> *Then he showed me **a river of the water of life**, clear as crystal, coming from **the throne of God** and of the Lamb.*
> *(Rev. 22:1)*

> *I kept looking until **thrones** were set up, and the Ancient of Days took His seat;*
> *His vesture was like white snow and the hair of His head like pure wool.*
> ***His throne** was ablaze with flames, its wheels were a burning fire. **A river of fire was flowing and***

149

coming out from before Him.
(*Dan.* 7:9-10a)

So in John's gospel we learn that the river of life flows from a person's innermost being. In Daniel and Revelation, we see that the same river flows from God's throne. When the Shulammite looks at Jesus she is seeing both of these realities colliding together. She is being given a vision of the reign and authority of God, which operates and flows by the Holy Spirit. In other words, Jesus's rule is marked by the flow of His Spirit. While human leaders sit on their "ivory thrones" and exert their power through military or intellectual strength, Jesus exerts His strength by the Spirit of holiness and grace. The "sapphire" reign of God is embedded within Him. This is the only true way to lead and reign. And, according to Revelation and Daniel, this reign simultaneously operates as a purifying fire of righteousness as well as a stream of life-giving water.

Now the passage in Daniel also says that multiple "thrones" were set up. Even though there is one true throne, we know that we have been raised and seated with Christ and are now called to co-reign with Him. We are given access to participate in His kingship. His one throne of righteousness is now multiplied through each one of His children! Therefore, out of our innermost being flows the same river of water and fire that proceeds from the very throne of heaven!

Recall again that the Shulammite is now describing the very body of Jesus. Thus, these descriptions include the church just as much as they speak about Him. All of this imagery reveals *why* Jesus made the statement about rivers of living water flowing from our innermost being. John wrote that when Jesus was glorified the Spirit would be released (look again at Jn. 7:39). Jesus's "glorifying" was when He sat down victoriously upon the throne of God after

His ascension to heaven. What's absolutely astonishing is that Jesus was not alone in this glorification. We were all glorified with Him!

> *(God) raised us up with Him, and* **seated us with**
> **Him** *in the heavenly places in Christ Jesus.*
> *(Eph. 2:6)*

Let's recap all of this and hopefully crystallize its meaning in our hearts...

Jesus reigns over heaven and earth. As the Christ, He is the true King of the earth. As the Son of the living God, He is the true King of heaven. This is seen in the imagery of ivory and sapphire. Jesus uses His authority to release a river of life, which is also the fire of His Spirit. Jesus's authority brings about life, healing, justice and righteousness. But since we have been raised and co-seated with Him, we are now privileged to release a river of healing and righteousness to the world as well.

Wherever we go, the throne of God is present!

Therefore, every prayer we pray and every action done in the name of Christ is done with the same authority behind that sapphire and ivory throne. The evils of the earth will burn up before our prayers and the pains of the earth will receive refreshing water through our courageous and grace-filled deeds! Hidden right within the Song of the Ages is a glorious revelation of our true authority in Christ.

7: Two Pillars

Though the Shulammite has encountered dark contradictions to the word of grace, as well as intense persecution and doubt, there is an undeniable sense of triumph that is building as she turns her attention away from herself and puts it on the glories of Jesus

Christ and His death, resurrection, and ascension. The Shulammite has been giving a full survey of the Lord's body. She started at the crown of His head and will now conclude with His legs and feet before giving the final overview of everything said thus far. This is her final "trumpet blast" before that great summarizing shout.

She compares His legs to "pillars of alabaster set on pedestals of gold." We'll start unpacking this by first looking at the alabaster legs, which is better translated as "white marble." Marble pillars were the hallmark of grand and exquisite structures during Solomon's era. They were a symbol of strength, fortitude, and beauty. Such pillars would be found right in the temple that Solomon built for the Lord.

In our last study of the Song of Songs, we discussed the connections between the temple of Solomon and the Song of Solomon. King Solomon oversaw the physical construction of the temple, which was a prophetic image of God in union with His people. He also oversaw the poetic construction of this union through the writing of his most important Song. Both these elements come together over and over again. The temple was a foreshadowing of Christ's body just as this portion of the Song is a foreshadowing of His body.

Interestingly, the temple had two key pillars leading into the Holy Place. These pillars are singled out so much that they even received their own names. Look at the account of Solomon's construction of the temple:

He erected the pillars in front of the temple, one on the
right and the other on the left, and named the one on the
right Jachin and the one on the left Boaz.
(2 Chr. 3:17)

152

The two pillars of the temple are indeed the legs of Jesus. Jachin means "He establishes" and Boaz translates to "in Him is strength." This speaks to the absolute, sovereign strength within Jesus. Everything He does is sure and steadfast. As the Shulammite meditates on these things, all doubt concerning His ability to fulfill His promises fades under the weight of these marble pillars. She goes on to say that these two pillars are "set on pedestals of pure gold." Once again, the metaphor of pure divinity comes into play. She began with pure gold on the head and ends with pure gold on the feet. From beginning to end, through and through, Jesus Christ is divine. More than divine, He is God Himself. And in Him is perfect strength to carry the weight of everything said thus far.

What's truly powerful is when we tie together the revelation behind this verse with the previous verse about His abdomen, the place of His throne. In the physical structure of the temple, right beyond the two pillars, there was a literal "throne" deeper inside the building. This throne was the Mercy Seat, which was a part of the Ark of the Covenant. Because of its location, you could actually say that this throne was in the "innermost being" of the building—the belly of the temple. Then, right outside of this place were two pillars, which are like the two legs of God. Amazingly, the temple's construction painted the same image that the Shulammite gives us! It's a picture of a human body!

In the last verse we also pointed out how a river flows from the throne of God and from the innermost being. It is amazing to see even more connections with this when we look at Ezekiel's vision of the temple. In Ezekiel 47, he was shown a life-giving river flowing out of the temple, finding its source in the innermost room where the throne of mercy was situated. Once again, we see all these symbols interlocking into one grand tapestry of truth. Solomon's construction of the temple and his composition of this Song were getting at one reality. The Song is describing the glory of Jesus, which is manifested through His spiritual temple—the church. In the Song, the Shulammite is describing both Jesus Christ and herself! The power of these truths is what will break down every wall that has stood in her way.

And with all of that, she will now give a final shout of His glory.

11

A Sweet Tree of Friendship

—— • ❖ • ——

His appearance is like Lebanon
Choice as the cedars.
His mouth is full of sweetness and he is wholly desirable.
This is my beloved and this is my friend,
O daughters of Jerusalem.
(5:15)

The Song of the Ages triumphantly plays on. Even when sorrow and contradiction rear their discordant notes in an attempt to drown out the Music, these things only provide a dark backdrop for even more of its brilliance to be revealed. Throughout the Song, we have been following the Shulammite as she confronts a wall that has haunted her from the beginning of her awakening, keeping her back from diving headfirst into the realities of grace. Earlier, we saw as she began to come into a true agreement with the work of the cross, leading her to finally wake up from the bed of deception. But like the Israelites confronting the walls of Jericho at the shores of the Jordan, she was immediately confronted by an outward experience that stood against her embrace of the truth.

It was there that she once again questioned her unbroken union with Christ by confessing that He had "turned away" and "had gone." Thus she continued to "search" for her Beloved. Yet this search led to a defining question from the daughters of Jerusalem, one that was probably motivated by the Spirit of Grace Himself. One that would bring forth another wave of truth upon her heart. The Shulammite's response to this question was like the Israelite response to the walls of Jericho. She blew the trumpet of the Gospel and now she prepares a final shout as she summarizes everything said up to this point. The wall of inharmonious sounds and fears will now become the canvas upon which the bright painting of the Song of the Ages will emerge.

Experiencing True Growth

The Shulammite gave a detailed description of the glories of Jesus from His head to His feet and now she sums up everything by speaking of His whole "appearance." She compares this appearance to the strong and beautiful trees of Lebanon (the same trees that were used to build Solomon's temple). Her words here carry a hidden reference to the very beginning of the Bible where the Hebrew word for "appearance" shows up for the first time. This was in the book of Genesis when it describes the *trees* that grew in the Garden of Eden. Genesis says the trees' appearance were *pleasing*. Most translations word it by saying they were "pleasing to the sight."

> *Out of the ground the Lord God caused to grow every tree that is pleasing to the sight and good for food; the tree of life also in the midst of the garden...*
> *(Gen. 2:9)*

Before the fall, Adam and Eve are pictured as being in a perfect condition and yet they were still dependent upon the food that grew from these trees. Some might say that the food was only for enjoyment, but I think God still used food to fuel the energy of the bodies He created. God loves to constantly remind us of the joy of absolute dependency upon Him, and our need for food is one of the prime examples of this. Some might argue this means low energy levels or even death was possible before the fall. But even if that were the case, it was not something that would cross the minds of the first humans. Lack of food was never a possibility. Food was in abundance and the trees were uncorrupted, pure, and always available.

This relates to us today. It has been made resoundingly clear that we have been redeemed and brought back to Eden through the work of Christ. Our redemption and identity is complete and perfect. Yet we remain completely dependent upon Jesus and His work. Perfect as we are in Him, we can still lose our energy if we cease to feed from the fruits of His labor (or if we feed from the wrong tree). Jesus is indeed the Tree of Life who is both pleasing to the sight and good for nourishment. Thankfully, the fruit on this Tree is just as abundant and pure as the trees of Eden and so there is no need to worry about lack. The believer need never suffer from a malnourished heart in view of Christ's abundance. We are well-fed sons and daughters of the house and no longer need to act like orphans who stand outside the home hoping to find scraps in the garbage. Christ came to give us nourishment, and to give it to us abundantly.

In this last section of the Song, the Shulammite rose up in worship and ate once more from the Tree of Christ. Each description of His nature was her embrace of the feast that hangs from this glorious Tree. This is where true growth always comes from. Hence the reason that the apostles called the church to "*grow in the grace and knowledge of our Lord and Savior Jesus Christ*" (see 2 Pet. 3:18). Many Christians receive their nourishment through weekly

Bible teachings that are essentially self-help messages with Bible verses attached to them (as though the Bible were an encyclopedia of right living). Or some churches pride themselves in expository teaching that goes line by line through the books of the Bible like the rabbis of old would go through the law each week and give lessons about God's commandments. But this is not where to find true nourishment. If it were, the church would be unbelievably healthy, strong, and united.

The Bible is a book filled with hidden bread and wine—the fruits of Jesus's suffering—and growth comes by feasting on the glories of Christ and His finished work as we are regularly reminded of it all. Unfortunately, many Christians are simply reminded weekly of what they are lacking in and what they need to do, whether in their marriage, their prayer life, their evangelism, or in some other area of "right living." In reality, the method of Bible teaching, whether expository or topical, does not matter. The only issue is whether or not the teaching points the believer to the knowledge of their Beloved and His abundant grace. According to the apostles, *that* is what brings true growth.

But there are other layers of revelation to this comparison of Christ's appearance to trees...

The True Tree of Life

Back in the Garden, the first two humans would have encountered something absolutely mystifying and spectacular in their experience of trees. This encounter, as amazing as it was, is actually something we have all continued to experience since then—we just take it for granted. The encounter I'm talking about is the actual process of a tree coming into existence. To the first humans, this process of growth must have seemed totally wild and crazy—even mystical.

A Sweet Tree of Friendship

Try to think about this as though you are watching the process unfold for the first time and you have no previous frame of reference to anything agricultural. First, you take a little, hard, rock-like item that fits between two of your fingers and place it on the ground and cover it with dirt. You then gather water (or wait for it to fall from these white and gray mountains that float through the sky) and pour it over the spot where that pebble-like thing is hiding. You do this in an act of absolute trust, hoping that this audacious activity with all of its required time and patience will actually lead to something.

You then watch as something does indeed happen. An entirely new entity, twisting and living, stretching and bending, begins to break through the dirt. Over time, this little thing becomes a big thing with beauty, fragrance, and edible fruits hanging from its stretching limbs, all of which connect back into union with one large stalk (which appears permanently fastened to the ground). This is something Adam and Eve witnessed when "out of the ground the Lord God caused to grow every tree." It must have been a completely breathtaking experience.

What's even more intense than this sheer miracle of nature is what the whole miraculous process points to: God's design of trees is a blatant signpost of the Person and work of Christ. He was the true seed that was placed into the ground through death and burial (see Jn. 12:24). Afterward, the rain of the Spirit fell from heaven and a Tree of Life emerged through His resurrection. That Tree was beautiful and perfect and yet it was destined to grow with more and more branches—*which is what we are*. We are now the growing branches united to the central trunk with the fruits of love and joy growing upon our lives as we find our nourishment in Him. During the days of His earthly ministry, Jesus made a wonderful promise about this Tree. He said that one day it would become the largest in all the earth (Matt. 13:32).

159

And so think about this as well. Before the fall even occurred, God gave a poetic picture to Adam and Eve of His plan of redemption. Even in the trauma and rebellion of that moment, when the God confronted Adam and Eve in their sin, He had automatically begun talking about a "seed" that would come from Eve (see Gen. 3:15). This seed is of course the Messiah. Planted in the ground through death and rising through resurrection, this seed would bring about a new entity on the soil of the earth, twisting and turning, breathing and living.

This entity would be the true Temple of the Spirit. Christ and His Bride. The true Tree of Life.

The love, sovereignty, and wisdom of God are unfathomable.

Sweetness Itself

She builds on this summary by then saying that His mouth is full of sweetness. As we have seen before, the mouth simply speaks of the Word of Christ. She is returning to this feature of the body because it defines everything else. This is the shout that encompasses all of the previous trumpet blasts.

Jesus is the Word. The Word is also the message of His grace and the work that He has accomplished. This is the summarizing message of all that has been said thus far.

The Hebrew actually seems to communicate that His mouth is "sweetness itself," which is how the NIV renders it. In other words, His Word is the very essence and origin of sweetness. Every "sweet" thing in life is but a drop or reflection of this original Word. Another way to look at this is to realize that every taste of honey, every sweet encounter with another person, every enjoyable experience of the good things that this world gives us, all of it is but a little drop from the ocean of God's Word—Jesus Christ and the truth of our co-crucifixion and co-resurrection with Him.

Jesus Christ is sweetness itself and thus He is "wholly desirably." That means that He is everything you could ever want or crave. He is completely and utterly satisfying and liberating. In fact, all of mankind's sins are just a settling for lesser fulfillments of this intense craving and desire for "sweetness itself." Sin is basically settling for poisoned fruit on dry bushes when a lush garden of abundance lays before us. This is why the prophet Haggai said that Jesus is "the Desire of the nations" (Hag. 2:7 NKJV). Every single person is craving the honey and fruit flowing from the true Tree of Life. When they finally encounter Jesus and His Word, this craving is forever satisfied and they can begin to feast upon it for all eternity. And unlike the things of this world, you can never tire of this feast.

The idea of unending satisfaction seems impossible to most of us, because all we've ever known is the fleeting nature of life's pleasures. But this is purely an issue of design. God purposely created the world in such a way that its pleasures and wonders will fade if we overindulge or focus on them too much. This fading element is not to diminish or demonize life's pleasures, but to teach us more about our dependency on God—even for things like wonder and delight. The desire for pleasure is godly and pure, and there is a true fulfillment in Christ. God uses the things of this world to propel us toward something of infinite sweetness. It may seem impossible that we could feast on one Tree for all eternity, but that is because we do not understand the source of sweetness itself. We do not understand that every good thing we taste in this world is but a ripple from the ocean of complete Goodness. As hard as it is to comprehend, this ocean is infinitely satisfying.

What's also important to glean from this is the fact that you can taste the true Gospel by testing (discerning) how sweet, intoxicating, and delightful it is. Such adjectives are behind the Hebrew word that Solomon uses to describe the Beloved's mouth. Thus, any "Word" of the Gospel that feels dry or methodical, one that does not lighten the heart and sweeten the soul, is either a complete non-Gospel or one of mixture. Any word that reeks of the bitterness of separation, judgment, and self-introspection does not proceed from the sweet mouth of our Lord. In all likelihood, someone else simply took the sweet message of Jesus and added their own sour ingredients to it. Such a mixed Gospel can never capture someone's heart and free them from the false pleasures of sin. It can only offer an allusive hope of freedom and pleasure in the far distant future.

Unfortunately, this is how the Gospel is so often presented. The "dessert" will come after this life, but now is the time to work through a meal of bitter herbs in order to get there. Yet that is not the truth of the Gospel. Jesus took away the bitter herbs and left His followers only with sweet wine and bread (see Ex. 12:8 & Matt. 26:26-28). This is because Jesus ate the bitter herbs of the Passover on our behalf.

Our time to enjoy the dessert is now. And our future will be layer after layer of increased icing on the cake.

My Beloved and Friend

It is important to remember exactly who the Shulammite has been speaking to this whole time, because the "daughters of Jerusalem" fit an incredibly expansive category of people. Remember that Solomon, the king of Jerusalem, is writing about Jesus, the true and eternal King of Jerusalem. He is in fact the true King of all heaven and all earth. "All authority in heaven and on earth has been given to Me," the King once spoke (Matt. 28:18). Even if all other authorities have not yet bowed before Him, Jesus is the still the true King of the entire earth. So from a spiritual perspective, Jerusalem can be thought of as the capital city of the entire world.

Therefore, these "daughters" represent everyone who lies under His domain. Of course, they may not know who their King really is. They may not have experienced "eternal life," which the Bible says is to *know the only true God, and Jesus Christ whom He has sent* (Jn. 17:3). Or perhaps they have experienced it to a certain measure, but there is so much more for them to see and understand.

So the Shulammite is responding to them all. And now she ends her triumphant declaration of the Person and message of Christ with a penetrating and timeless statement. You can imagine her looking the daughters of Jerusalem directly in the eyes as she says this, roaring with a shout of absolute confidence and authority.

"*This* is my beloved and *this* is my friend, O daughters of Jerusalem!"

If you listen closely, you can feel the weight of passion behind these words. It is as though she is forcefully correcting centuries upon centuries of incomplete understanding about the true King of Jerusalem. We might read her closing words in the following light:

> *If you've ever thought of the King of kings in a lesser way than how I've just described Him—the One who is the perfect God in a human frame, a Person who is sweetness itself and whose work of redemption is fully satisfying and eternally complete—well, now you know otherwise!* **This** *is who your King is...* **This** *is my Beloved and Friend!*

The Song of the Ages: Part II

After illuminating these fellow children of God to the wonders of Jesus, she then brings the description of Him into the most intimate of terms. She does not close her trumpeting speech by referring to Him as a Shepherd or King or even as God. Of course, Jesus can be described by any of those titles. But she has already given many glorious descriptions of Jesus's divinity, power, and faithfulness through the different features of His body. In the end, she chooses to sum up everything in the context of an intimate relationship.

Jesus is certainly God and King, but He is also our Beloved and Friend. Such words bring His kingship and divinity into the safest and most pleasant setting. There is no room for even the slightest amount of fear with this kind of knowledge. The God of the universe is the One who draws near to us as a true friend draws near to his companion or as a beloved husband draws near to the love of his life. Any worry of things like judgment, rejection, hell, or defeat crumble under the weight of this truth.

And thus these words are truly her final shout, dreadfully powerful and infinitely sweet. They are spoken with a convicted heart, rising as a victorious wave of sound that stands against any prior sense of abandonment or isolation. The seed sown in her heart at the Summit of Truth has finally begun to break through the soil. That returning wave of glory has pummeled the shore, washing away the walls on her soul like a raging tsunami overtaking a child's sand castle.

With this glorious declaration, the previous lie that Jesus "turned away and had gone" is completely demolished. All that is left is a Promised Land of union and fruitfulness—free for the taking.

12

The Revelation of the Ages
Pt. 1

Where has your beloved gone,
O most beautiful of women?
Which way did your beloved turn,
That we may look for him with you?

My beloved has gone down to his garden,
To the beds of spices,
To browse in the gardens and to gather lilies.
(6:1-2 NIV)

The Shulammite is no longer half-asleep. The Trojan horse of the Gospel has been fully unleashed within her soul and its contents rush inward and outward, overflowing from her heart and pouring out of her singing lips. While the Bride had previously sung with clashing pitches and different lyrics from her Beloved, harmony has now been redeemed. The deception and intimidation of the wall lies in clumps of broken rocks and pebbles under her feet. The Song of the Ages is now being released with perfect clarity.

But the Bride is no longer just singing the Song.

She has become the Song.

Because of this, the poetry of her life has made quite an impact upon the hearts of those around her. For the first time since the beginning of the journey, the ever-observing daughters of Jerusalem want to join the Bride on her quest for Christ. These young Shulammites-to-be now want to leave their own vineyards of religion in order to search for the One who brings true rest. They have sensed something of Eden through her life and now they ask where they too can taste of this perfect Sweetness.

The Bride's answer to the seeking daughters will come as the crowning note and most transcendent part of the entire poem. In this redeemed harmony, we are able to listen to the Song in its purest form. The shout is over and the walls are fallen, leaving behind a crystal-clear picture of the Gospel. This is the greatest revelation mankind has ever been given. It is the revelation of the ages. We are now like Joshua standing upon the ruins of Jericho and looking westward. This is the clearest look at what the "Promised Land" has always been about...

The Doorway of the Word

My beloved has gone down to his garden!

This brisk and straightforward answer to the daughters' question is actually the entirety of the Song summed up in a single phrase. This is the moment where the Bride finally joins with the full Song of her Beloved. It is where the eternal Song of heaven becomes the Song of the earth.

Earlier, the Bride had questioned the whereabouts of her Beloved. She believed that He had turned away and gone. She then searched for Him through the city streets and other places. Thankfully, after a time of reflection and worship, she came back to reality—to *Amana*. After a season of denying her Beloved's presence, she was questioned by the daughters of Jerusalem and returned to the Gospel's sweet truth. Now she declares that He "has gone down to His garden."

Commentator after commentator throughout the centuries have acknowledged that the garden is a clear symbol of a person's inner being and heart. Therefore, the meaning of this verse is quite clear.

Where has He turned away and gone? the daughters ask.

He has not turned anywhere, she responds.

He is within me!

The Shulammite finally trusts that she and her Beloved are one. Circumstances may not have changed on the outside, but her heart is radiant and alive with this mystery and truth. The Shulammite's response to the daughters of Jerusalem is a timeless piece of Scripture that serves as the door-hinge of the entire Word of God. Now this is a pretty dramatic statement to make about this verse's significance within the Bible, so let's attempt to back up this assertion.

First of all, the written Word is a doorway into the Word Himself—Jesus Christ (Rev. 19:13). This is another way of saying that the Bible is a lamp unto our feet (Ps. 119:105). It is a glorious light that guides our steps ever closer to Christ. Thus, the Scriptures serve as a true doorway into a deeper encounter with Jesus. The problem is that throughout Hebraic and Christian history many people have worshipped the door in and of itself—but it is the Person to whom the door leads that is its real purpose. Without that purpose, the door is just a dividing piece wood that can be the source of wars, schisms, and denominationalism. But when its purpose is truly engaged, the Word opens the way to peace and righteousness. As Paul said to Timothy, the Scriptures are God-breathed and are completely effective in leading us to righteousness. Let's just remember that righteousness is a Person. It is Jesus Himself (compare 2 Tim. 3:16 and 1 Cor. 1:30).

Now like any other door, the written Word has a frame that surrounds it. The beginning, middle, and end of the Bible are all edged in similar imagery—the imagery of a garden. The Old Testament starts in a place called Eden. There we see the essence of our origin and the beginning of our destiny. Eden reveals what was in the heart of God when He established creation and birthed mankind through the kiss of His Spirit. Afterward, in the middle of the biblical story, we come to the New Covenant. This covenant starts to take shape when Jesus enters a garden called Gethsemane and surrenders Himself to the will of the Father. This is where His betrayal and suffering begin. The work of Christ is then completed when Jesus emerges from a tomb that was also located in a garden (see Jn. 19:41).

After Eden and Gethsemane, the Word of God ends in the book of Revelation with vivid portraits that bring us back to the Garden of Eden. Though the story concludes with the beautiful city of the New Jerusalem, the last two chapters of Revelation are filled with images that are drawn straight from the first few chapters of Genesis, such as the Tree of Life and the flowing river. And so the beginning, middle, and end of the written Word are woven together and framed by a garden. On the left is Genesis, on the right is Revelation, and in the middle are the gardens where Jesus stood before and after His crucifixion. Like the top part of a doorframe, these garden scenes with Christ connect the beginning and end of the Bible. And like the Hebrew people's doorframes in Egypt, they are smeared with the blood of the Lamb (see Ex. 12:7).

Now a door won't properly swing open and allow entrance without a hinge of some sort. But thankfully, there is a hinge that the Word of God rests upon. This is the way by which the Word opens wide and becomes a living reality for us—not just a book of religious ideas and concepts. This hinge is encapsulated in the words of the Shulammite in this second verse of the sixth chapter of Solomon's Song. This hinge ultimately unveils what the Garden imagery was always all about. It uncovers the true meaning of both Eden and the New Jerusalem. As said before, it also reveals the full meaning of the Promised Land.

All of these beautiful images and verses speak to the reality of union. The garden is the human heart united with the heart and Spirit of God. This is not a union that we simply look at and study (or just hope for), but one that is already accomplished and present, which we boldly enter into by trust.

Paradise Now

God's plan was never to just plant a literal garden in and of itself. Nor did His heart envision a literal building of precious stones surrounded by golden streets. His great plan was also not about populating a small plot of territory called Canaan. All these things are only meant to point us to something greater. Something for which the whole world is searching. Like the Shulammite in the beginning of the Song, and the daughters of Jerusalem now, all of us are seeking after our origin and destiny—Genesis and Revelation. This is our Alpha and Omega. It is Sweetness itself. In essence, all of us are seeking after the true Kingdom of God, which is wrapped up in oneness with Christ. His reign is established through the garden of our hearts.

Multitudes of people are waiting for a physical garden or city to come out of the sky and plop on the earth. But Jesus's plan was always to establish Eden from within. This is why the Kingdom of God is described as righteousness, peace, and joy (Rom. 14:17). This is also why the book of Romans does not say that the earth is groaning and waiting for the physical return of Christ. Rather, it says that the earth is waiting for the manifestation of the *sons* of God! True Eden will manifest first in the hearts of His people. And so the hope of glory is *Christ in you*—not Christ in physical Jerusalem! (See Rom. 8:19 & Col. 1:27)

Now please know that this is not an assertion that Jesus won't physically return one day. He will surely come back in the same body He had when He walked the earth for 40 days after His resurrection. We must never get duped into thinking that Jesus is only Spirit. He is both perfect Spirit and perfect Man. Nonetheless, there will be a surprising and offensive mystery of the "end-times," which involves the return and revealing of Christ *in us*, even before a physical return of a singular Man named Jesus.

Once again, the people of God will be confounded by the purposes of heaven. Like the Jews in Jesus's day, many Christians are expecting a conquering Messiah to come and kill all the rebellious people in the world and enforce a new government on the earth. They believe this will happen as He comes out of the sky with a literal bloody sword that extends out of His mouth (Rev. 19:15). They will then be waiting for a physical paradise to come out of the clouds with streets of gold and literal trees of healing that line those streets. But like many of God's people in the first century, Christians will be extremely surprised, and perhaps offended at the real manifestation of these prophecies.

They will learn that the Messiah's conquering sword comes out of His mouth for one reason. It is because it is the same "sword of the Spirit" that Paul referred to as the Word of God (see Eph. 6:17). It is the revelation of the Gospel, which destroys the false nature of man by the Holy Spirit. Moreover, paradise does not primarily descend out of physical clouds. Paradise comes out of the innermost being of the awakened church.

This is what John saw at the end of Revelation...

> *Then one of the seven angels who had the seven bowls filled with the seven last plagues came to me and talked with me, saying, "Come,* **I will show you the bride, the Lamb's wife.**" *And he carried me away in the Spirit to a great and high mountain, and showed me the great city, the holy Jerusalem, descending out of heaven from God.*
> *(Rev. 21:9-10 NKJV)*

The city represents the Bride—which is obviously *people*. People are the precious stones that make up the temple, and that temple is *already* being raised up and established on the earth (see 1 Pet. 2:5 & Eph. 2:22). In other words, paradise is already coming out of the heavens because the Song of the Ages is merging with human hearts. Even now, the Spirit is kissing the dust of our being and forging a new creation in the midst of the old one. Like a sword, the Spirit is cutting away our sinful identity and conquering our guilt and fear. We are *now* becoming the leaves that bring healing to the nations, as John the apostle also saw (Rev. 22:2). We are branches united with the Tree of Life Himself. As the Psalmist says, we are like trees planted by streams of water and our leaves do not wither (Ps. 1).

This is part of the great mystery of the ages. To the beloved daughters of Jerusalem, the awakened Bride reveals that the King is not far away in outer space nor is He located in some bloody future. Jesus is nearer to us than our own breath and He is already covered in blood—His own—for man's wickedness was crucified with Him. The fruitful and fragrant Promised Land is not purchased by our sweat and blood, but by the drops of blood and sweat that fell from Jesus in the garden of Gethsemane and on the hill of Calvary.

The Promise now lies within. The paradise of righteousness, joy, and union begins now. The Kingdom is at hand—within reach—waiting to overflow from our trusting hearts in order to bring healing to a broken and unbelieving world. The sacrifice, joy, and love of the awakened church are the fruits of the Spirit that feed the nations with the life of Christ. Every day this Kingdom is advancing whether our eyes are open to it or not. The seed of Christ's death is becoming a mighty tree that will fill all nations, even before the King physically returns.

What Jesus Said

The daughters of Jerusalem are looking for the way to the King and His sweet, desirable Kingdom. When the Shulammite finally responds by saying that He has gone down to His garden, she is giving a response that blows every other religious answer out of the water. She is basically saying that they need to stop *waiting* for His Kingdom (and that they shouldn't try to attain it by their own efforts like she had been doing).

You'll find that this is a similar response that Jesus gave to another group of lost "daughters of Jerusalem"—the Pharisees. Some of these Jewish leaders had questioned Jesus about the Kingdom, wanting to know signs and direction to it, as well as its timing. But do you remember Jesus's response?

It was very similar to the Shulammite's answer to the daughters of Jerusalem...

Now when He was asked by the Pharisees when the
kingdom of God would come, He answered them and said,

*"The kingdom of God does not come with observation; nor will they say, 'See here!' or 'See there!' For indeed, **the kingdom of God is within you."***
(*Lk. 17:20-21 NKJV*)

So let's make it explicitly, abundantly, and redundantly clear. The Song is not talking about a literal garden at King Solomon's palace nor is it referring to the garden of the Shulammite's physical body and thus making a sexual allusion. As we've noted in the last study of the Song, this Song is not about physical marriage. Any kind of sexual metaphor is only meant to lift our eyes unto the greater reality of divine oneness. This is the heavenly glory to which the marriage bed points. Physical intimacy is like the star of Bethlehem pointing to the manger. The Christmas story was about the birth of Christ, not a guiding star. The star is only a bright signpost leading to Immanuel—the One who unites God and man. This great union is what the Shulammite is singing of.

She has awoken to the central mystery of the Word when she says that the Beloved has gone down to His garden. Of course, we have seen this all along, especially at the Summit of Truth. We have been extrapolating and unfolding this mystery since the beginning of the Song, so its unveiling does not come as much of a surprise. However, it is surely meant to be a surprising and beautiful crescendo within the lyrics of Solomon's Song. The only problem has been the clouds of distraction and contradiction that have billowed up in her vision. Nonetheless, Christ continued to pursue her with wave after wave of His love and truth, calling her to awaken to this great mystery even when she accused Him of turning away.

The Song of the Ages: Part II

Here and There

For a moment, let's put aside the door analogy and instead describe the Word of God as a delicious meal that the whole world has been invited to feast upon. When a meal is prepared, salt is often added to bring out its full flavor. The chemical properties of salt actually hide certain bitter flavors and enhance others. In like fashion, God has cooked up the delicious meal of His Word and has sprinkled salt throughout its pages to bring out its full flavor and meaning. This salt is found in many of the stories of the Old Testament, which we have been unpacking along the way. We have looked at Genesis, Exodus, Joshua, Isaiah, and many other portions of the Bible. We will now look at the book of Jeremiah and pick up one more piece of salt that will enhance and confirm what we're currently seeing in the Song.

Jeremiah 31 is a significant chapter of the Bible. It boldly and victoriously declares the coming of a New Covenant even in the midst of a dark period within Israel's history. The chapter is like its own star of Bethlehem with one particular verse that expresses the deepest mystery and flavor of God's Word. It is a verse that we will find powerfully connects with the Song of Solomon.

> *How long will you **go here and there**, O faithless daughter? For the Lord has created a new thing in the earth—a woman will encompass a man.*
> *(Jer. 31:22)*

Earlier, when the Bride accused Jesus of *turning away*, she was using a Hebrew word that also shows up in this verse in Jeremiah (although it is translated differently into English). When God asks His faithless daughter how long will she "go here and there," He is using this same word for "turning away." In other words, He is asking, *how long will you turn this way and that?*

174

For Israel, this meant God was asking how long they would turn to different idols and other systems of religion and security, pursuing their rest in a multitude of ways outside of the Way Himself. For the Shulammite, her turning and wandering looked like a constant trip back into the "city" of religion and to the watchmen of the walls who guard the ideologies of separation and religious works. For the church throughout history, this back-and-forth wandering has happened from its earliest beginnings when the churches in Jerusalem and Galatia began to fall away from grace. The faithlessness of God's people, no matter what biblical time period or region it occurs, always comes down to a distrust in the saving love of God, and a rejection of His finished work.

So this is quite ironic considering the Shulammite was accusing God of being the One who had "turned away." She had lost a sense of His presence as she faced the darkness of a world, which seemed to contradict the beautiful truths she had seen at the Summit of Truth. She had opened the door of His Word through Her confession of the truth, but was continuing to use her natural eyes as she moved forward. Perhaps she was looking more for a physical garden of Eden to appear before her eyes and for her outward circumstances to align with the truth of Christ's words. But she was only losing sight of Eden within. She doubted once again who she was and who Jesus is.

All of this connects back to the book of Isaiah, where we saw how Israel was crying out for God to wake up from His slumber and deliver them with His mighty right arm. As was already covered, God responded and told them that they were the ones who needed to wake up. He called Israel to come away from fear and illusion and to see that His deliverance has already come. He then told them about a suffering servant. The exchange between God and His people in Isaiah 52 led to the revelation of the cross in Isaiah 53. This was yet another grain of luminescent salt sprinkled on the Word. Every piece of salt is the same, although each carries its own unique geometry. There are different riddles and mysteries all throughout the Word, but each brings out the full flavor of Christ's work.

Now in this one verse of Jeremiah 31, a similar pattern follows. But God's response to the people of Jeremiah's day is much stranger. God calls them to stop faithlessly turning this way and that, and then calls their attention to something quite mysterious, something that almost seems contextually out of place. He says, "For the Lord has created a new thing in the earth—a woman will encompass a man."

At face value, this statement makes little sense and has thus been a point of much debate for both Jewish and Christian commentators over the millennia. God is telling the people to stop wandering and living in faithlessness and then He gives the reason *why* they should stop all of this "turning away:"

> *For I have done something new... A woman will surround a man!*

What?

It's an incredibly confusing statement until you realize that salt is not what we're having for dinner. It's only a complement to the meal that is meant to bring out its full flavor. The real meal of the Bible, including the law and the prophets, is the message of redeemed union—the garden of oneness. And so the "new thing" in Jeremiah 31 speaks of the new creation in Christ. A woman surrounding a man is a word picture. God has joined us to Himself through Christ and we are now His Bride. A woman (the church) now encompasses a Man (Christ).

It is Christ in us, the hope of glory!

God has given this same answer to the listeners of Isaiah and Jeremiah, the daughters of Jerusalem, the Pharisees, and so many more. It is the Song He has been singing all along, even before the foundation of the earth. This is the eternal music that sets all people free, if they would only listen and believe. And thus we have this glorious shift occurring in the sixth chapter of the Song where the Shulammite declares that her Beloved has gone down to *His garden.* She understands and believes that Jesus never really turned away from her. In reality, she was the one who had turned away and gone!

A Stable and Heavenly Vantage Point

Think about a sunset for a moment. What is really happening when the sun begins to set? Even though it appears as though each evening the sun slowly makes its escape from us, we know that this is not true. The earth is turning away from the sun, not the other way around. This of course is a solid fact in our minds and so we do not doubt its truth. However, to the natural eye, this really isn't common sense. Because of this, mankind has long thought, *even for the majority of our time on the earth,* that the sun revolved around us. We firmly believed this because our everyday experience, our *perceived* reality, was that we were stationary and the sun was moving. And so we accused the sun of turning away.

All mankind collectively lived in a false belief that the sun would regularly abandon us and leave us in the dark dampness of the night. However, in due course, some revolutionary thinkers came along (no pun intended) with new instruments and startling ideas. Men like Copernicus and Galileo began to challenge our "common sense" and preached a new message, one that contradicted everything we thought we knew. Ironically, the religious leaders of the day, with their limited understanding of the Bible, persecuted and fought against those who were heralding this new message.

But this revelation could not be stopped. Once the telescope was fine-tuned and enhanced, no one could deny that we were the ones who were actually turning away from the sun, not the other way around. This was a "new thing" to humanity that yet had been true from the beginning.

In a similar fashion, the Lord has been continually enhancing and lifting up our own spiritual perceptions. The telescope of His Word helps us lift our eyes to a higher reality and the Song of Solomon is like a mighty lens that helps us focus into this truth. It lifts us up above the natural experiences of pain, sin, and darkness to a higher and more stable reality of identity and redemption. This heavenly vantage point is far above the religious ideologies and fears of mankind. It reveals the all-encompassing work of the Son. There we see that His light is all-present and His love is unfading. Our union with Him is unbroken and true.

Now much like the religious crowd of Galileo's day, there are those with small-minded views of the Word that will persecute others who hold to this truth. They persecute us with the Bible itself, which can sometimes hinder us from fully accepting the words of our Beloved. For Galileo, this persecution made him water down some of his own beliefs for a period of time. But the truth will always prevail. The Song of the Ages will play on. Like the facts of our sun, one day the truths of the Song will be common knowledge amongst the church (and eventually amongst the entire world).

Today, few would dare question that the earth revolves around the sun. This is because it's common knowledge that has been generationally rooted into our minds. Fortunately, there is a day coming when no one will question the realities of the finished work of Christ and the perfect union we already have with Him. People will be taught this from the youngest of ages and it will trump any earthly experience. Worship songs, sermons, and prayers that carry the language of separation and delay will fade into the archives of Christian history, like the indulgences people bought to secure salvation in the Middle Ages. As we move forward into the truth, people will still experience darkness for a season, but they will rest upon a higher reality. Like John the apostle, the church will boldly decree that "the true light is already shining and the darkness (deception) is fading" (1 Jn. 2:8, parenthesis mine).

What's happening is that the Bride is learning to repent—to change her mind. This has been the church's progression all throughout history and it has been the Shulammite's progression through the Song. She is finally accepting the "new thing" that God has done once and for all. She realizes that she encompasses a Man. She is fully one with Christ. Though the darkness of the night makes it seem like this is not always true, she has let go of the illusion of shifting sunlight. Her trust is rooted in the reality of unfading love and eternal grace. Whether she feels it or not (or understands it or not) the truth remains more faithful than the sun. Her beloved has gone down to *His* garden. She now surrounds and embodies the very glory of God.

The Bride has come into agreement with a truth that was once communicated to a church that was also "turning away" and losing sight of grace. It reads as follows:

> *I have been crucified with Christ; and it is no longer I who*
> *live, but Christ lives in me; and the life which I now live*
> *in the flesh I live by faith in the Son of God, who loved me*
> *and gave Himself up for me.*
> *(Gal. 2:20)*

All along, this message found blatantly revealed in the book of Galatians has been playing like hidden chords dancing along the score sheet of Solomon's Song. We now see these secret chords emerging from the shadows through the Bride's response to Jerusalem's daughters. As we said in the very beginning of the Song, the Shepherd's plan was to lead her on a journey to reveal what was already hers. He would lead her to an intimate knowledge of the Truth. Though she once thought otherwise, the rest and righteousness of Eden could never be earned. The Gospel is an equal playing field for all, whether the baby in the womb or the missionary on the field. The only thing we can do is awaken to its glory and bask in its light.

And so the Shulammite finally *gets it*. She is resting and basking. And thankfully, she is a picture of the rising church all over the world. Solomon's words are sourced from a place outside of time, revealing the full journey of the Bride throughout history. Thus we can rest in the fact that *we will all get it*. Just like humanity has come into a true knowledge of the sun, one day we will "all come into the unity of the faith and the knowledge of the *Son* of God" (Eph. 4:13).

13

The Revelation of the Ages
Pt. 2

I am my beloved's and my beloved is mine;
He browses among the lilies.
(6:3 NIV)

If the previous words about the Beloved dwelling in the garden were the crown jewel of the Song, then this next verse is its sparkle and shine.

I am my Beloved's and my Beloved is mine.

This is perhaps the most famous verse of the Song, having found its way onto modern bookmarks, devotionals, greeting cards, wedding ceremonies, and a host of sermons and teachings throughout the centuries. However, in many of these instances, people have only stayed at the base of this verse without ascending to the full heights of its meaning and implications. So, by the grace of our Beloved, we will attempt to go a little bit higher than usual in approaching this beautiful lyric.

In order to climb its heights, we are going to approach this verse as though it were a massive building of light filled with many different stories, each of which is a whole "floor" of revelation that builds upon the previous floor. By taking this verse at face value, many people have entered the first floor of its meaning, but there are indeed many more floors after that. In fact, if this were truly a luminescent building made up of different stories, it would rise high into the clouds and go far off into infinite space. But we are going to keep things simple and imagine only three main "stories" to this verse.

Each of these stories are key truths that encompass the heart of the text. Now even though we are simplifying it into these three areas, there is no intention of stripping away its infinite dynamic. Instead of the building extending into unending heights, this perspective allows it to extend outward into boundless width and length. There is still an incalculable amount of "rooms" within each floor of truth, and each room contains a unique insight or facet of the overall message of the floor. Accordingly, this chapter will read like a general overview and map of the building. However, the hope is that the Spirit of God would touch you as you read, and that long after you've finished this chapter you would be compelled into an endless exploration of the Shulammite's radiant words.

The First Story

This first story of this verse involves its first four words—*I am my Beloved's*. This is the Shulammite's declaration that she belongs to Another. It is the acknowledgement that her life is no longer her own and that her heart fully belongs to Jesus. To borrow once again from the words of Paul, the Shulammite sees herself as a "bondservant" of Christ. Paul often referred to himself as such, because in the Hebrew culture this often referred to a slave who willingly gave up his freedom to stay with his master. Such a bondservant would forever belong to his master not out of economic need or control, but out of love (see Ex. 21:1-6).

The Shulammite has abandoned an independent life in order to give it to Jesus as her perpetual Master. She does not make this statement of surrender out of some dry obligation, but out of her encounter with the love of Jesus. Her journey has been one confrontation after another with the goodness of God. Even in her darkest hour, Jesus continually affirmed His love for her. Not once did He speak in harsh or condemning tones and He was always there to remind her of her identity as His spotless one. On top of this, the Lord also poured out the deep contents of His heart and made Himself completely vulnerable to her, unveiling more and more of what He did at the cross. The myrrh-laced scent of His death has invaded her nostrils and infused her head with a new paradigm of God. Thus, she has not surrendered her life to an ugly slave-master or to a controlling and abusive husband. She has said *yes* to the most pleasant and sweet Person alive.

Surrendering your life over to another is certainly seen in the Hebraic image of a bondservant, but it can also be seen in the context of marriage. In fact, it is the marital dimension of this verse that stands out the most. Hence, Jewish and Christian weddings throughout the millennia have often utilized the words of the Shulammite. In Solomon's day, a woman truly let go of everything when she came into marital union with her husband. Much of this still carries into our modern culture. When a woman was married, she was not only leaving her father's household, but she was leaving her father's name behind as well. She was surrendering herself fully to her husband's care and taking on his name and identity. She fully belonged to her spouse and was called to continually serve him in love. In this ancient context, she was even considered his property. (Of course, this is a concept we would look at with disgust today, because of the abuse and inequality mixed in with it. However, let's not dismiss this cultural insight just yet—we'll come back to its significance in a little bit.)

Some readers may still be uncomfortable with being called the "Bride" of Christ. Even if you've come this far in the Song, that language may still be awkward to you. But the image of marriage, especially when it is taken from the Hebrew culture, is so vital in understanding our relationship to God. We have highlighted the idea of "union" more than anything else throughout the whole course of this study and now it has reached its glorious climax in these recent verses. Of course, this is all because the entire Song points to the reality of union with God. It is the Song of the cosmos, the Song of all ages and time periods. It is the meaning of all creation and it is where everything is headed. However, it's important to know that we are not just talking about an ethereal idea of union with an invisible force.

There is certainly a mystical reality to our divine union. God is Spirit and there is a divine oneness we share that cannot be put into human language. Nonetheless, we need to recognize something incredibly important. When the Lord set about to communicate the central message of the cosmos and the meaning of life itself—*union*—He chose to explain and memorialize it through something very specific; something the vast majority of mankind would physically and tangibly experience. He chose to do this through the imagery of a husband and wife. Though there have been Gnostic tendencies in the church to super-spiritualize the concept of union, God has explained this cosmically important message through the very real and earthly picture of human marriage.

*"For this reason a man shall leave his father and mother and be joined to his wife, and the two shall become one flesh." **This is a great mystery, but I speak***

184

concerning Christ and the church.

(Eph. 5:31-32 NKJV)

From the Garden of Eden, where the first marriage took place, to the wedding caravan of Song of Songs 3, where the marital purpose behind Moses's tabernacle was discovered, to the New Jerusalem descending out of heaven as the *Bride* of Christ, everything in the Word points to a wedding. This is the bright sparkle and shine upon the garden revelation from the last verse. Everything is about union—that is the hinge, the frame, the door, and the destination of the Word. But this union is most deeply described by the covenant of marriage. And this should be obvious considering Jesus came to inaugurate a new "covenant." His shed blood was the sealing of this divine marriage.

So when people talk about divine oneness in deep theological or mystical terms, it always needs to come back to this. The covenant of marriage is a bedrock and foundation to our understanding of union with Christ. Hence, this is the foundational first floor of this timeless verse. We are in union with Christ just as a bride is in union with her husband. This involves a practical life of surrender, of intimate relationship and dialogue, of service and care, and of re-prioritizing one's life around Another.

The Second Story

Once the preceding truth is established, we are able to go up a flight of stairs and behold another level to this glorious verse. This second floor comes with a revelation that is absolutely staggering. It is the second part of the Shulammite's statement—*my Beloved is mine.*

Now think about that for a moment. Just pause. Take a breath into your lungs and take this truth in with it. I understand it's like a paper cup on the beach trying to take in the ocean, but at least let part of that ocean water into your heart for a moment...

Your Beloved, the Creator, *is yours*.

That is what she is saying. He belongs to her. He has given Himself to her. He is just as much hers as she is His. So if we are to be considered the property of Jesus, then He is our property as well!

This verse is not just talking about our bondservant relationship to God. The Gospel is also rooted in God's bondservant relationship to us! Do not think that this is some new or strange teaching. This is found all throughout the four gospel accounts. Jesus said over and over again that He came not be served, but to serve. Please understand that this was not just about a one-time act of sacrifice on the cross so that He could return to a heavenly dictatorship where He would no longer serve us anymore. The cross was a manifestation of His eternal nature, which is to *always serve*. The very essence of God is to put others before Himself.

Let's not rush past this truth. This is a section of the second floor where there are numerous rooms of light that will illuminate your heart beyond your wildest dreams as you peer into their luminous corners and closets. Take this into consideration once more: The cross was not a singular event where Jesus would serve us and, now that it's done, we have to serve Him all the time because He's Lord and Master, the eternal tyrant of Heaven and Earth.

No.

The cross revealed Who God Is. Who He has always Been. Who He will always Be.

God's very nature is to serve and give of Himself for the betterment of others—of us. He is truly Lord and Master, but He is the most benevolent and other-centered Master you could ever imagine. (And, in fact, you can't imagine it. The love of God is beyond comprehension, according to the apostle Paul. Like the paper cup in the ocean, you can only take in a little bit at a time, and those little bits are unending.)

So we are not talking about a typical bondservant relationship. Nor are we discussing a typical marriage that is rooted in the cultural weaknesses and abuses of this world. Instead, we are talking about a willing and loving two-way relationship of service and care for one another. This is what marriage is supposed to be. Marriage was always meant to be a mirror of divine realities, but it has gotten extremely shattered and fragmented after mankind's descent into darkness. Outside of our brokenness, however, marriage is an amazing image that showcases a loving equality between a man and a woman, with mutual love and shared service (see Eph. 5:21).

Preachers spend a lot of time talking about how we need to surrender to Jesus and serve Him. Much of this teaching is rooted in a good place, for it comes from that first floor of revelation. This is a level of understanding our relationship with God in terms of our service and surrender to Him. Paul and other apostles often used the word "slave" to describe this relationship to Jesus. They understood that their journey involved giving up their own rights and even their whole life to Jesus's lordship. The Holy Spirit has thus led many people to understand the Christian life in these terms. It is a foundational level and there is an incredible amount of blessing on that floor. Sacrificial obedience to Jesus, rooted in love, is a beautiful place to be. Some people who intensely preach a message of grace miss the centrality of the first floor as well as the loving obedience that is supposed to flow from the inner garden of our hearts.

And yet there are so many more people throughout the church's history who have chosen to stay on the first story of this verse and have not boldly stepped into its next part. They may have seen the staircase leading up to the second half of this lyric, and they may have even pointed it out from time to time; however, many believers choose to stay in the place that focuses on our own servanthood and sacrifice.

But we need to walk up those steps.

We need to see that Jesus continually surrenders Himself to us. He is fully ours. He has given up His own life for us, and seeks to serve and care for us on a regular basis. In fact, every day we can wake up with the expectation that Jesus is caring for us and meeting our needs. He serves us even when we ignore Him. He is the perfect Husband. Again, this service was not limited to the historical event of Calvary. The cross simply revealed the constant truth of His heart.

And so the first floor is incomplete without the second. The first four words of the Shulammite are religiously empty without the last four. As we've said numerous times before, Christianity is not ultimately about our sacrifice and obedience—but His. To truly enter into loving servanthood, we have to see Jesus in the purest form of what a Husband is supposed to be.

One of the best scenes in the Gospel accounts that communicates this aspect of our relationship with Jesus is when He spoke to His disciples at the last supper. He made it very clear that they were far more than servants:

> *No longer do I call you slaves, for the slave does not know what his master is doing; but I have called you friends, for all things that I have heard from My Father I have made known to you.*
> *(Jn. 15:15)*

188

We are talking about something far more beautiful than the earthly images of masters and servants or husbands and wives. This is why the Song has taken so long to penetrate the heart of the Shulammite. Like all of us, she has grown up among the shattered mirrors of earth's broken relationships. She has not known what a perfect image looks like. As a result, the Song has been easy to dismiss because it doesn't line up with our everyday perspective. Its melodies declare an intimacy that transcends all that we've seen and experienced. Nonetheless, the broken fragments of life can give us short glimpses into this intimacy from time to time. There are moments in life where the divine image shines forth on the small pieces of glass amongst our family and friends, where we lose sight of the rigid edges and cracks, and instead see a beautiful picture of the divine. This is what the world is looking for and it is why the Song is the greatest thing that could ever pierce the human heart.

This image of mutual love and belonging between God and us is breathtaking. This is what the Shulammite has woken up to. This entire floor or revelation lifts up the heart and fills it with an uncontainable joy. To understand that you belong somewhere is powerful. But to understand that you belong to God Himself *and that He belongs to you*...that is a whole other story.

The Third Story

And yet there is a whole *other* story to this building. The third level of this verse unites the previous two revelations and brings something else out of them. Now we must first issue a warning before we go up this next flight of stairs. Though it's only the third floor, it is still very high and people who fear heights may have a tough time with it. There are those who put up a lot of caution tape and fences around this third floor, because they're afraid of people flying off the deep end into heresy and strange teaching.

The Song of the Ages: Part II

Surely, there are a lot of good intentions behind these barriers; however, they can often prevent those who are genuinely seeking the Lord from seeing the beauty of this third floor with all of its panoramic views. Just because there are dangers of falling off and just because there have been abuses of this revelation in the past does not mean that we neglect what the Word is communicating. If a person is deeply established in the first two stories of the building, then they should boldly and confidently engage this final piece.

I am my Beloved's and my Beloved is mine.

If you look closer, you will see this entire statement is not just about belonging, surrender, and relationship. Hidden within these words, the Shulammite is also making a declaration of identity. If you listen closely, you can hear her singing something to this effect:

I am my Beloved and my Beloved is me.

Did you catch that?

In other words, she sees herself *as Jesus*. She has taken the reality of being *in Christ* to its furthest and highest conclusion. She understands the full implications of having received His name. She knows that this is far more than a legal transaction. His name is now hers in the sense that His life is now hers. It is no longer her, but Christ.

And so she begins this statement with two very important words—*I am.* This is in fact the name God gave for Himself when He came to Moses and to the young nation of Israel.

> *God said to Moses, "I AM WHO I AM"; and He said, "Thus you shall say to the sons of Israel, 'I AM has sent me to you.'"*
> *(Ex. 3:14)*

190

I Am is a mysterious name that comes from a Hebrew word that simply means "to be" or "to exist." It signifies the eternality of God. He is the One who simply *is*. This was different from every other name given to God in the Bible and it is thought to be one of the earliest times that the Hebrew people understood God's personal oneness. Amongst Jewish thought, the name was often rendered as "the self-existent One." Such honor and holiness was ascribed to this name that when scribes would copy the Scriptures onto new scrolls, they would have to stop and wash themselves every time they came to this word.

When God gave His name and introduced Himself to Israel through Moses, this was more than a simple hello. He was beginning the process of entering into a covenant with the people, which was the first part of His unfolding plan of restored union with humanity. When this covenant with Israel finally came, there were certain commandments attached to it, one of which was "thou shalt not take the name of the LORD thy God in vain" (Ex. 20:7 KJV). The King James and other translations capitalize all the letters in "Lord" to signify that God is using the personal name that He gave to Moses. Now we need to understand that this particular commandment is not about using the words "God" or "Jesus" as a curse word. The commandment to not take God's name in vain was is in reference to the covenant. The people were literally "taking His name" through a type of marital ceremony. And so the Lord is saying, *Do not take My name—I AM—in vain. Do not take it as though it means nothing. Honor My name and show yourself a people who are set apart by their covenant with Me.*

Of course, we know that the first covenant was incomplete and was only preparing the way for the final covenant of Christ. Now, because of the myrrh and wine of the Gospel, and because of the One who dwells in our garden, we have returned to union with the I Am. We have taken on His name in a deeper way than the Israelites in the Old Testament. God's name speaks to His nature, His eternal being, and His Spirit. We have taken His very being into ourselves. We are now one spirit with the Lord. Think about that statement again. *"He who is joined to the Lord is one spirit with Him"* (1 Cor. 6:17).

This means there is no delineation between your spirit and His. Your spirit, which is the essence of your being, the life of your life, is one and the same with God's. It is like you have mixed your earthly green with His heavenly blue and created an eternal aqua. Our green earth has united with blue heaven and a new creation has emerged. There is no separation between green and blue in a splash of aqua. So too, through the splash of Christ's blood, there is no separation between us and God. The I Am is the fabric of our being. This is far from blasphemy. This is both the spiritual and logical conclusion of the terminology that the Bible itself chooses to use—terminology of oneness.

In the Passion Translation, Dr. Brian Simmons points out something fascinating in his commentary on the Song of Solomon. He explains that the words "Shulammite" and "Solomon" are essentially the *same* Hebrew word. One is the feminine version of the word (Shulammite), while the other is the masculine (Solomon). Think about the beauty of this insight. The Holy Spirit actually moved King Solomon to pen this great love Song after he fell in love with a woman who shared a reflection of his own name. Today, it would be similar to a man named Jesse meeting and falling in love with a woman named Jesse and writing a song about it.

Herein lies a reminder that we ourselves come from the I Am. That is our true name and God has fallen in love with us according to the truth of who we are. We reflect Him, and it is through Christ that the fullness of this divine reflection is restored. King Solomon and the Shulammite woman continue to paint a beautiful picture of Christ and His Bride, who both share the same essence and being.

He Who Has Seen Me...

Let's think back to when the Bride lost sight of Jesus's presence and began looking for help. She cried out to the daughters of Jerusalem who responded by asking about the One she was so passionately searching for. The Shulammite's answer became the turning point of the whole Song as she gave a poetic description of Jesus's entire make-up and frame, beginning at the head. The description of His head gave us a strong reminder of the perfection and divinity of Christ. This was coupled with the truth that Jesus is the One who stands out among ten thousand. He is totally separate and beautiful. He is the *I Am*—holy and other and true.

But remember that she continued these worshipful descriptions and began going further down His body, describing His arms and hands and legs and feet. Something was happening at this point that has led us right to the Bride's full awakening where now we see the great revelation of the ages. She had been describing the glory of God, but then she began describing the glory of His body. As she shouted these things forth, a realization began to dawn on her: *The body is seamlessly connected to the Head.* You can imagine a holy moment in her heart when this realization emerged...

Hold on. I am the Body of Christ! I am one with the Head!

In other words... *I AM my Beloved's and He is mine!*

Her very description of Christ led to her to realize she was describing herself! Thus, when the daughters of Jerusalem asked where to find this glorious Man, she gave the following answer:

The Song of the Ages: Part II

He has gone down to the garden! He is within me! I am My Beloved's! If you are looking for Him, then look at me!

Do you see it?

This is why this portion of the Song is the very door hinge of the Word and the essence of the music of all creation. There is no greater realization than this. In times past, the church has not always embraced the full extent of this mystery, but the Holy Spirit is highlighting the Song of Solomon and other books of the Bible to help us see the fullness of who we are—and Whose we are. When the world looks for Jesus in the days ahead, the church will more confidently say, "Look at me! If you have seen me, you have seen the Lord."

And such is the life Jesus modelled to His disciples. At one point, toward the end of His ministry, the disciples wanted to see the Father. They were like the daughters of Jerusalem asking how to find God. Jesus's response to them was just as strange and wild as the Shulammite's. He said, "He who has seen Me has seen the Father" (Jn. 14:10).

From here, Jesus began to unfold the Father's plans for the disciples, which was to send them out in the same way that He was sent. They were to reveal Christ in the same way that He revealed the Father. It was during this same conversation that Jesus began to teach them about praying and acting in His name. This was far more than tacking "in Jesus's name" at the end of their bedtime prayers. This was a statement of absolute union and a full identification with God Himself. Speaking of His resurrection, which would mark the completion of this new identity, Jesus said the following words to His disciples:

In that day you will know that I am in My Father, and you in Me, and I in you.
(Jn. 14:20)

194

There it is. Plain and clear. We have been called to share in the same union and oneness that Christ has always enjoyed with the Father. This is what "taking His name" truly means. And in this same discourse with His disciples, Jesus promised that by truly taking His name, they would do even greater works than Him! This is an unbelievable statement, but He said it, and it's true. Historically, there have been those who've stepped into its truth. A good portion of the early church woke up to this revelation and they entered into world-changing "greater works" as a result. This is why the people around them ended up calling them "Christians." That is a word that amazingly means *little Christs.*

And is this not the purpose of the church—to manifest Jesus Christ? To be a living temple of the Spirit? A branch on the central vine? The physical Body of Jesus still walking the earth, healing bodies and souls and setting the captives free?

True Humility

Some will agree with this, but then assert that these conclusions unite us and Jesus too closely. They may be uncomfortable with the response of the Shulammite, who told the daughters of Jerusalem that if they wanted to see Christ then they should just look at her. They will say that this kind of language is misguided and we must point away from ourselves unto Jesus.

There are two responses to this.

First of all, there is no *us* to point away from.

We died.

When people talk about pointing away from themselves, they sometimes do this out of a continued sense of *self* in the first place. They feel that there is still a dark self that needs to be put down and discarded. This is why the "dark versus lovely" revelation was the first part of the Shulammite's journey and it continues to wind its way throughout the whole Song. Jesus has been trying to awaken her to the fact that the darkness is gone and their oneness is closer than the air she breathes. She is lovely, not because of anything she has done, but because of the One who made her lovely—the One who *is* her loveliness. The Shulammite has obviously come to grips with this and so she knows the old self is dead. All that is left is Christ.

Earlier, it was like she was singing, *I belong to sin and sin belongs to me.* Her words were out of key and the songs of heaven and earth had not been brought into true harmony. But now she has changed her tune. She sings, *I am my Beloved's and my Beloved is mine. The old is gone and Christ is now my life!*

Look again at the words of Paul:

> *...there is no distinction between Greek and Jew,*
> *circumcised and uncircumcised, barbarian, Scythian, slave*
> *and freeman, but **Christ is all**, and in all.*
> *(Col. 3:11)*

Christ *is* all.

He *is* all of us. The One Who Is, the I Am, is the breath and life of our being. We are Him and He is us. This is the revelation of the "third floor."

Now please understand that none of this should write off the utter importance of humility. This is the second response to the issue of pointing away from ourselves. We should certainly point away from any of our own efforts or contributions to these truths. We would do well to remind ourselves that this union is all because of Him—it is by Him and through Him and for Him. Jesus is the Creator and Sustainer of it all and without Him we are just clay vessels. There is no place for pride in this revelation.

But there is certainly no place for false humility either. Jesus Himself never watered down the full glory of who we were created to be. One time, after offensively revealing Himself as the I Am (see Jn. 8:58), Jesus spoke about our divine origin. To the Pharisees, He said the following words:

> *Jesus answered them, "Has it not been written in your*
> *Law, 'I said, you are gods'?"*
> *(Jn. 10:34)*

The problem comes when people try to jump to this third floor without traversing the first two. Numerous religions, cults, and philosophies do this by recognizing the inherent truth of our divine origin and destiny, but then negate or ignore the centrality of the Gospel. Satan doesn't outright feed poison to the masses; he mixes it in with divine truth. And some of the worst poison out there is hidden in some of the sweetest revelation of the Bible. That's why millions of people swallow up the deception in these cults and ideologies, because they can taste a little bit of the truth for which their spirit was designed. As a result, many become content with an idea of a nebulous oneness with a divine force or some broad spiritual teaching that says we are gods and creators in and of ourselves. But these realities are empty and pointless without first waking up to the mutual love and surrender of the Gospel.

We are not talking about an esoteric philosophy of beings "gods" apart from intimate relationship with Jesus and faith in His finished work. We cannot skip over those foundational levels of love and belonging. We are not *just* gods. We are first and foremost dependent beings called to surrender our lives in love to the One who surrendered His life for us. This is both the first and second level together. When these things are fully apprehended, it is then that we can begin to wake up to the third story of our membership within the Trinity.

Yes, you read that correctly. We are *members of the Trinity*.

The third story of the verse is our oneness with the Triune God.

A Part of the Trinity

If you believe that Jesus is God then this phrase should not scare you. For you are *members* of Christ (see 1 Cor. 12:28). Therefore, you are *members* of the Trinity. Christ is not separate from the Trinity. So if you are a member of Jesus, you are a member of the Triune God.

Perhaps you can think of it this way. We are a part of the Godhead (Father, Son, and Holy Spirit) like branches are part of a tree. We are the branches of the eternal Trinity, extending into time and space and bearing the fruit of His nature and being. When somebody thinks of a tree, very rarely do they separate the branches in their mind as a unique entity. When you think of a tree—you just think of a tree! Branches, bark, trunk, and all. It is the same with God and us. We are one entity. And yet we know that branches are indeed a unique part unto themselves (and a lifeless part unto themselves). A branch by itself is not a tree at all. In the same way, human beings in and of themselves are *not* God. But yet in and through Jesus...

Obviously, all of this is a mystery that goes beyond our rational either/or ways of thinking. But it is true nonetheless. This is the mystery of the ages and the awakening that is sweeping through the Body of Christ. From the glory of this truth, the greater works that Jesus promised will flow forth from His disciples like never before. Once again, the name "Christian" will take on its original meaning.

We will now begin to enter a new phase of the Song where we will see the victorious aftermath of this awakening. The Bride is now on a collision course with the greater works of Christ. From here on out, everything will be different.

14

A Tale of Two Cities

———•◆•———

You are as beautiful as Tirzah, my darling,
As lovely as Jerusalem,
As awesome as an army with banners.
Turn your eyes away from me,
For they have confused me;
Your hair is like a flock of goats
That have descended from Gilead.
Your teeth are like a flock of ewes
Which have come up from their washing,
All of which bear twins,
And not one among them has lost her young.
Your temples are like a slice of a pomegranate
Behind your veil.
(6:4-7)

The tidal wave of the Song has crashed. The shores have kissed. Free from the lies of the wall, the Shulammite is fully awake to the bliss of union. Everything is now just the overflow of that revelation as more and more waves pummel her. For the first time in a while, Jesus makes His presence known to the Shulammite and begins to speak to her again. Notice here that He does not say to her, "Finally! What took you so long?" Nor does He come and say, "Ok, now that you got it, let's get a move on. You've been wasting time, so let's get to work!"

No. He comes with the same love that He had when she was stuck on the bed of lies. Whether she's standing in the light of truth or in the shadow of darkness, His love does not change. He is the same yesterday, today, and forever. And so He comes again without any shame and without putting any new expectations or conditions upon her. Of course, Jesus would have every right to remind her of the things she could be doing. But now that she has woken up to the unfading realities of grace, He simply pours even more grace upon her! And this is exactly who He is...

> *For out of His fullness [the superabundance of His grace*
> *and truth] we have all received grace upon grace [spiritual*
> *blessing upon spiritual blessing, favor upon favor, and gift*
> *heaped upon gift].*
> *(Jn. 1:16 AMP)*

The more one pursues the grace of God, the more they find and the more they enjoy. The waves do not stop. As one rolls in, another wave is right behind it. "Whoever has will be given more, and they will have an abundance" (Matt. 13:12 NIV)! So let's continue to drink of the superabundance of grace being poured out from the lips of Jesus.

The Great Divide

The Beloved first compares the Shulammite to two cities. "You are as beautiful as Tirzah, my darling, as lovely as Jerusalem."

A Tale of Two Cities

"Tirzah" is a name that means pleasant or acceptable. Jesus continues to affirm how pleasant and enjoyable she is to Him; how He does not just "love" her, but He actually likes her and *enjoys her*. He then speaks of Jerusalem, a city known as the "joy of the whole earth" (Ps. 48:2). His comparison to Jerusalem attributes a sense of grandeur and holiness to His Bride. It bears repeating over and over again that this is how God sees us—not only delightful, but also full of splendor and majesty. The true church is the very throne of the Almighty, the place where His royal palace is set up upon the earth. Such truths realized in the heart change the way you live.

Now, as usual, there is a lot more going on in this passage. We'll continue to see that this is far more than an earthly love poem, for it would not be common to compare a woman you love to a city of buildings and governing bodies. There is a higher purpose to this comparison that we will unpack, which will first require a little bit of background on the cities being mentioned.

Jerusalem was of course the capital city of Israel and the home of Solomon's temple and palace. Shortly after his reign, Israel fell from the glory of Solomon's kingdom and the unified nation split into two. Toward the end of Solomon's life, the seeds of civil war were sown, which eventually blossomed when his son Rehoboam took over. A large portion of Israel rebelled against the king and formed their own nation under the leadership of a man named Jeroboam.

Jeroboam had been a key official under Solomon and was in charge of the king's workforce. He eventually led a revolt of the people who had felt that Solomon and his son were too oppressive in their labor demands. This led to ten tribes of Israel breaking away from Jerusalem and forming their own kingdom in the north. The southern kingdom stayed with Rehoboam and became known as the kingdom of Judah. Jerusalem remained the capital. In the north, Jeroboam initially set-up camp in the town of Shechem, but then shifted over to the city of Tirzah. As we can infer from the Song, this was a place that Solomon had dearly loved and admired. Now it had become the capital city of the rebellion (see 1 Kgs. 15:33).

Through of all this, remember that Israel was elected by God to speak to the nations of the world. The story of Israel throughout the Old Testament became a representative parable of humanity's fall and redemption. The split of the northern kingdom from the south is thus a picture of mankind's separation from the Lord. As the Son of David, Jesus is the Lion of the tribe of Judah and the true King of Jerusalem. It is fairly obvious that the southern kingdom of Judah would point us to God. The northern kingdom then represents the children of rebellion, those who have walked away from the Lord and from their true home in Him. (This also speaks to the southern winds of Songs of Songs 4:16, which are associated with warmth and paradise while the northern winds speak of bitterness and cold.)

All of this came about because an angelic deputy of God stirred up a rebellion in the first humans, which led us to form our own "city" (an organized way of life outside of the reign of God). The tower of Babel and the city of Babylon are two other representative pictures of this, which show mankind operating independently from the Creator. As this independence grew, so did the dividing wall of unbelief and fear in the minds of men. A new fleshly "nation" of separation and religion was firmly established throughout humanity.

When Solomon wrote his Song, Tirzah was a beautiful city that was part of the unified kingdom. It was never meant to be separate. Solomon probably would have never imagined that Tirzah would become the home of a rebellious nation within his own kingdom. This parallels the tragic rebellion of humanity, who was originally created as "pleasurable" and "acceptable" to God and was fashioned to walk in the fullness of His kingdom.

And yet herein lies the great hope hidden within the lyrics of the Song. The Shulammite is a picture of redeemed humanity—a spiritual nation and a royal priesthood. The Scriptures refer to her as *one new man* (Eph. 2:15).

The World Re-United

We have discussed this title before when we first looked at the dividing wall, behind which the Bride was still hiding in fear. This phrase is from the second chapter of Ephesians, a book that declares many other truths about the Bride of Christ. The "one new man" describes a re-united humanity in the Person of Jesus. It is Jew and Gentile coming together through the work of the cross, having moved past the lies of separation and fear. The New Jerusalem seen at the end of Revelation is another spiritual picture of this beautiful city and nation. This one new man is ultimately about Christ, the Jewish Messiah, being united with the people of the world.

The comparison to these two cities shows what the church fully represents. She is Tirzah and Jerusalem together—the northern and southern kingdoms united—God and humanity brought back together as one! This is glorious, majestic, and breathtaking—not only to us, but to Jesus Himself. When God looks at the church, He sees Jerusalem (Christ) and Tirzah (mankind) shining together and fulfilling the good pleasure of His will (see Eph. 1:9-10). This is a sight that continues to take His breath away.

"Turn your eyes from me," He says again. "They overwhelm me!"

It is still hard to imagine something that would cast awe and wonder into the heart of God. But that's just how incredible He is—an infinite God can accomplish a work that could even stun Himself! What's amazing is that this awe is rooted in the full unveiling of the church. This brings us back to the image of the rainbow from earlier when we discussed how God glorifies His own glory. God is like the white light of the sun with a rainbow hidden within. In the third chapter of Ephesians, Paul talks about a mystery that "from the beginning of the ages has been *hidden in God*" (Eph. 3:9). This great hidden rainbow of glory is now popping out through the prism of Jew and Gentile, the nations of the world, coming together in Jesus. An expanse of color was hidden within the light of God from before the foundation of the world, but now it is shining out through the awakened Bride.

The Bannered Army

In the midst of the imagery of two cities, there is also a statement made about a bannered army. Here is where we finally start seeing the advancing and conquering nature of the awakened church. The unity found in the spiritual picture of Tirzah and Jerusalem snowballs into a military metaphor. The idea of a bannered army speaks of a gloriously united force. Jesus describes it as "awesome," which is a word that could be translated as *terrifying beauty*. Think of a black hole of unfathomable size surrounded by a whirlpool of starlight slowly sucking you into itself. It's something that would hypnotize you with its splendor while causing your soul to tremble beyond words.

He specifically calls this a "bannered" army. In our earlier study of the Song we saw how banners were used as a rallying point for troops. They held the identifying crests of the army's nation and would be stationed in specific areas on the battlefield so that the troops could gather toward them in particular formations.

Jesus is now comparing the church to the world's finest armies. He is describing a body of people who are truly unified and moving forward. He is not seeing an ineffective and irrelevant church splintered into different denominations and factions. This is the true church, a seamless entity that conquers darkness with the unstoppable force of love.

So we see here that the Bride's awakening to divine union will overflow into true unity within the church. The truth of the Beloved dwelling in her garden has led her to this place. And surely the global church cannot move forward in unity without first coming to rest in our eternal union with Christ. Ecumenical movements and evangelistic initiatives will only produce a small measure of fruit without the realities of the cross placed at the center. This is why the true "advancing" nature of a unified church has been a rare thing throughout history. The greater works of love, unity, and power can only flow from a people who know who they are and who the I Am is. Global advancement and the destruction to darkness are fruits that arise out of our love for one another—something that won't happen apart from truly abiding in the love of Jesus.

This comparison to a terrifyingly beautiful army comes up again a little later, and so we will look at it in more detail then.

The Truth Again

Jesus then begins to marvel at the beauty of her hair, comparing it to "a flock of goats that have descended from Gilead." He then sings of her "teeth" and "temples." Here He begins reiterating previous truths that were already spoken in the Song. We will not spend as much time on these verses since we already unpacked many of them in our last study. There is, however, something important to point out at this juncture of the Beloved's praising words.

The Song of the Ages: Part II

First, a quick recap from the previous study. We found that the hair is an image of wisdom and its comparison to a "flock of goats" shows that the Bride's wisdom is rooted in sacrifice; particularly, the sacrifice of Jesus. The teeth speak of understanding and their comparison to a "flock of ewes" reveals a similar thing. Understanding is the practical application of wisdom. So not only does she carry the wisdom of the cross, but she has the spiritual understanding of walking it out. When Christ-centered wisdom and understanding are coupled together, they "bears twins and not one among them loses her young" (verse 6). This shows an innate fruitfulness within her—a fruitfulness that remains. The Messiah was anointed with both the "Spirit of wisdom and understanding" (Isa. 11:2). Here we are reminded that His Bride has that same Spirit within her (see Rom. 8:11). The "temples" then speak of her cheeks and the symbol of pomegranates shows her holding and speaking the message of Christ's blood. The temples can also describe the head, which would show that she has the mind of Christ.

In this season of the Shulammite's life, these attributes are becoming more outward and obvious. These qualities were not being exhibited in full force when she was still hiding in her bed and stuck behind certain lies. Yet what is amazing is that Jesus still praised her for these qualities back then. Nothing has essentially changed about who she is. The only difference is that now these elements are budding upon the branch of her life as she rests in the Lord.

So once more, this portion of the Song highlights the fact that our journey is not about changing into something we're not. Rather it is about realizing and growing into who we already are. Back in the fourth chapter of the Song, Jesus was already affirming these things, even while she was in a place of self-focus and fear. This was long before she confessed that the old was gone and then

208

opened the door of her heart. This was before she truly awoke to the Lord within her garden, the One whose very Name she shares. The fact that these verses are being spoken again are a deeper affirmation of how He has *always* seen her, even when she was not walking it all out.

Even in the northern kingdom of unbelief and isolation, Jesus still sees the truth of who we are. His eternal perspective never changes. We are still "Tirzah" to Him—acceptable and pleasurable. What wonder and joy comes from seeing the hope laden within this Song, a hope that reaches far beyond the walls mankind has erected. A hope that sees mankind joined together as one! The Shulammite's journey has brought her beyond the deceptive walls of separation into the Kingdom of peace and everlasting union. As we will see in the next verse, all of humanity is called to see and embrace these truths as well. Yet it is the rising Bride who has learned to say yes to it all. She is the one who begins to embody the message.

And the whole world will begin to notice.

Fifth Selah

Grace upon grace upon grace upon grace.

Gift upon gift, favor upon favor. Unfailing love upon more unfailing love.

And even more, and more, and more...

The waves do not stop. Love does not relent. Truth does not eclipse when you understand it. The grace and truth of Jesus is not something you "get" so that you can move on to other things. It is the heartbeat of the cosmos with an infinite expanse of life-giving arteries to travel through. It is the everlasting mountain that rises above all others. As soon as you reach one vista of the love of God, there are more cliffs to explore and more terrain to enjoy. The table of the love feast has been set and this table is the spaceship that carries you into the cosmic heartbeat. It's the climbing gear that brings you into the eternal heights of love.

Let's pause our hearts and just be. Let's *recline* at the table. We are creatures who often fall under the illusion that we are bound and controlled by time. We often feel stifled and limited by it. But we forget that eternity is a sovereign reality that does not wax and wane with our temporal experience. Time itself is only a gift whereby we can appreciate and grow in the glory of eternal truths.

But either way, the fullness of God's grace is ours for all eternity. And so it is quite okay to pause and reflect and come away.

"Coming away" in the Song of Solomon is really about coming away from an old identity into the new creation life of Christ. But it can also mean to come away from the pressure to have everything figured out, as well as the pressure to perform and get stuff done. The pressure to do. Time is on your side when you rest in God. It's a paradox, but it's true. It's like a Chinese finger trap where you counterintuitively give in to the trap in order to find release. As you waste time on grace, your personal time is redeemed.

It's okay to just be. God's unfolding plan is not dependent on you. You can sit back and just let the waves carry you. In fact, you may find yourself drifting into places you could not paddle on your own when you were so focused on time and personal responsibility.

Selah.

15

The Difference Between a Queen and a Bride

There are sixty queens and eighty concubines,
And maidens without number;
But my dove, my perfect one, is unique:
She is her mother's only daughter;
She is the pure child of the one who bore her.

The maidens saw her and called her blessed,
The queens and the concubines also,
and they praised her, saying...
(6:8-9)

Once again, there is more to these verses than meets the eye. The mention of "sixty queens," "eighty concubines," and "maidens without number" carries incredible meaning, hidden and kept for those who would draw near to the Lord and listen to the whisper of His singing heart.

There are many reasons why we should recognize that there is a deeper message to this part of the Song. First of all, these are not accurate numbers from Solomon's life. In 1 Kings 11, we find that Solomon had far more marriages than this. In fact, he had about 700 wives and 300 concubines. There is a specific reason the Holy Spirit moved Solomon to pen these particular numbers. "Sixty" and "eighty" are used strategically and spiritually to communicate something of a greater meaning. (Now perhaps the Song was written at an earlier time in Solomon's life when he did in fact have sixty wives. But this would be no less spiritually significant, for the Holy Spirit would have moved Solomon to write this Song at that exact moment in his life. He could have written the Song when he had 400 wives or 230 concubines, but he wrote it at this precise moment, thus highlighting the importance of the numbers sixty and eighty.)

We need to go back to what was said in our first study of the Song and realize that we must look at this writing with the Hebraic model of interpretation called *sod*. This was the way the apostles and even Jesus Himself often interpreted Scripture. It involves pointing out the spiritual mystery behind a passage. A big part of this interpretative method involves finding the meaning behind certain numbers. This is not to be confused with people who claim that there are hidden codes within the numbers of the Bible that forecast specific events. We are simply talking about symbolic meanings, such as the story of Jonah's three-day visit in the belly of the whale, which represented Jesus's three-day descent into the belly of the earth (Matt. 12:40).

First, let's take a step back at the look at the Song of Songs from a natural and unspiritual perspective. The Song is a lyrical poem written by an earthly king who had married a multitude of women and who had numerous concubines as well. As the nation's ruler, he was also entitled to any of the unmarried maidens within his kingdom, which were far more plentiful and thus "without number." This is from a polygamous society where it was common for kings to have such a multiplicity of relationships. Most of

Solomon's "queens" were the daughters of foreign kings who had been espoused to him for political purposes. Concubines were simply for sexual pleasure or for producing an heir. The overall poem and song was then written to one of the king's brides, whom he loved above all other queens, concubines, and maidens. This was a woman with whom he shared true intimacy and friendship. She was someone from the region of Shulam who had romantically captured his heart.

Now let's make something very clear. In all of His blessings to this literal king of Israel, God was never condoning polygamy. God has patiently and graciously walked with humanity through our immaturity and deception. The Lord made it clear in Genesis that marriage was between one man and one woman. Nonetheless, in our descent from our original design, the Lord has worked within our broken societies and tolerated things like polygamy and divorce, though never once declaring them as right and just.

Therefore, like any other part of Solomon's Song, it is important we see this with spiritual eyes. God is speaking to us through the writings of Solomon, even in his fallen lifestyle as an earthly king. Just like Jesus (the living Word) took on human flesh, the Bible (the written Word of God) often takes on the fallen flesh of man to communicate an eternal message of truth and hope. In the words of Joseph, God makes something good out of what man intends for evil (see Gen. 50:20). God takes Solomon's polygamous lifestyle and brings out an amazing revelation through it. That is what we will unpack in this chapter.

The Number of Man

In the book of Revelation, the apostle John is given spiritual understanding into the meaning of a particular number—six. This is the only time that the Scriptures blatantly explain the meaning of a specific number. Oftentimes it takes deeper study and prayer to discern numerical interpretations, but John makes it very easy for us in this case. He is first shown the infamous marking of "666" and is then given insight into its spiritual meaning. He tells us that this is the "number of man" (Rev. 13:18). This interpretation of six shouldn't surprise us for man was created on the *sixth day* (Gen. 1:31). Six relates to anything regarding humanity. Whether six or sixty (or 600 or 666), all of it points to the same general meaning.

So with our spiritual eyes wide open, we can start to see that Solomon is writing about "sixty queens" for a specific reason. There is a symbolic connection between this statement and the number of man. Now before we look more closely at Solomon's words, let's look at a few other instances in Scripture where this number shows up. This will help give us a more thorough understanding of its meaning as well as the amazing revelation hidden in Solomon's poem.

In the Pentateuch, the first five books of the Bible, Moses uses the number "sixty" when giving directions for sacrificing a peace offering to God. Today, we understand that these sacrifices were never about the animals themselves, but what they were pointing to—the ultimate sacrifice of Jesus. As our true peace offering, He is the One who restores harmony between man and God. Moses specifically instructs the priests to offer "sixty" innocent lambs as a sacrificial peace offering. He also instructs them to sacrifice sixty rams and sixty goats (see Num. 7:88). Seeing that six is the number of man, Moses's instructions reveals that the true Lamb of God took upon Himself the sins of *all mankind.* All of humanity's sin—sin itself—was absorbed into the body of Jesus and crucified. As John the Baptist said, "Behold, the Lamb of God who takes away *the sin of the world*" (Jn. 1:29). The law was symbolically prophesying this through the sixty lambs of the peace offering.

Later, in the book of Deuteronomy, Moses recounts the defeat of a wicked king named Og. This man had sought to destroy the Israelites in the same way that Pharaoh wanted to destroy them at the Red Sea. Og is a satanic figure who wants to steal, kill, and destroy. By the help of God, the Israelites defeat this king and go on to conquer all of the cities that were under his control. There were "sixty cities" to be exact (see Deut. 3:4). This also symbolically points us to the work of Christ. Jesus has completely defeated the enemy and has regained authority over the entire earth (Matt. 28:18). This means that Jesus is now the true king over the "sixty cities" of the world. In other words, He is the true King over all mankind. Not everyone kneeling and bowing before the King, but that does not nullify the truth of His reign.

Going backwards in the Old Testament, the number six shows up in a fascinating way in the story of the flood. The Scriptures recount that Noah was exactly 600 years old when the floodwaters covered the earth (Gen. 7:6). This speaks of two things. First, it conveys the universal judgment that came upon mankind's sin through the flood. Yet there's another side of that coin. In the story we find 600-year-old Noah entering the ark with his entire family and thus all of future humanity with them. At that point, every single person who has ever lived since the flood was hidden in the loins of Noah and his sons. Therefore, this is also a picture of the mercy that was released upon all of mankind. All of the world—represented by 600-year-old Noah and his family—would be hidden in the ark of Jesus Christ, the true Lamb of God who took the sin of the world upon Himself (just like the ark took on the floodwaters of judgment as they enveloped and beat against it).

When you get to the story of Israel's exodus from Egypt, this number shows up in a different way. As we've discussed before, Israel is a light to the nations and gives us a representative picture of God's purposes for mankind. Interestingly enough, the Bible points out that 600,000 men left Egypt after the Lamb's blood was put on their doorposts (Ex. 12:37). The meaning of this should be more obvious by now. After His blood was spilt, Jesus raised us up out of the spiritual Egypt of sin. His resurrection presented mankind innocent before God. Because of this, He is "not counting men's trespasses against them" (2 Cor. 5:18). The 600,000 men leaving Egypt represents humanity being taken out of the condemnation of sin. It like 600-year-old Noah leaving the cursed earth to hide in the safety of the ark.

The number "sixty" shows up again during the construction of Solomon's temple. Throughout our studies of the Song, we have made it abundantly clear that the temple represents the church. We are indeed the true temple of His Spirit. Remarkably, Solomon's temple was built "sixty cubits" high (1 Kgs. 6:2). Its height (or stature) is the number of man. This is fitting considering human flesh was chosen to host the presence of Jesus. Therefore, mankind (symbolically represented by sixty cubits of height) was designed to be the true temple of God's Spirit.

Long after the construction of the temple, we are told an interesting accounting fact about Solomon's wealth. The Scriptures tell us that 666 talents of gold were annually brought into his treasury from the surrounding nations (2 Chr. 9:13). This was a huge amount of gold that came into the kingdom from all over the earth at the height of Solomon's reign. The spiritual meaning of this is similar to the other instances. Humanity is the true "wealth of the nations" that God longs to come into His spiritual temple (Isa. 60:5). They are the lost "coins" who truly belong to God (see Lk. 15:8). Therefore, the 666 talents of gold coming into Solomon's kingdom spiritually represent mankind being brought into Christ's Kingdom.

Much later in the history of Israel, after they are divided, conquered, and exiled into the surrounding nations, this number shows up yet again. When the exiles finally return from slavery, one of the heads of an Israelite clan named Adonikam brings 666 people with Him in order to rebuild the temple (Ezra 2:13). The name Adonikam means "Lord of rising." This is yet again a picture of Jesus Christ who is the true Head of humanity. Through His death and "rising," Jesus has brought mankind back to the Father in order to rebuild the temple of His Spirit.

One last example. There is something we didn't point out in our previous study of the Song when discussing the "sixty men" surrounding King Solomon's travelling caravan (see Sgs. 3:7). We mentioned that this caravan gave us a picture of Christ seated upon the Mercy Seat of heaven. We then connected the sixty armed men with the angelic host that surrounds the presence of God, bringing us strength and protection in our own journey. But like so many other Scriptures, there are even more layers to this verse.

The King being surrounded "sixty men" is also a picture of Jesus being surrounded, or clothed, with humanity. Think back to Jeremiah's mysterious prophecy about a woman encompassing a man (Jer. 31:22). This is a similar word picture of humanity surrounding the Christ. Jesus is clothed in flesh, which is again what the number six represents. This mystery of the incarnation is hidden all throughout the Scriptures. Jesus's union with humanity is indeed one of the greatest messages of the entire Bible.

Sixty Queens

Unpacking the meaning of different symbols in Solomon's Song is much like playing a hidden object game where one looks for concealed items within a crowded picture. The hidden item is technically right there in front of you, and yet it's very difficult to see unless you know what you're looking for. That's why hidden object games usually have a key or a list so that the viewer knows what they're searching for. If they know they should be on the lookout for a pail or a shovel, then their eyes can pick it up more easily when they come across it hiding in a bouquet of flowers.

Understanding the biblical meaning of the number "sixty" is like receiving one of those clues. As we let our eyes scan over this verse again, the strategic message behind Solomon's "sixty queens" is opened up to us in a new way. Now that we know the biblical meaning of that number, we find here in the sixth chapter of the Song that God is speaking about something quite spectacular. We can now see the concealed message. In Solomon's mention of sixty queens, God is speaking to us about His marriage to *all of mankind*.

Now before you dismiss that statement and say that God is *only* married to the church, please understand the full context of what is being communicated. We will find in a moment that there is a great difference between a queen and a *bride*. But first, let's get some more understanding into who and what a "queen" represents. A queen is obviously someone with royal power and authority. More specifically, a queen is the feminine side of a nation's reign. This connects to God and humanity. In Genesis 1, man is fashioned after God's image and is then immediately given authority over the earth. And so mankind has always been like an earthly "queen" to the King of heaven.

Besides this queenly identity of mankind, there is another key element to consider when discussing God's marriage to humanity. It is important to remember that through the incarnation, Christ has united Himself to *everyone*. This is why His death was the complete end of the old man—the corporate Adamic race (read Romans 5 and Romans 6:6 *together*). Paul clearly taught that "one died for all, therefore *all* died" (2 Cor. 5:14). The same "all" that

He died for is the same *all* that actually died. There is not a single person that Jesus did not represent in His death—and He could not represent them and die *as* them without being in some form of union with them.

The apostle John also taught that Christ's blood tangibly applies not only to the church, but to the entire world (1 Jn. 2:2). The apostle Peter went so far to say that the "spirits in prison"—people who lived and died long before Jesus even entered the earth—had this same good news preached to them as well. Thus they were also able to be released from the prison of death (1 Pet. 3:19 & 4:6). All of this brings us back to John the Baptist's famous words about the Lamb of God who took away the sin of the world. This was an accomplished work! It is not just a potential hope for those who intellectually believe it. All sin was atoned for at the cross, for Christ was united with the sin of all humanity, whether past, present, or future.

A Complete Atonement and a Loving Bride

Bear with this quick detour on the atonement of Christ for it connects very powerfully with the story of the Shulammite and the people she is beginning to impact.

The Gospel of Christ's work on the cross does not become true when a person believes it. It is already true and our faith is simply an acceptance and awakening to that reality. Therefore, the Gospel is not bad news for the masses of humanity with a condition of surrender attached to it that makes it potential good news. The Gospel is an exceedingly joyful announcement of a finished victory, which is why it's called *news*! The word "Gospel" in the Greek (*euagelion*) does not signify an offer, but a clear announcement. This is why the angels at Jesus's birth proclaimed *good tidings of great joy for all people* (Lk. 2:10)!

In reality, Jesus drew all humanity to Himself and reconciled all things by His blood (see Jn. 12:32 & Col. 1:20). Salvation is the result of the pure grace of God alone. But here's something incredibly important: The benefits and experience of this salvation come *through* faith. Our salvation is by grace *through* faith (Eph. 2:8). But again (and this is so important), faith is simply agreeing with what has already been accomplished. It is resting in something tangible and solid. You can't lay your head on a pillow that doesn't exist. You lay your head on a pillow that is present and available. A person coming to faith is someone who has rested their head on the pillowy rock of Christ—a rock that was already present on the bed of their existence. All of this is why Paul says that "Christ is the Savior *of all men,* especially those who believe" (1 Tim. 4:10).

This is absolutely central in understanding the wine, the myrrh, and the apple tree of the cross—that central message of Solomon's text and of the whole Bible. Everything is about the New Covenant, which is a covenant that was enacted between the Father and the Son. We had no part to play in this. We had already thoroughly failed in the covenant-keeping business. This is why the Father extended His own arm and worked out salvation all by Himself (Isa. 59:16). This happened through the Son who represents all of humanity, not just an exclusive club of people who do or say the right things. This is why the unborn, the mentally ill, the unreached, and those who died before Jesus's coming are all included in the Gospel's pronouncement. Jesus Christ is the obedient response of humanity to the Father!

In the end, there will be no boasting among men. We will not even boast in our *faith* or *decision.* Jesus has done it all and in eternity we will marvel at this for ages and ages (and I expect we will look back and have a hearty laugh over man's self-aggrandizing doctrines about gaining or losing one's own salvation, as though we had any part to play in this glorious work). All people are brought into the covenant, because that covenant was enacted between the Father and the Son on behalf of all. Some may insist on rejecting the wedding party or stand outside the celebration like the older brother in the parable of the prodigal son—but that does not negate the fact of their initial invite and welcome.

Our belief in the truth does not make the truth real to God—it makes it real to us. And that changes everything. So we are not talking about some forced universalism. The problem is that not all have woken up to this glorious message and said "yes" to it in their own hearts. All are under the shade of the apple tree, but not all have laid their heads down under that tree and found rest. The issue really comes down to what was mentioned at the beginning of this discussion. There is a difference between a queen and a bride. Both are included in the King's love and in His saving work, but it is the bride who truly knows Him and draws near to the inner chambers of intimacy and friendship.

Let's paraphrase Solomon's statement here. "I have sixty queens…but my bride is unique" (we'll talk about the "concubines" and "maidens" in a moment). Here's what this translates to: Though God is united with all of humanity through the incarnation, only *one* has awoken to that love and union. As the Father of all creation, He is good and all-powerful and has brought salvation and redemption to all. And yet He is not looking for a forced relationship. Hence the reason for the Bridegroom's continual words, "Do not awaken My love until she pleases!" The Lord wants a relationship of mutual love. He is looking for the "one" who will wake up and joyfully receive this amazing grace (and then manifest its beauty to a world still asleep). He is looking for a companion of love, not a servant or a political partner.

As we mentioned before, a queen in Solomon's day was often espoused to a king for reasons that had very little to do with love.

In fact, the queen could be one of the most distant people from the king in his palace. Oftentimes, a queen was just a political pawn or a way to produce an heir for the kingdom.

So let's think back to the human perspective of this poem. A Jewish king named Solomon had numerous women all around him. He had sixty queens espoused to him through a real covenant of marriage. Yet, for the most part, it was all loveless. And yet there was a young maiden from Shulam who had stolen his heart. She is the one who had fully received his love and desired to rest in his presence. This is why the word *bride* is so important. A bride is an intimate term that signifies a true connection and a two-way relationship. The espoused queens of humanity are called to become *brides*—that is what God is looking for and that is how heaven truly invades the earth.

But in all of this, it is important to remember that our faith is not a work. Faith is an effortless response of joy—it is gleefully drinking from the cup of covenantal wine that Jesus has already poured out for all. At the cross, God knelt down on one knee and proposed His love to all of us. At that same cross, Jesus said "I do" to the Father. We get to simply stand in awe over it all and drink it in by faith. We get to join in with Jesus and also say "I do" as we taste and see how kind and gracious He is. This is how we continually enter the House of Wine, which is ready and open for all!

In the days ahead, be ready to open your gaze even wider to the wonders of the cross. Get ready for any religious thinking to be stretched by the all-encompassing grace of God. More than ever, we need to guard our hearts from the deep offense that often comes as God reveals more of His goodness to His children. There are realities within His finished work that will shock us to our core as we see how powerful and far-reaching it is.

Concubines and Maidens

Solomon goes on to talk about how he also has "eighty concubines and maidens without number." This statement gives us further understanding into the people of the world and their relationship with their Creator. They are those within the "queen of humanity." Symbolic language does not often follow a logical structure. Solomon begins by talking about sixty queens, but then expands the spiritual meaning behind it by discussing concubines and maidens. This shows us that within the queen of humanity there are different types of people and different layers to people's knowledge of God.

We'll look at the eighty concubines first. The number eighty is not as well-defined in the Scriptures as the number six. While many correctly point out that eight is the number of new beginnings, there are a lot of other references that suggest another aspect of it. Solomon had "80,000 stonecutters" for the work of the temple (2 Chr. 2:18). A righteous priest named Azariah once brought "eighty" men with him to challenge a wicked king. These men were known as valiant priests of God (2 Chr. 26:7). Later on in the history of Israel, a faithful king named Jehu brought "eighty" servants with him to destroy the false priests of Baal (2 Kgs. 10:24).

As we see in these stories, the number eighty can speak of those who are in service to the king. The imagery of eighty concubines is thus a graphic and stark metaphor that gets a deep point across. When the Song mentions Solomon's concubines, it is talking about those who serve the true King of heaven but do not have the same type of trust and intimacy as the rising Bride. Indeed, a concubine was someone who did not share a deep relationship with the king. She certainly engaged in one level of physical intimacy with him (which is a symbol of "knowing" someone), but this did not transcend into a heart-felt relationship.

The Song of the Ages: Part II

A concubine can be a symbol of someone who "knows" about God and may even produce spiritual children for Him, yet it is usually surface knowledge with a relationship based on works. They often lack a deep intimacy and knowledge of their own identity—and God's. This is what Solomon's eighty concubines point to. They may be servants of God, but they have not plumbed the depths of intimate friendship and oneness with Christ.

Now as we continue in this study of the Song, please understand that we are not talking about a hierarchy within humanity or saying that some people are better or more special than others. That is very important to recognize. Even our deeper knowledge and intimacy with God is a gift. It is all by grace and no one can claim any merit of their own in the depth of their relationship with the Lord. In looking at this verse, we are simply discussing the varying degrees of people's awakening to the Gospel. God loves all His children with the same love, but there are those who have truly awakened to that love and have entered into a closer relationship because of it.

In regard to maidens, Solomon says that they are "without number." This shows an even wider extent of the queen of humanity—those who do not even "know" the true God at all. The word "maiden" is synonymous with the word "virgin." From that natural standpoint, a virgin maiden was a woman in the kingdom who had not yet been with the king or any other man for that matter. It is thus speaking of someone who does not *know* God yet and does not even consciously serve Him.

Throughout the queen of humanity, there are an abundance of concubines who know God to a certain extent and even serve Him, but there are far more who are "maidens." These speak to those who know even less of the Lord's love and have not heard the fullness of His Gospel. These are the maidens without number.

And yet they are still longing for Him. They are still seeking after Him in a hidden way. This is why the Song begins by declaring that the maidens "love Him" (Sgs. 1:3). Even as spiritual maidens, their hearts are still hungering and longing after the true Desire of the nations, Jesus Christ (Hag. 2:7).

The Embodiment of the Song

We then come back to the description of the Shulammite Bride. Solomon says, "But my dove, my perfect one, is unique: She is her mother's only daughter; she is the pure child of the one who bore her."

The Bride is the one who is fully identified with the dove of the Holy Spirit and with the perfecting work of Christ. Yet as we've seen over and over again, this glorious identity is not the result of any work of her own. She is unique because she has truly awakened to the work of the cross. She is the one who reflects God's own perfection because of her ascent to the Summit of Truth. This is what the entire journey has been about. And so it is absolutely vital that we understand *the truth is true even before a person believes it*. Even when the Shulammite was hiding behind a wall of doubt and fear, Jesus still referred to her in these amazing terms.

As we've pointed out before, our journey isn't about climbing a spiritual mountain by our own sweat and blood in order to attain some glorious victory. The scandal of the Gospel is that the mountaintop was already brought to us and our journey of climbing is really about discovering and receiving that free gift. But when we truly understand this, we must then come to terms with the fact that this has serious implications for the "queen" of humanity, including all the spiritual "concubines" and "maidens" out there.

The Song of the Ages: Part II

Think again of the Bride's own journey. It began with her being somewhat like a maiden, not even fully knowing the King or the way to find Him. Thus she was led on the path of grace as she came to the King's table in order to receive His sacrifice into her heart. That is where all true spiritual discovery takes place.

One could argue that at the beginning of the Song the Shulammite was also like a spiritual concubine. She appeared to have some knowledge of Jesus, but did not know Him intimately. She was serving in the vineyards of religion, but was tired and burnt out and ridden with a false identity. As a type of maiden and concubine, she was led into a greater understanding of the depths of His love. First, she found Him as the Shepherd of the lost sheep, but then she began to find Him as the gentle lover of her soul.

The Bride's journey is the journey of all humanity, no matter where they are. Every single person is a potential temple of glory, but that glory is hidden behind a veil of unbelief and deception. However, that doesn't mean that the glory isn't there. As Isaiah said, the whole earth is *full* of His glory (Isa. 6:3). It is when the truth shines in and God's love is received that the veil over our spirit is torn and Christ in us, the full image of God, manifests. This is why Paul teaches that when a person simply *"hears and understands* the grace of God in truth" that they bear the fruit of His glory (see Col. 1:6).

The Bride is not more "special" than others. And yet she is, because she has believed His Word and allowed that "specialness" to come forth. She is perfect and unique, because she has said yes to the wedding wine and has fully received the perfection that was already hers. She is the one who has said yes to the eternal love that is ever flowing to the earth. And this is the clear call to every single person—to let go of all fear and striving and discover a righteousness that was there from the beginning.

This is the Song that all creation is called to awaken to. For those whose eyes are opened, whose hearts believe, they will experience its full power and effect. And as we receive this truth, we begin to "embody" it. We literally become the "Body" of Christ, who already fills and sustains all things. Perhaps all of this will bring more understanding into this mysterious passage from the book of Ephesians...

> *The church, which is His body, is the fullness of Him who*
> *fills all in all.*
> *(Eph. 1:23)*

The church is the *fullness* of Him who *fills all in all.* This is somewhat of a confusing statement that is often glossed over as a person goes from the first chapter of Ephesians to the second. But this small statement is hinting at something beyond comprehension. The church is the *embodiment* of the One who already fills all things.

When Solomon says that his Bride is "unique," the word for *unique* can actually be translated as "one." *My Bride is one.* In other words, the Bride is embodying union. She is manifesting the incarnation between God and humanity in the person of Jesus. Her life is now showcasing the One who already *fills all things.* And this is indeed the ultimate dream and pleasure of God. This was Jesus's great prayer in John 17, that we would come into true oneness with God and one another. The Bride is the one who has come into the experience of this prayer. She has transcended spiritual ignorance, religious head knowledge, and dry servitude in order to taste the pleasures of God and become the fulfillment of His dream. In other words, *she has moved from maidenhood to bridal love.*

The Song of the Ages: Part II

The Bride represents those who have heard the Song of the Ages, the Song of infinite grace, and have learned to dance to its glorious music. Her dance will now start to awaken a world of queens, concubines, and maidens, who are still deaf to it all, caught up in lesser tunes and darker light. But as the Bride dances to this music, she *becomes the music*. And in becoming the music, she begins to manifest Christ within. The Shulammite is a queen of Solomon like everyone else. But she is different in that she has embraced the fullness of her Bridegroom's love. And now she is catching the attention of everyone around her. This is why the Song of the Ages manifesting through the church will change the whole landscape of the planet. The entire world will see the church and "call her blessed!"

The next portion of the Song will unravel one of the most triumphant descriptions of the Bride yet. But this time the description does not come from Jesus. Now it is the entire world who begins to speak of the Bride.

16

Who is She?

———— •◆• ————

Who is this that grows like the dawn,
As beautiful as the full moon,
As pure as the sun,
As awesome as an army with banners?
(6:10)

Something has transpired in the heart of the Shulammite that has translated into her outward and visible life. No longer is this the fearful young maiden questioning her identity and going back and forth in the love of Christ. This is now someone who has found her rest in the pastures of grace, who will never turn back to the city of religion and fear. Her verbal confession of union with the Beloved now matches the inner confession of her heart, and the alignment of the two has brought a deep awakening in her body, soul, and spirit. The veil of unbelief has been put away and now the light that was always hiding behind it is radiating out. As a result, the nations of the earth are beginning to take notice. In this scene of the Song, we will see a fulfillment of Isaiah's prophetic word about God's people:

The Song of the Ages: Part II

Arise, shine; for your light has come,
And the glory of the Lord has risen upon you.
For behold, darkness will cover the earth
And deep darkness the peoples;
But the Lord will rise upon you
And His glory will appear upon you.
Nations will come to your light,
And kings to the brightness of your rising.
(Isa. 60:1-3)

Who are those kings of the earth? They are the symbolic "queens" of humanity, especially its rulers and leaders. But this extends to the concubines and maidens of the world as well. Young and old, rich and poor. All the nations are being drawn to the glory of the Lord that is shining out through His awakened temple—the Bride of Christ and the jewel of His heart. The jewel that calls out to all other jewels that are still exiled and hidden behind their own veils of unbelief.

This has always been the call to the church—to arise like the sun and shine like the moon that reflects it, so that all might be pulled toward the beauty of Christ. This is our destiny: to be a worldwide signpost of glory that will ultimately draw all nations into God's Kingdom. There is a day coming when the church will be so alive to the Gospel of grace that it will manifest in a light that will transform the *entire world*.

There is a strong biblical foundation to this hope. Jesus's commandment to disciple "all nations" is something He planned on seeing fulfilled (Matt. 28:19). His metaphoric "mustard seed" that grew to become the biggest tree in all the land is a sure reality as well (see Matt. 13:31-32). Daniel's "rock" that became a mountain that filled the whole earth is getting at the same promise (Dan. 2:44). Isaiah said something similar:

Who is She?

*Now it will come about that in **the last days** the mountain of the house of the Lord will be established as the chief of the mountains, and will be raised above the hills; and all the nations will stream to it. And many peoples will come and say, "Come, let us go up to the mountain of the Lord... For the law will go forth from Zion and the **word of the Lord** from Jerusalem."*
(Isa. 2:2-3)

The apostles told us that we are presently in the "last days" time period (see Heb. 1:2, 9:26 & 1 Cor. 10:11). Therefore, Isaiah's prophecy is not about some future reality *after* Jesus returns. This involves the current age of time that we are in right now. The "word of the Lord" and the "law" of love went out from Jerusalem in the first century and now its destiny is to transform the entire earth—here and now. The fate of the church is to be the largest "mountain" to which all peoples "will stream." In the same way, the church is the leaven that will eventually work itself into the *entire* dough of humanity (see Matt. 13:33).

Washed in the Blood

Deception runs thick through the theology of the church, like black mud coursing through a silver pipe. The apostles referred to this as "doctrines of demons." One of these darkened doctrines involves a hopeless and catastrophic view of the future. A view that says the church will grow weaker while the world grows more wicked until we get to a point where the church is called up to the mother-ship in a "rapture" that will leave the earth abandoned to destructive fire. How it must satisfy the pride of God's "saved ones" to consider themselves safe from this divine terror and rejection (though they will often say that they teach these doctrines with "a heavy heart." I'm sure the Pharisee Saul casted his vote of stoning Stephen with a *heavy heart* as well).

There is something else on God's timetable before any physical rapture and before the second coming of Christ. This is absolutely central to understand as we look at the story of the Shulammite, the representative figure of the Body of Christ. What this story shows, as well as numerous prophetic Scriptures and apostolic teachings, is that there is a massive awakening growing within the Bride that will one day awaken the rest of the world—the "sixty" queens of Solomon.

Earlier we took a detour into discussing the atonement and now we take a bypass through some eschatology, the study of the "end-times." These are not irrelevant discussions. They are key facets of the Bride's journey throughout the Song. The central message of the Song is the blood of Christ and it is His blood that washes and purifies every "doctrine" of the church, whether soteriology (the study of salvation), ecclesiology (the study of the church), or eschatology. Indeed, all of our "ologies" need to be bathed in the waters of the cross, which run through the entire Bible and flood Solomon's Song with a rush of clarity. Ultimately, it is "theology" itself, *the study of God*, that needs to be washed in the blood of the Lamb—for it is Christ who came to perfectly reveal the Father (Heb. 1:3).

Church history is unfolding in Solomon's poetry and we are reaching the climax of the journey in the sixth and seventh chapters of the Song. Therefore, let's continue down this road of the church's impending destiny.

The Manifestation of God's Children

All creation is groaning and waiting for something. Interestingly, Paul doesn't says that creation is groaning and waiting for the return of Christ. Rather, it is waiting for the "manifestation of the sons of God" (Rom. 8:19 KJV). This is not denying that there is a physical return of Christ on the horizon of human history. However, His return will happen after "we all come into the unity of the faith and the knowledge of the Son of God, *to a mature man*, to the measure of the stature which belongs to *the fullness of Christ*" (Eph. 4:13). That's a statement Paul made when discussing five-fold ministry. He said that the work of ministries like pastoring and evangelizing will continue *until* those realities are in place. If evangelizing continues until the "mature man" of "the fullness of Christ" comes forth, you can be certain that Jesus won't be returning before that. (Read Eph. 4:11-13 as a whole unit.)

Christ died so that a crop of resurrection life would come; one that would lead to a corporate body walking in the full dimension of sonship that He walked in. The earth is waiting for the full reward of His suffering to manifest itself in a church moving in true unity. This is the emerging Bride who is "unique" and walks in the full measure of her Beloved's stature. And so the earth is in labor with a hidden fetus that is growing and developing. That is the journey of church history: transformation from the womb of faith into the birthing of manifestation and fullness. As a global church, we are going from glory to glory in this journey.

Now here's something important to understand. There are principles of truth here that are not just about the future of the entire church. This is not only about a coming epoch of glory for the church. It is also about a hopeful epoch in the life of every believer who chooses to go down the rabbit hole of grace. Awakening to the love of Christ will always lead to an outward manifestation of His glory. Every individual is invited into the Shulammite's journey, to open their eyes to God's grace so that the hope of glory within can radiate out.

Nonetheless, this also speaks of the journey of the whole Shulammite Bride and a global awakening of grace that is near and, even now, is upon us.

Greater Works and Greater Fulfillment

In one sense, the Isaiah 60 promise of the nations being drawn to the light is already fulfilled. It was fulfilled with the birth of Christ and His subsequent life as the glorious Messiah of Israel. Look at verse 6 of that prophecy:

> *A multitude of camels will cover you,*
> *The young camels of Midian and Ephah;*
> *All those from Sheba will come;*
> *They will bring gold and frankincense,*
> *And will bear good news of the praises of the Lord.*
> *(Isa. 60:6)*

The glory of Israel and the light of the world came to the earth as a baby named Jesus, and wise men from other nations brought him literal gold and frankincense. As this King grew up, many other people came to Him, being drawn to His light as Israel began to shine with hope like never before. Soon after Christ's resurrection and ascension, His disciples saw an influx of people from many different nations coming to salvation at the feast of Pentecost (see Acts 2:5). This is a picture of "the abundance of the sea" being turned over to God's Kingdom (Isa. 60:5). All these different elements of Isaiah 60 were fulfilled in the birth, death, and immediate resurrection of Jesus.

Yet any honest reader can recognize that there is more to the promises of Isaiah. Like many other prophetic words in the Old Testament, there are several layers of fulfillment to it. The nations coming into the church on Pentecost was a sign of something greater to come. This is why Pentecost is called the Feast of *First-fruits*. There is always a greater harvest after the "first-fruits." As we've mentioned before, Jesus was our "forerunner" (Heb. 6:20) and He said we would do greater works than Him. It is the church rising into her union with Christ who will bring about the full promises found in Isaiah's hopeful words. The church will one day shine so brightly and with such unity that *all nations* will bring their praise and glory into it.

The Multiplied Seed

When He walked the earth, Jesus actually turned away many of the people from other nations who came to see Him, which, at first glance, seems like He was hindering Isaiah's prophecy. An example of this is found in the book of John. Toward the end of Jesus's ministry, Greeks had come from other lands to visit the temple of God during the Passover season. These were "foreigners" like the ones mentioned in Isaiah 60:10, who were being drawn to the light of Israel. They requested a meeting with Jesus through some of His disciples, but He did not allow the meeting to take place.

Now think for a moment how this would seem to be a lost opportunity. You can imagine the disciples' letdown after they had excitedly ran to tell Jesus about the Greek's request, and then He immediately turned it down. Jesus had the chance to start preaching the Gospel to the nations beyond Israel. This was an amazing opportunity to get the message out to a dark and hurting world. Yet Jesus did not take the opportunity. Instead, He gave a mysterious response to His disciples. Look at the full account of what happened:

> *Now there were some Greeks among those who were going up to worship at the feast; these then came to Philip, who*

*was from Bethsaida of Galilee, and began to ask him, saying, "Sir, we wish to see Jesus." Philip came and told Andrew; Andrew and Philip came and told Jesus. And Jesus answered them, saying, "The hour has come for the Son of Man to be glorified. **Truly, truly, I say to you, unless a grain of wheat falls into the earth and dies, it remains alone; but if it dies, it bears much fruit.***
(Jn. 12:20-24)

From here, Jesus denied the meeting with the Greeks and continued down the road to Calvary. But when we listen carefully to His words, we find insight into heaven's long-term plans of fulfilling the greater reality of Isaiah 60.

Jesus's agenda was not to gain followers so that He could form a "Jesus club" that lived and acted a certain way. He did not come to start a religion or a new geographical nation built on a certain philosophy. He also did not want people coming to Him as a ruling king who would dictate a new set of rules and teachings for them (even if those rules and teachings were godly and perfect). As the Son of Man, Jesus came to be glorified *within us*. That's why He said "unless a seed dies, it remains alone." The whole world could have come to sit under the reign of Jesus, but He would have been the only One in true union with the Father. Everyone else would have been slave-like disciples with unchanged hearts still held captive to the power of sin.

But if the grain of wheat dies—which it did—then it bears much fruit...fruit after its own kind and likeness.

Jesus died to reap the fruit of mankind redeemed to the image and likeness of their Father.

Who is She?

That is one of the key reasons for Jesus's suffering. To multiply His own life in humanity and restore God's original purpose for humanity. We find later in the book of John that Jesus died and "went away" so that the "Helper" of the Spirit would come (see Jn. 16:7). The Helper is so much more than an empowering force for ministry. The Helper was and is the gift of His very presence being released into the world again.

Jesus died so that a collective "Jesus" would arise. What began in His own body on the hills of Israel was destined to continue through a corporate body on the hills of all nations. Thus, you have the Shulammite Bride. She is the one who shares His name and essence, like the Shulammite woman shared and reflected the name of Solomon. This is she who would one day *arise and shine like the dawn,* bearing the light of a new day for a world still covered in deep darkness. In union with her Beloved, this Shulammite Bride would be the one to freely reap the greater harvest of *all nations.*

This was Jesus's great inheritance and hope, the joy set before Him on the cross.

The Sun and the Moon

In this part of the Song we find the world looking at the rising Bride and they immediately compare her to the dawn. She is the budding light of the coming full day of redemption that will sweep through the whole earth. As such, she is a literal "hope of glory" (Col. 1:27). The people of the world go on to say that she is as beautiful as the full moon and as pure as the sun. These are absolutely staggering analogies. And remember that these are descriptions about the Bride from those who do not fully know God yet! Again, this is the fruit of an outward transformation after an inward journey of faith. At last, the Bride is entering into her destiny.

The Song of the Ages: Part II

The first comparison to the brightness of a full moon is rich with revelation and insight. First of all, the moon itself is a cold rock filled with dusty craters. It hovers above the earth and continually encircles it like a constant companion. But that rock, as massive and big as it is, is completely invisible to the people of the earth—until it is positioned in such a way that the sun can shine on it.

In reality, the church is called to be a faithful friend to the people of "earth." Unfortunately, we have often been like a cold rock to the world, filled with craters and holes, wounds and scars, division and emptiness. We have acted like dust-based beings instead of the glorious children of God. The church's light has waxed and waned throughout time as she has gone through periods of oscillating radiance. But despite this, our great calling and identity has often been invisible to the earth. As a result, the church is often seen as distant and irrelevant—as irrelevant as a hovering rock would be to a world without sunlight.

But when the moon is correctly positioned in front of the sun, the earth takes notice. And at one specific moment of its positioning, the moon reaches a full and complete reflection of the sun's rays. In that moment, the beauty of the moon (which is really the beauty of the sun; the moon can take no credit) comes out in full blast. All of a sudden, the night is lit up and a glow is cast upon the earth that impresses it with a deep touch of wonder and peace.

Such is the case with a church that is fully positioned before the light of Jesus. As the church reflects Him, our irrelevancy and coldness vanishes at light-speed. We become a true beacon of hope for the world, declaring that even though a night season is at hand, the "sun" has not left us. The moon is the evidence of a faithful sun still facing a sleeping world. Even if that world has turned from the sun, having rotated into rebellion and unbelief, the sun is ever shining with love and warmth.

Who is She?

Now let's not miss the greater implication of this particular verse. This lyric is speaking of a "full moon." It is talking about a church that *fully* reflects the Son. And remember, this is no longer the hopeful and prophetic words of Jesus to His doubting Bride. These are now the words of the queens, concubines, and maidens of the world who are literally seeing a full reflection of God in the church. The weight of this statement is indescribable. This is talking about a full reflection of Jesus made visible to a world that is still lost in the darkness of sin. *This* is what is on the horizon of church history (and our own personal lives as we wake up to the Song of the Ages).

This verse is speaking of a day when the same glory that manifested through Jesus will shine out through His whole church. It is the coming crop, full and mature, that will have the same quality wheat as was produced by the original seed of grain. So let's think about the original grain Himself—Jesus. He was and is gloriously beautiful. He walked in transformative love and brought hope wherever He went. He had divine authority over sickness and death. Jesus was fully confident and yet totally humble. Demons submitted to His word and men had no power over Him other than what He granted them. Jesus knew who He was and exhibited His identity in unrestrained splendor. *This* is the kind of stuff the entire world will see reflected in the church.

In the Song, the other maidens are no longer seeing a cold judgmental rock filled with holes and dust, where criticism is easy to pile on, along with skepticism and avoidance. Now they are seeing the beauty of Jesus in full radiance. In other words, they are seeing the light of His glory rising upon the earth through His multiplied Body. This is the dawning of a new day for humanity through the manifestation of Christ in His church. No longer is it all about one grain of wheat stuck in religious history books. Now we are seeing a whole harvest of wheat—*little Christs*—who have risen as well. This is the great plan of the Father, which is hidden from many eyes, including doom-and-gloom theologians that have populated the pulpits of this world.

And there is even more to the analogy. We are not just reflections of Christ. Again, Christ is *in us*. We are carriers of Him. Therefore, after the Shulammite is compared to the full moon, the onlookers then say that she is "as pure as the sun." No metaphor is perfect and therefore new analogies need to be given in order to describe the full essence of the church's identity. In reality, the church is not a hard rock. While she certainly can't take credit for the glory rising upon her, that glory is not in distant outer space, millions of miles away. This description is not speaking of a glory from the outside, but that which is from within. She is as pure as the Son Himself, because within her true nature is the full glory of God.

All of this was a gift from the very beginning, which she has been joyfully unwrapping throughout her journey. This unwrapped gift of identity is now meant to be shared with the entire world. And that is exactly what's happening at this point in the Song.

Setting Free the Orphan

The whole world is suffering from an identity crisis. Nevertheless, as the church manifests her true identity, that will in turn awaken the world to theirs as well. Out of this, the people of the world will also be drawn to the intense love of the Father, which is the great longing of mankind.

One of the deepest issues within the broken soul of society is the inner lie that we have been rejected and abandoned by our Father. People might not articulate it as bluntly as such, but this is at the core of many people's struggles. Since our original fall from glory, mankind has wrestled with an orphaned mindset that both longs for and rages at the heavens. This rage and longing leads people into completely horrible places as they seek to fill the void or quench the anger of their souls. Many people outright reject God or arrogantly demand miracles and proof to show that they have not been abandoned. Other people hide behind religious formalism and repetition, believing that we were visited by God for a brief period of time, but are now left with only traditions and holidays. All we have in Jesus's place is an upgraded religious system called Christianity, which can be utilized in order to earn our way into seeing Him again. Thus, people have a hope of being united with the Father in the distant future, but this is contingent upon behavior, personal faith, and other factors. At the end of the day, this sense of abandonment pervades both the atheistic and religious corridors of the world.

But God has not left us. He is Immanuel—*God with us*—and that will never change. Jesus "went away" in His glorified physical body so that He could hug the orphans of the world with a greater, glorified, spiritual body. It is the church arising in the full identity of Christ who are meant to settle this issue in people's hearts. This is perhaps why James said that the purest and truest religion is that which cares for the orphan and widow—those in society who have experienced some of the worst feelings of abandonment (Jms. 1:27).

God has not abandoned us. He absolutely longs for the world to be rescued from this lie. And all along, the church has been His true vehicle to reveal His faithful mercy and presence. It is the church who manifests *the truth* for people. Like the faithful moon, they show the earth that the "sun" has not left us. Though we do not fully see Him now, the "moon" is the proof that He is present nonetheless.

Indeed, the Bride *is* His presence. The Lamb now dwells within His people. We are like a tree whose leaves bring healing to the nations (Rev. 22:2). We are destined to be an overcoming army that lays waste to the deceptive forces keeping people in the dark about the love of the Father and the truth of their original sonship and daughterhood. Earlier, it was Jesus who described the church as being like "a bannered army." Now it is the world who is beginning to see this as they are impacted by her love. That is the final metaphor that comes after the brightness of the moon and the purity of the sun. Because of this awakening to her identity, there is a conquering explosion of grace being ignited through her. No army of men and no demon in hell can stop the momentum that is occurring. All are stunned by the glorious Shulammite Bride, which of course means that they are stunned by her Beloved and her Friend—Jesus the Christ.

Even now, this incredible power is in the church, which Jesus has always seen and continues to patiently declare. But as the Bride awakens to His Word (the kisses of His mouth), she will let go and allow that power to come forth. This is the promise for individual believers, and it is the ultimate hope for the entire church. We are and will be a terrifyingly beautiful and gloriously united army, who sets free the orphan and illumines the world with grace.

Who is This?

Remember that earlier in the story the daughters of Jerusalem weren't that impressed with the Bride. This was during her doubt-filled stage as she crawled like a caterpillar through fear and unbelief. Nonetheless, they were impressed by her devotion to Jesus. In response to this unrelenting devotion, the daughters asked her a different question back then.

"Who is He?"

In that moment, the Bride began to re-discover the Gospel and the great revelation from the Summit of all Truth. During that time, she released a mighty torrent of praise even in the midst of contradiction, persecution, and defeat. And in her songful declarations of Christ, the Son of the Living God, she described the glory of His head and the equal wonders of His body. It was then that she came to understand her seamless union with Him as His body. Her praise of Him led to an established understanding of her own identity. It was here that any remaining walls of religion and fear finally broke. Then, her innermost being poured forth a river of healing that had always been resident within her.

We cannot overstate how much this reflects the historical journey of the church throughout the centuries (as well as her looming future). Slowly, the music of the Song has been progressively restored to the church and has begun to infiltrate pulpits and hearts like never before. All of this is leading to a global confession of the true Gospel—the complete reality of union and grace.

Today, in the 21ˢᵗ century, the overall church finds herself somewhere between chapters 5 and 6 of the Song—that great transition when the Bride began to turn her attention toward the head and body of her Beloved, releasing wave after wave of praise. In recent decades, there has been a massive movement of prayer and worship to Jesus that has been building and growing throughout the world. The global Bride is beginning to praise the glory of Jesus like never before. On top of this, the Bride is connecting more than ever via the internet and through new forms of communication. But like the Bride in the fifth chapter of the Song, this global movement of intensified worship and connection is all leading to a greater revelation of union. As that happens, the queens, concubines, and maidens of the earth will no longer recognize the church. Instead, as they gaze at her growing luminescence and her bannered beauty, they will say "*who is this?*"

This will be like seeing something totally different than before. The Bride will no longer be a cratered rock, but an illuminating force of love. The church will move from being a crawling caterpillar to a soaring butterfly. Like the turning of the full moon, there is indeed a "butterfly" metamorphosis coming to the church. While that metaphor isn't found in the Song of Solomon, it is certainly found in the song of creation and adds even more layers of understanding to what we are seeing in the Shulammite's story.

Just imagine for a moment that you have never seen a butterfly before. Imagine that even the idea of it is completely foreign to you. Next, think of the wonder that would capture your heart if you were to behold a brightly colored winged creature emerging for the first time from a dry cocoon. A question similar to the queens' might come to your own heart:

What is this?

This is the drastic nature of the transformation that is at hand. Even now there are multitudes of people who are long done with the caterpillar forms of church, so much so that they are leaving it in mass droves. This is because their hearts are set on a pilgrimage to something deeper and truer. Many are in a state of intense struggle and confusion in this metamorphosis process, and some are questioning their fidelity to God while experiencing infidelity to the religious systems of the world. But it is all part of the great transition that is upon us. It is because we are nearing a corporate experience of Song of Songs 6:10. We are in the days of transformation and illumination even now, and the story is only going to get more intense as the church continues to move forward in the lyrics of the Song.

To reiterate, the awakening of the Bride is available to every believer, right here and right now. Don't limit yourself by waiting for a future day to experience the realities we've been discussing. This is speaking about who we already are. Yet, when contradictions appear to abound, we can rest with a deep hope that this is the ultimate trajectory of our lives—as well as the whole body of Christ. We will taste and see the goodness of this Word in this present age. So cast off the burden of gloomy theology and faithless expectations of some global evacuation plan called "the rapture." We are not evacuating. We are illuminating, mobilizing, and transforming the nations.

And yet there is indeed a rapture coming.

An inner rapturing of the glory of Christ within.

"Christ in you" is the glorious hope ahead of us all—for each of us personally, for the larger church, and indeed for the entire world.

17

The Journey in a Nutshell

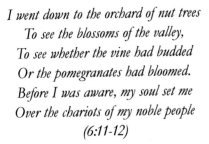

I went down to the orchard of nut trees
To see the blossoms of the valley,
To see whether the vine had budded
Or the pomegranates had bloomed.
Before I was aware, my soul set me
Over the chariots of my noble people
(6:11-12)

After being showered with praise and admiration from the people around her, the Shulammite gives a response. Ever desiring that others taste this same love as well, she starts to explain how she arrived at this place of glory and light. She wants to teach and disciple the world around her, even as her Beloved taught and discipled her. She begins this by talking about how she "went down to the orchard."

The word *orchard* can also be translated as "garden." In the Scriptures, the word is often used to particularly describe a king's garden. King Solomon used this word himself when he gave an account of some of his personal ventures in the book of Ecclesiastes. We've looked at this reference before: "I made *gardens*

249

and parks for myself and I planted in them all kinds of fruit trees" (Ecc. 2:5). The book of Esther also uses this word when it talks about the "palace garden" that belonged to King Xerxes of Persia (see Est. 1:5).

It is quite clear that the Shulammite is talking once more about the garden of her own heart, which belongs to the King of all kings, Jesus. Recall her earlier words, which brought forth that great revelation of the ages, when the Bride exclaimed that her Beloved "has gone down into *his* garden..." (Sgs. 6:2). She is now describing the garden of her inner being as an orchard of nut trees with vines and pomegranates. It is still referring to that wondrous Promised Land for which Jesus gave His life to redeem.

Giving an Answer

To the adoring queens and maidens, she reiterates that all of the glory in her life flowed from a place of union and from there it continues to flow. Earlier, the Bride said that Jesus "went down" into the garden. Now she says that she is the one who "went down." It is there that she has put her life's focus. She is now explaining to the seeking world how she took hold of the divine light. The Shulammite is thus recapping her own journey of faith as she learned to accept her identity and believe in the finished work of Christ. This is where the light and glory came from. Out of this, the splendor of the sun and moon arose and a new day dawned for those around her.

This scene in the Song is actually a picture of true evangelism. People were drawn to the light within her and she is now leading them to where and Whom it came from. The most effective evangelism is when people are pulled to the love and light within us. This is similar to how Jesus evangelized the sinful tax collector Zaccheus. Zaccheus was drawn to the light of Christ, so much so that he climbed a tree so he could get a better look at Him as He walked through a large crowd. Jesus saw this man who was already drawn to Him and engaged in a deeper relationship with Him. He went over his house for dinner, which led to Zaccheus's own awakening to love and forgiveness. This is when Jesus affirmed that He "came to seek and save that which was lost" (see Lk. 19:1-10). The seeking often comes by attracting the lost through the fragrant fruits of the Spirit manifesting in our lives.

This is why Peter said we should always be ready to give an answer "to everyone who asks you to give an account for *the hope that is in you*" (1 Pet. 3:15). Peter is referring there to the hope of glory—Christ within. As people see the light of Christ in us, they will ask questions (like the queens of the world did to the Shulammite). We will not need to seek them as much as they will seek us. And like the Shulammite, we are then called to give the "answer" of the Gospel. In the Song, the Shulammite takes no credit for the light that is shining out of her. She says that it all came from the garden of her heart where she finally realized the great truth of the Song: *I am my Beloved's and He is mine!* She is heeding the words of Peter and giving the ultimate answer for the shining hope within her.

She goes on to explain how this trek into the garden led her to a place of authority and power. She says, "Before I was aware, my soul set me over the chariots of my noble people." Without even being *aware* of it, the Bride came into a place of unassailable power. In other words, she became that awe-inspiring "bannered army" without even trying. It came about by simply going "down to the garden" where her Beloved already rested and dwelt. Here, she is giving a map to the queens of humanity so that they may discover these same things as well...

The Journey of the Shulammite

It is of great importance that we look at the mention of "nut trees," which brings a new depth of insight regarding the inner garden of her soul. As with every verse of the Song, these words are not spoken flippantly. Instead, we will find that this poetic imagery continues to paint a unifying picture and message.

Most commentators believe that the referenced nut trees were most likely walnut trees, which may have been common in a king's orchard. The walnut—or any nut for that matter—has a hard and unappealing exterior. It has grooves and cracks and an overall rigid form. To an unassuming onlooker, it could appear like a dirty and porous rock without any kind of nourishing fruit inside. (In case you were wondering, a nut is technically a type of fruit.)

In describing her inner garden as an "orchard of nut trees," she is first saying that her heart and life has been planted by the King of creation—the owner of this royal orchard. This is a garden or orchard that has great and nourishing fruit inside of it; however, the fruit is often hidden behind an unsuspecting shell. Indeed, we were formed and fashioned with the clay of the earth and our journey of experiencing the glory of God often comes through much contradiction and outward hardness. What we see on the exterior very often runs opposite to the treasure that lies underneath.

Yet the Bride is one who has seen the truth and has taken hold of it by faith. She believed in hope against hope that the glory of Christ was within her, even after times of stumbling in defeat. She came face to face with the walnut-like cracks and grooves of her life's experience. But despite all of this, she learned to rise up and "see" with the eyes of her heart. She "went down" to the garden of promise "to *see* if the vine had budded or the pomegranates had bloomed" (v. 11). She trusted Jesus's words of hope concerning her true identity. In other words, she looked down from the Summit of

The Journey in a Nutshell

Truth and beheld the true glory within her. As you can see, all of this imagery continues to point to the same essential truths.

The Shulammite is basically recapping her own journey of awakening. At this point in the Song, the queen of humanity—the masses of both religious and non-religious peoples of the world—are beginning to see the great light within her. They are now being drawn to that light and are praising her for it. Here then is a paraphrase of her response to them:

> *Let me tell where this glory comes from! It is all from Jesus—my Beloved and Friend. Despite my failings and my unbelief, I "went down" past the surface of my experience and looked deeper into His eternal Word. I saw the truth of who I am beyond the shadows and cracks. I learned to trust that my entire being was like a walnut—a hard exterior that is filled with good fruit. I learned to persevere and "see" with the eyes of my heart, holding to the truth of my Beloved's words, believing that an inner vineyard of multiplying life dwelt within.*

> *Without even trying, power and grace erupted from within my soul. As I entered into His rest, an overcoming authority emerged. It was like being set over the chariots of a royal army, where I began to ride on the winds of heaven as an awakened Queen reigning at the side of Jesus Christ. This is who I am and it all comes from finding my rest in the sweet garden of oneness.*

Once again, the Bride shows herself as a picture of redeemed humanity, living out the life that is offered to every single person. Remember that mankind originally dwelt in a kingly orchard called Eden, the garden of God. From there we were called to co-reign with the Lord, subduing the earth and bringing everything into alignment with the beauty of Eden. This reigning authority flowed out of Eden, a place of pleasure, rest, and intimacy. It is there that we walked with God in the cool of the day. Out of that pleasurable walk, we were called to ride upon the chariots of heaven (perhaps without even being aware of it, like our friend the Shulammite).

But all of that was lost. So, a Redeemer came to seek and save that which was lost. As we've seen all along, Jesus came to redeem this "garden life" of deep rest and humble power. In the Song of Songs, we find the Shulammite church taking hold of this redemption and coming back to that place of rest and pleasure. Out of this fragrant place, she finds herself walking in that original calling to subdue the earth through love. All of this is encapsulated in the Shulammite's simple poetry about going down to the orchard and finding her soul set over chariots.

The Rise of Joseph

The first time the Hebrew word for "chariots" shows up in the Bible is in Genesis 41. This is when Joseph, the son of Jacob, is exalted to the right hand of Pharaoh after spending years in prison and slavery. Most of us know this story very well. While in prison, Joseph is given the opportunity to interpret a dream for Pharaoh. Upon getting the right interpretation, Joseph lands a new job position. He is released from prison and given great authority over the land of Egypt. Joseph is automatically called to ride in the "second chariot"—second only to Pharaoh.

> *Then Pharaoh took off his signet ring from his hand and put it on Joseph's hand, and clothed him in garments of fine linen and put the gold necklace around his neck. He had him ride in his second **chariot**; and they proclaimed*

before him, "Bow the knee!" And he set him over all the
land of Egypt.
(Gen. 41:43-44)

We will find that this is yet another Old Testament story that parallels the work of Christ on our behalf as well as the hidden journey of the Shulammite. First of all, Joseph is a type and shadow of Christ. He was the beloved son of his father Israel (Gen. 37:3), persecuted and beaten by his brothers (Gen. 37:23), sold for pieces of silver (37:28), and thrown into a pit (37:24). But from that pit of death, Joseph eventually rises to the right hand of the king (Gen. 41:40). While still subject to the king, he is seen as an equal to him, and even becomes his mouthpiece (Gen. 41:55 & 44:18).

The parallels between Joseph and Jesus are amazing. Jesus was of course the beloved Son of God (Lk. 3:22). He was persecuted and beaten by His own brethren in the nation of Israel (Lk. 22:63). He was sold for silver and His body was thrown into the grave (Matt. 26:15 & 27:60). Yet from that pit of death, Jesus arose and ascended to the right hand of the Father. Jesus is of course equal with God (Phil. 2:6), but as the eternal Son of God He lovingly subjects Himself to the Father (1 Cor. 15:28). Finally, Jesus is the Word of the Father and is thus His perfect mouthpiece (Jn. 1:1).

As we've said over and over again, the key to understanding the work of Christ is realizing our union with Him in that work—the reality of our co-crucifixion, co-resurrection, and co-ascension with Jesus. All of these events happened to us, and we are called to trust in that truth. So we are now like Joseph, raised out of the prison of death and given a signet ring of authority. We have been clothed in the fine linen of Jesus's righteousness. We have been seated with Christ in heavenly places. We now co-reign with Him through our union together. Jesus was beaten and killed so that we could freely inherit these things. His goodness is beyond comprehension.

Here's how all of this connects to the journey of the Shulammite, and thus the journey of each individual believer. Going "down to the orchard of nut trees" is learning to see beyond the rough shell of our exterior lives and setting our gaze upon the greater reality of union with the risen Christ. We are called to see ourselves united with Him in His ascension to the Father's throne. Remember that the Shulammite went to "see" if "the vine had budded." Jesus *is* the Vine and we are the branches. She went to *see* her union with the Vine, from where all true life flows. She also went to see if the "pomegranate had bloomed." As we said in our previous study of the Song, Jesus's blood is symbolized by the red seeds of the pomegranate fruit. That is also what the Shulammite went to see. She began to focus on the blood of Jesus, trusting in its inherent power to release life and fruitfulness in her own soul.

As we join with the Shulammite in this "seeing," we will also find ourselves riding on the "second chariot" like Joseph. We will reign in life at the right hand of the Father, where we have been freely seated with Christ. We will find ourselves flowing in a new dimension of spiritual authority and influence without even being aware of it. Or, in other words, without even trying. "Before I was aware" is a statement that shows us the Shulammite did not go searching and striving for promotion and authority. She did not struggle her way into a place of spiritual power and influence. She only went into the garden of union to walk with God in the cool of the day. She learned to just enjoy His abiding love and saw herself as a participant in His life and accomplishments. In seeing Jesus as dead to sin, she saw herself in the same way. In seeing Jesus risen with joy and power, she saw herself risen with joy and power. In seeing Jesus seated in authority and favor, she saw herself also seated in that same place. All of this is a gift that flows from the Vine of His being.

In our own day and age, there is a generation of influential "Josephs" on the rise. These are people who will suddenly and often effortlessly find themselves in places of great influence. This influence will not come from the ways that man typically seeks power. Instead it will come as an overflowing side-note from a life of rest, humility, and joy. When asked about this overflowing glory in their lives, they will boast only in the finished work of Christ and their union with Him in His death, resurrection, and ascension. Like Joseph, they will joyfully wear the coat of many colors (Gen. 37:3), which is the free and unmerited favor of the Father. This is the rainbow of His glory manifesting through their lives. Light will crack through the rugged walnut shell of their lives and give hope to other broken shells around them—those who do not believe such glory is possible for them.

A House of Bread and Light

The story of Joseph continues to parallel what we are seeing in the Song. Like the Shulammite, Joseph also saw the nations of the world being drawn to him. This is because Joseph was the overseer of a massive storehouse of grain that had been built for a time of famine. When the famine finally hit, people came from all over the world to receive grain for bread.

The people of all the earth came to Egypt to buy grain from
Joseph, because the famine was severe in all the earth.
(Gen. 41:57)

This should remind you of the words of Isaiah that we looked at in the last chapter. Isaiah promised that the nations of the world, lost in deep darkness, would come to the light rising upon God's people. This is where we see how the story of Joseph and the prophecy of Isaiah all point to the journey of the Shulammite and the destiny of the church. The world around us is lost in a famine of spiritual darkness and they are looking for true light and true bread.

Jesus of course is the Light of the World and the Bread of Life. He is what humanity is seeking. So as the Bride rises up in her full identity, the world will come to the bread and light manifesting from within her. Remember, we *are* the multiplied "grain" of Christ arising from His sacrificial death (Jn. 12:24). We are food for the world, teaching them to partake of Christ's life for themselves.

All of this happens as we go down to the Garden of union and sees our lives hidden in Christ. This is where we awaken to the signet ring that is *already* upon our hand; the fine linen *already* upon our shoulder; the gold necklace *already* upon our neck. For all those things are already upon Him, and we are truly *in Him*. Like the Shulammite, we need to "see" this and embrace it, which leads to its eventual manifestation in our lives. It is then that we become a storehouse of grain, providing bread for a hungry world.

And as the world draws near to us, we will learn to take no credit for it. Like the Shulammite, we will simply explain the journey of awakening—of seeing beyond circumstances and hard exteriors and by trusting in the love of Jesus. This will then spawn new disciples from the queen of humanity, whether it's those who already somewhat know God or those who have no knowledge of Him at all. We will call and disciple people into this same journey of love. Out of this, people will discover the light and bread of Christ for themselves.

For all people are a walnut of glory, even though many have not cracked open the shell of their minds by embracing His death and realizing His grace.

Everyone's a Nut

This brings up one last point in our study of this verse. Some people interpret this part of the Song as though it were describing the Bride going down into the orchards of humanity to labor in new vineyards outside of herself. They say that it is a picture of the Bride now going into the world to minister to others. Since there are layers of truth to the Song, this is an entirely valid way of looking at this verse. The Bride would then be going into the world and looking beyond the hard and cracked shells of *other people*. She would be looking to bring out the hidden image and glory of God resident in everyone.

This is a good reminder that when we minister to other people, we are actually ministering to Christ. Whether they are a hardened prisoner, or a mentally ill person in poverty, or someone without enough clothes to keep warm, Christ is hidden in each person and situation (see Matt. 25:35-26). This is because our labor in the world is a labor amongst hardened walnuts hidden with the glory of Jesus. These are lost sons who never stopped being sons—they just lost sight of home. This is partly why Paul was so successful in his ministry. He learned to no longer see any man according to the walnut flesh. He said, "Therefore, we recognize *no one* according to the flesh" (2 Cor. 5:16). Please understand that Paul was not speaking only of "Christians." No one means *no one*.

The illuminating, life-giving, and satisfying Bread of the Word is not far from anyone. This truth is available to all, waiting to be discovered and unwrapped. Paul said, "the Word is near you, in your mouth and in your heart" (Rom. 10:8). That Word *is* the Song of His heart, the kiss of His mouth, and the wine at His banqueting table.

And so this verse that speaks of going down to the orchard is really the whole sum of the Shulammite's journey—in a nutshell. And it calls everyone else to the same journey as well.

18

The Mystery of Mahanaim

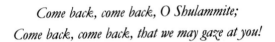

Come back, come back, O Shulammite;
Come back, come back, that we may gaze at you!

Why should you gaze at the Shulammite,
As at the dance of the two companies?
(6:13)

I want to encourage you to move through this chapter slowly and thoughtfully. There is much terrain to cover and it will be best to pace yourself as you walk through it. We'll start by giving you a lay of the land and then explore it piece by piece. The focus of the Song is rapidly shifting. Now that the Bride realizes who she is, there is a natural and effortless overflow into a place of light and strength. She is becoming a true city on a hill that is drawing the nations to the Lord. The Song has found the perfect instrument to play its enchanting chords to the sleeping world. It has found the strings of a childlike heart. The very veins of life within the Shulammite are being plucked as joyful blood beats through her chest.

The Shulammite's soul has been "set over chariots" and she's no longer the same person. In fact, the Shulammite is gone. It is no longer her, but Christ. This of course has been the truth all along, but now that truth is visible and bright. The world responds to this by saying, "Come back! Come back!" They want to continue to gaze upon her. Yet all they see is the dust kicked up by the chariot wheels of glory with the Shulammite nowhere to be found.

Not I, but Grace

As the Bride rises and shines, maturing into the full harvest of wheat that Jesus embodied, she will come across something that Jesus also experienced. When He walked the earth, people often wanted to make Jesus a literal king or make Him their new Moses who could mediate between them and God. Now of course, Jesus is our King and Mediator. But He is a different kind of king and mediator than the one people were used to. His mediation brings us into a deep and personal intimacy with the Father. He is not a liaison that passes messages along to God. We find throughout Jesus's life that His purpose was to bring everyone into the same access to the Father that He enjoyed. He did not come to create a new religion, but to awaken His sleeping brothers and sisters.

And so the Bride is experiencing something similar here. People are awed by her and want to gaze at her, but they do not necessarily want to enter into the same place of intimacy as her. If you remember from our last study, the Shulammite had to learn this lesson for herself. Earlier on, the Shulammite went into the "city" to search for her Beloved, which we found represented organized religion. She did not find His abiding presence there. Instead, she found a system that kept her ever seeking, but never truly "finding." Eventually, when she found some watchmen, which represented spiritual leadership, she moved past them and quickly found her Beloved at the outskirts of the city.

We discussed how this isn't meant to devalue the importance of teachers and leadership, but rather highlight the fact that true shepherds and watchmen point away from themselves. They teach people to find a personal rest and intimacy with Christ, helping them realize that we all have equal access to our Dad. Such leaders live according to the old adage of teaching a man to fish instead of catching the fish for him. Thus, this scene reveals that many people in the world are beginning to be influenced and taught by the Shulammite, but she is calling them to awaken to love for themselves.

In the book of Acts, there is an interesting encounter between Paul and Barnabas and the people of Lystra. The two apostles enter as missionaries to the city and immediately begin to embody the works of Christ. They walk in tangible love and release the power of the Spirit by healing a man who had been lame from birth. The crowds see this—the "queen, concubines, and maidens" of this Greek city—and they start declaring that the gods have come down to them in human flesh (Acts 14:11-12). They rename Paul Zeus and give Barnabas the title of the Greek god Hermes.

In this encounter, the people were onto something true and yet they were greatly perverting it. We were certainly made to be partakers of the divine nature and to embody the glory of God. That's exactly what Paul and Barnabas were doing as awakened sons of God. The divine Spirit of Christ had manifested in their human bodies. And yet, as we've profusely discussed, this is all about bringing the glory back to Jesus. Paul and Barnabas rebuked the people for their worship of them. Like the Shulammite, they pointed away from themselves. They told the people that they were men just like everyone else. It is here that Paul begins to preach the Gospel to them and attempts to open their eyes to the truth that this same union is available to all.

Paul made statements that backed up this point in several of his letters to the churches, such as his famous words to the Galatians: "It is no longer I who live, but Christ who lives in me; and the life I live in the flesh I live by faith in the Son of God" (Gal. 2:20). In his first letter to the Corinthians, Paul talks about the amazingly divine and powerful works he had accomplished and says, "I labored even more than all of them (the other apostles), yet not I, but the grace of God with me" (1 Cor. 15:10). As the church taps into the same realities as Paul—as they wake up to the fullness of the grace within them—they will encounter this same thing and need to make the same point. Though people will intently gaze at us, we will need to point away from ourselves and keep the focus on the Person and work of Jesus.

The seeking ladies ask the Shulammite to come back, and then a response is given. It is the Beloved Himself who speaks back to them. In fact, it is the Beloved *within* His Bride responding. Jesus is speaking and teaching the hungry people of the world through the Shulammite. It's her lips, but His voice. He responds with these mysterious words:

Why should you gaze at the Shulammite as at the dance of the two companies?

This is one of the most mystifying passages throughout the entirety of the Song. Many commentators and translators have struggled tapping into its meaning and thus the interpretations of this verse are dramatically varied. But we can be sure that such a shrouded verse contains priceless treasure for those who continue to search out its depths. As Solomon said, the glory of kings is to search out that which God has concealed (Prov. 25:2). God never conceals anything to keep us away, but rather to entice our hearts into a greater journey of wisdom and understanding.

And so, by the grace of God with us and within us, let us also search out the depths of this verse. All of this has been an overview of the land, but now we'll set our feet to hike it out. We will find that within this passage is a land of wisdom flowing from the heart of Jesus toward a thirsty and seeking world.

The Response

In order to understand this response, let's first reexamine the context of our present point in the Song. The Shulammite Bride is now blossoming with the fruits of divine love and power. As she rises into a new place of influence and authority, the world is finally taking notice and they are gazing at her beauty. However, in some way, she turns from them and does not allow them to continue in this gazing. She wants them to come into this same glory for themselves through a relationship with Jesus. They beg her to "come back," but Christ within responds with a statement about "the dance of the two companies."

Now take notice that Jesus is asking them a question. As He often did with both His disciples and accusers, Jesus asks pointed and mysterious questions in order to help the genuine seeker come into a deeper revelation for themselves. Jesus asks them, "Why would you gaze at the Shulammite as at the dance of two companies?" It is the phrase "two companies" that unlocks the meaning of this question. The number "two" can often represent a divide or separation. So here is another way of looking at His response:

Why are you staring at the Shulammite as though she were separate from Me—as though you were staring at "two companies." Don't you see that she is one with Me? This

glory and beauty you see in her comes from Me.
And I long to bring forth that same glory in you!

Jesus is drawing the world to Himself through His Bride and He is now teaching the Gospel to them, helping them to understand the realities of relationship and union. That is the essence of Jesus's response. He wants to take the focus off of *just* her and put it on the both of them together.

That being said, this verse is a rabbit hole that goes much deeper than this. The Hebrew word behind the phrase "two companies" is like a key that pops open the full treasure box of this question. It is the word *Mahanaim*. The New International Version and several other Bible translations choose to simply use this Hebrew word in the actual verse instead of translating it as "two companies." This is because it is referring to an actual region in the land of Israel called Mahanaim. So the NIV puts Jesus's response to the seeking world in the following way: "Why would you gaze on the Shulammite as on the dance of Mahanaim?"

Mahanaim was a place named by Jacob at a major turning point in his life, which was in fact a turning point for the entire Bible. The story of Jacob and the life-changing events that transpired around this region give us the meaning and power behind this phrase. We'll need to spend some time looking at that story in order to capture the full beauty of this revelation...

The Journey of Jacob

Jacob, the son of Isaac, left the land of his birth and the territory of his inheritance after an event that brought a great deal of shame and fear into his life. Jacob had stolen the birthright of his older brother Esau and then went on the run. Jacob's very name meant *deceiver* or *supplanter*, which matched many of his actions in his early days, including what he did to his brother. Jacob was sent off by his father to the land of Paddan-aram to stay with relatives, particularly with his uncle Laban, and it is there that he remained for about 20 years. During this time, Laban became Jacob's father-in-law after he married his two daughters, Leah and Rachel.

Throughout this time, Laban took advantage of Jacob over and over again. Jacob was deceived into working for Laban much longer than he had originally bargained for. This was difficult labor and his father-in-law often cheated him in his work by changing his wages. Even though God was helping him prosper, Jacob was miserable in the land of Paddan-aram and soon set his heart to return to his homeland in Canaan. Knowing that Laban would disapprove of this, Jacob made preparations to leave secretly with his family and servants.

Three days after he left, Laban discovered what had been done and gathered all his men to come and overtake Jacob. He pursued him with the intent of capturing him, but was then warned in a dream not to bring any harm to Jacob. Because of this, Laban and his son-in-law decided to enter into a covenantal agreement together, which safely separated the two of them. They took a rock and set it up as a pillar and then piled up a heap of other stones before entering into the covenant. Standing by these rocks, Laban declared, "This heap is a witness, and the pillar is a witness, that I will not pass by this heap to you for harm, and you will not pass by this heap and this pillar to me, for harm" (Gen. 31:52). Jacob was let go from his father-in-law and they shared a celebratory meal together. Jacob was forever released from Laban's grasp and could now return to the Promised Land of Canaan, the place of his birth and inheritance.

This moment in Jacob's life became a convergence of confrontation and revelation. Not only did he have to deal with the present situation of Laban's control, but he would also have to deal with his past. Jacob was now safely leaving Laban's territory, but on the way into Canaan he knew he would have to come face-to-face with his older brother, who he had not seen since the time of his treachery. As he safely departed from his father-in-law and crossed over into Canaan, Jacob camped at place just outside the Jordan River to the east. It is here that he began to encounter a whole company of angels. Because of this, he named that place *Mahanaim*, the Hebrew word for "two companies" (or "two camps"). This referred to his own company of people as well as the company of God's angels.

Here in this region of Mahanaim, Jacob's fear of his older brother reached a boiling point and he made preparations to face him. Out of this fear, Jacob ended up dividing his own camp into two:

> *Then Jacob was greatly afraid and distressed; and he divided the people who were with him, and the flocks and the herds and the camels, into* **two companies**.
> *(Gen. 32:7)*

Jacob was moved by such terror of receiving judgment and revenge from his brother that he divided up his family in order to spare some of them in the event that Esau attacked. He then begged God to continue to fulfill His promises to him, but he did this with a weary and worried heart (Gen. 32:9-12). Hidden within this scene we can start to see that Jacob, like all the sons of Adam at the time, saw himself separated from God. Thus the name Mahanaim, or "two companies." He did not yet know if God was on his side and if they were truly *one company* together. There he continued to wrestle with fears of the past, encompassed by a present sense of shame, and a great deal of worry about the future as his brother approached. Mahanaim became a collision point between all these issues that Jacob was wrestling with, even as heaven and earth collided together as well. But we find that this was indeed the breakthrough moment for Jacob as he finally stepped back into his inheritance and destiny.

A New Name

At night, Jacob ended up in a literal wrestling match, which is one of the stranger episodes of the Old Testament. The account says that "Jacob was left alone, and a man wrestled with him until daybreak" (Gen. 32:24). It becomes apparent that he came across one of the angels in "God's company" and began wrestling with him. Through his interaction with this being, Jacob discovered that it was actually God Himself in either angelic or human form. Many people believe that this was a pre-incarnate appearance of Jesus who had not yet been revealed as the Messiah (and thus He does not give His name to Jacob when asked for it).

Jacob was unrelenting in this wrestling match with God. Eventually, the Lord touched the socket of his thigh and dislodged it, leaving Jacob with a permanent life-long limp. Nonetheless, Jacob continued to cling to the Lord and wrestled on. God then said to him, "Let me go, for the dawn is breaking." But Jacob still did not let go. Instead, he asked that this mysterious Man would give him a blessing.

It is here that we come to one of the most defining parts of the history of God's people. The Man first asked Jacob to state his name. Jacob gave it. Remember that in the Hebrew it would be like making this statement:

"I am *Supplanter.*"

Or, "I am *Deceiver.*"

In giving his name, Jacob was confronted with his current identity and his tumultuous past. But it was at that moment that the real blessing came to him and he was given a new name. The Man declared, "Your name shall no longer be Jacob, but Israel; for you have striven with God and with men and have prevailed" (Gen. 32:28). Jacob was given a name that means "one who has striven with God." It can also be translated as "prince of God."

It is at this point that Jacob fully realized Who he had been wrestling with. He named this particular area "Peniel," which translates as "the face of God." He said, "I have seen the face of God, yet my life has been preserved" (Gen. 32:30). Jacob was surprised to see that he did not die in the presence of God. At that moment, the sun rose and the day broke. Jacob lifted up his eyes and saw his brother approaching him with an army of men. Jacob then entered into the final confrontation of this journey into the Promised Land.

In his panic, Jacob had decided to send gift after gift toward Esau to try to appease his supposed wrath. He then further divided up his wives and children and went ahead of them to talk to Esau personally. On the way, Jacob bowed to the ground seven times in order to show honor and reverence toward his brother. Up to the very last minute he was trembling with fear. Yet at that moment everything changed and Jacob was given the surprise of his life.

Esau ran to his brother and tacklds him.

With love.

Esau hugged and embraced his younger brother. He "fell on his neck and kissed him," weeping over this reunion with Jacob (Gen. 33:7). And Jacob lost it here. He too began to weep under this surprising fountain of forgiveness and mercy.

They continued to embrace one another and Esau told Jacob that his gifts of appeasement were completely unnecessary. Jacob responded to this with an eternally significant statement:

The Mystery of Mahanaim

*"No, please, if I have found favor in your sight, then take my present from my hand, **for I see your face as one sees the face of God**, and you have received me favorably. Please take my gift which has been brought to you, because God has dealt graciously with me and because I have plenty"*
(Gen. 33:10-11).

The True Face of God

We will look at that statement more closely in a moment. First, let's attempt to gain some spiritual perspective of Jacob's entire trek through *Mahanaim*. In this convergence of his past, present, and future, Jacob takes on a new identity. He is named Israel. Now let's also keep in mind that as Israel he represents the whole nation that would come from his loins. That being said, he also represents humanity, for the people of Israel were a priesthood to the nations, representing the whole world. All of mankind finds their journey coinciding with Jacob, the supposed Supplanter and Deceiver. Like we have seen in so many other texts, this story of Jacob is actually a parable that holds a glorious message for each one of us.

Esau does not usually represent something good in the Bible. However, in this instance, the light of Christ shines through the Old Testament text and we find something different here. In this particular case, Esau, as Jacob's older brother, represents Jesus—our older Brother. Esau essentially represents God in this story of Jacob's crossover. All along, Jacob had really been wrestling with the same thing that all of humanity has wrestled with—a fear of God and a growing sense of distance in the heart (which has also kept us from the land of our original birth and inheritance—our true identity).

271

All of us have been exiled in our hearts. We have spent time in heavy labor under the burden of our "father-in-law." Jacob laboring under Laban's control speaks to living under a temporary and incomplete understanding of God through the "law." But like Jacob leaving Laban for the land of promise, we are also called to leave our "father-in-law" behind, which entails leaving behind the law *and* our old name (as well as our faulty understanding of the Father).

It is amazing to see that a covenant set up with stones is what releases Jacob from the control of his father-in-law. Laban agrees not to go past this particular heap of rocks in order to bring harm to Jacob. The rock pillar and the heap of stones become a boundary marker that the father-in-law could not cross anymore. This is exactly what happened in the covenant of Christ. Christ is our Rock whose resurrected body has become the eternal marker of a New Covenant. Christ is our permanent boundary line whereby law and slavery can never again cross over and touch us! The weary life of laboring under the sun in order to "earn" something (or appease our own sense of shame) should no longer have access to us.

And yet *we* can always choose to go back to the law and put ourselves under its burdens and consequences. We can choose to stay in the shame of the past and live with a false identity. Realistically, Jacob could have crossed back into the land of Paddan-aram and there the covenant would not be valid. Laban could have legally captured him at that point. Yet if Jacob simply stayed beyond the place of the rock he would be in complete safety. The heap of stones remained a permanent boundary marker saying that Laban could not cross through there to bring harm to Jacob. So too, the covenant of Christ offers us complete safety from the law and its cursing threats.

This parable of Jacob's life becomes even more powerful as we continue in the story, especially when he passed through

Mahanaim and made a full return to Canaan. After the covenant is sealed, Jacob and his family immediately enter the borders of the Promised Land. But we find here that even though Laban is behind him, Jacob's heart is still ruled by fear. He is still terrified of his older brother's wrath. This speaks to us of "entering the Promised Land" but still feeling a sense of distance and rejection from God. We can be freed from the law, and understand the essentials of the Gospel, but still be bound up in our hearts to the lie of an angry God.

So it is here that we come back to the terminology of "two companies." Jacob sees both his and God's camp and makes a distinction between the two. This again speaks to that sense of division between humanity and God. The two have not truly become one—at least in Jacob's mind and experience. In this place of *Mahanaim*, Jacob's fear of his older brother is fully exposed. He sends gifts and sacrifices to his brother in hopes of appeasing his wrath and then releases a desperate prayer to the heavens after dividing up his family and livestock. It is here that he ends up literally wrestling with God, which typifies his whole journey.

This wrestling match is such a random story within the Bible that it stands out like a giant exclamation point highlighting something of great importance. Jacob wrestling with God is a picture of all our wrestlings with God. Jacob is trying to receive a blessing somehow. He is still trying to manipulate and force his way into the promise. He is still striving. And thus he is still living under the old identity. Jacob is embodying what he has done his whole life. He has experienced long years of heavy labor, bouts of deception and manipulation, and periods of great fear and exile. In the land of Paddan-aram, Jacob had to work fourteen years for the love of his life, Rachel. Now Jacob is worried that God will not come through for him and perhaps abandon him to the wrath of his brother. So he tries to wrestle his way back into more blessing.

The Song of the Ages: Part II

But it is here that everything changes and the light of grace shines through. God gives his wrestling son a new name as Jacob finally confronts the core issue of his heart. It is the same issue the Shulammite had to face early on as she too sought after her own land of inheritance. The Shulammite identified herself as "dark," but the Lord responded by calling her "lovely," even comparing her to the fine linen curtains of Solomon's temple. Jacob defined himself as a deceiver, but God gave him a royal name. He called him a victor and a prince of God. This is the source of all the blessing and inheritance we seek. It involves coming to terms with God's Word—the Song that He sings over us. It is discovering the Father's love and the truth of how He sees us—*how He has always seen us.*

After wrestling with God, Jacob is spared from death, which is something he expected to encounter in the direct presence of God (like everyone else in this time period). As a result, he names the place of this wrestling match *Peniel* because of the realization of having seen the face of God—a face that was kind and good. Truly, this is where all our wrestling ultimately leads us: to a greater revelation of God's beautiful face. Jacob is seeing something of God's goodness here, but it doesn't totally click right away.

From there, Jacob finally confronts his older brother and receives the surprise of his life—the "Gospel" of his journey—something that he has been headed toward for over twenty years. When he encounters his brother, he does not find an angry and vengeful man. Instead, he finds someone who deeply loves him, who embraces him warmly and passionately. The reunion of Jacob and Esua is a stark foreshadowing of the prodigal's return to the Father, who fell on His son's neck with joy and weeping. That is what we're seeing with Jacob and his brother. You can bet that this moment forever wrecked Jacob's heart with mercy and compassion. This is where things truly click and everything comes together in

Jacob's mind. This is what prepares him to move past Mahanaim and enter fully into the Promised Land. He says to Esau:

"I see your face as one sees the face of God!"

He gets it. Jacob now understands the full meaning of Peniel. He understands who God truly is. He sees the love of the Father, coinciding with the truth of his own identity. He understands that God is for him, not against him. He realizes that all along there was nothing to fear. Like Esau, God did not need his sacrifices and gifts to appease him. He had already forgiven him—and us—and He proved this forevermore at the cross of Christ.

Jacob, the Shulammite, and Us

Is this not the whole journey of the Shulammite? She too has wrestled and striven with God from the days of her own labor under the sun. Even when she came to the covenantal meal at the table (her own departure from "Laban" at the place of the cross), the Shulammite still continued hiding behind the wall of fear, worried about the rain and snow of an angry God, as well as a continued sense of darkness in her heart. It is this that she has wrestled with all along, preparing her for the ultimate revelation of love. She finally saw and understood the dawn of Christ's resurrection and she entered into that new day for herself.

So remember that when Jacob wrestled with God, the Lord told him that the "dawn was breaking." He told him to let go. In other words,

Stop wrestling, My son. Stop trying to earn My blessing.

And stop living in fear.

275

For the dawn is breaking. In My resurrection, the old is no more. There is no more shame. There is no more Jacob. Furthermore, My resurrection proves that your Father is not angry with you. In fact, He has never been angry with you.

He loves you with an everlasting love.

The dawn obviously speaks to the resurrection of Christ. He is the eternal Sunrise that brings a new merging between God and humanity. He brings forth the true face of God, revealing that our Father was never against us. As the Scriptures teach, even while we were still sinners living in the land of exile, Christ died for us and raised us up in His glorious body.

A Second Encounter at Mahanaim

One more quick note about the region of Mahanaim. This will hopefully tie a beautiful bow around the gift of insight that is pouring out from this biblical location. This area of Jacob's life-changing encounter shows up again at another juncture in Israel's history when the nation's power transitioned from King Saul to King David. Saul was the failed leader of Israel who David was divinely chosen to replace. Unfortunately, when the time came for David to reign, many people did not automatically embrace him as king. Instead, those who were still loyal to Saul made his son the king. His son's name was Ish-bosheth, which literally means *man of shame*. This happened in the region of Mahanaim (see 2 Sam. 2:8).

Once again, we can see a spiritual pattern at work. Though it's outside the scope of this chapter to explain, King Saul represented the old order and the works of the flesh. He was the controlling king that the people wanted, not the one who God had picked. Saul's reign speaks to the old order of law and fear, which came before the dawn of grace, represented by David. David was the one chosen by God whose name literally means *beloved*. So the law and the old system represented by Saul produces nothing but "shame." That is the fruit of its loins, so to speak. That's why Saul fathered a son whose literal name was Man of Shame. David, however, always represented the new. His life spoke to the true King of Israel who would enact a New Covenant of grace—Jesus.

But Saul was defeated and the old order was destroyed. And yet the people of Israel still continued to live under the influence of the old. They chose to live under the Man of Shame. As a result, much of the kingdom remained divided as Judah followed David and the northern kingdom followed the fruit of Saul's loins.

Ish-bosheth was taken to Mahanaim, which we've already noted is located on the border of the Promised Land, just outside the Jordan River. There he was anointed, which further established this divided kingdom. David was made king, but there was a long war between him and the house of Saul. Nonetheless, David was victorious and more and more of his enemies were made a footstool under his feet (2 Sam. 3:1). David eventually took over the entire kingdom, which had belonged to him the whole time anyway.

This parable signifies much of church history, as well as much of our own individual journeys. Jesus has fully conquered death and put away the entire order of shame and fear, but there are still those who cling to it. They still live under the reign of shame in the northern kingdom of unbelief. Thankfully, this false reign is slowly being defeated and Jesus's Kingdom of grace is gaining more and more ground. All the enemies of truth and grace are being turned into a footstool under the victorious feet of Christ.

In other words, the Song of the Ages is rising and the church is coming into her full inheritance.

The Meaning of Mahanaim

And so *Mahanaim* represents the struggle, the wrestling, the division; seeing ourselves separate and distant from God. It is a place of continued dualism and fear where we are still unsure of the Father's undivided word over us—that we are *His beloved*. It is a place of being caught between law and grace in a land of in-betweenness; where though we are set free from Laban and Saul, there is still the fruit of shame and guilt. So much of the Body of Christ still lives in this place today.

However, there is abundant hope here. Mahanaim is also a place of *crossing over*. It provides for the transition between any remaining fear and the full entrance and acceptance of the Promised Land. It is the place of realizing the love of God and waking up to the full dawn of the resurrection. It is the collision between earth and heaven, which every member of this planet is called to embrace.

With this in mind, let's go back and look once more at the Lord's question to the seeking ladies:

> *Why should you gaze at the Shulammite as though at the dance of Mahanaim?*

The Bride is no longer in the same place as the queens, maidens, and concubines of the world—the other daughters of Jerusalem who do not fully know Jesus like her; those who are still living under some form of the law. This is why they said, "Come back! Come back!" The Shulammite has permanently left their territory.

278

The Mystery of Mahanaim

And so the Bridegroom within her responds and poetically explains why she is no longer at that place anymore. She has moved past Mahanaim and is no longer in the dance of two separate companies. At this point, it's important to know that the Hebrew word for "dance" comes from a root word *chuwl*. Though this word can simply mean "dance," it can also translate as "twisting and writhing." Thus, it is often used for when a woman would twist and writhe in the pain of childbirth. So this "dance" can speak of the continued wrestling and writhing under the fetal period of law, like Jacob wrestling with the angel. It is the point that lies right before one is born into the full joy of the Gospel's truth.

Basically, Jesus is speaking the following in response to the queens, concubines, and maidens:

My dear queen, the Bride has gone deep into the land of Canaan. There is no way to reach her but to cross over into that same place—to cross the Jordan and be baptized into the fullness of My joy. The Shulammite has embraced My eternal friendship and has thus become one with Me in experience. She has truly accepted the beauty of My cross and the revelation of our Father's love. Now she shines with the joy and freedom that it brings. Receive this joy for yourselves!

The queens, concubines, and maidens of humanity are standing at the spiritual region of Mahanaim, beholding the beautiful church right beyond the Jordan River, to the west. They have perhaps already been taught and discipled to some extent, but they have grown content to just gaze at her and spectate. So the Lord within her responds to this and calls them further in. They are not meant to be spectators, but participants in the grace of Christ! Through His Bride, Jesus calls everyone to leave the land of Laban. To come out from every wall and walk past the leopards and lions of deception and defeat (see Sgs. 4:8).

He's also issuing the eternal call to embrace God as Father, whose face is like the surprise of morning light, filled with graciousness and peace. He urges them to leave dualistic philosophies and theologies where we see ourselves as half-evil and half-good or see God as half-angry and half-kind. This is the call to come into the full embrace of the Father while also receiving a new name as His son or daughter.

This is the journey of all humanity—for the queen is yet asleep in a false identity of her own. But even that will begin to change as we continue in this great tale of the Shulammite and her Beloved...

19

The Awake Tree

---◆---

How beautiful are your feet in sandals,
O prince's daughter!
The curves of your hips are like jewels,
The work of the hands of an artist.
Your navel is like a round goblet
Which never lacks mixed wine;
Your belly is like a heap of wheat
Fenced about with lilies.
Your two breasts are like two fawns,
Twins of a gazelle.
(7:1-3)

The dialogue continues between the people of the world and the Shulammite. Many commentators believe that these particular words of praise toward the Bride are now coming from the King. However, the context appears to show that this is the continued praise of the people around her. We will find later that this portion ends with them saying, "The king is held captive by your tresses" (Sgs. 7:5). This gives some good evidence that the queen of humanity is the one talking as they address the Bride and her relationship with the King.

Unimaginably Relieving News

Through the words of Christ within her, the people have been hit with a new understanding of her journey. Having learned about the dance of Mahanaim, they now know more about the true nature of the Gospel. Hearing all of this, the people exclaim, "How beautiful are your feet!" This would appear to be a random compliment until we understand that this phrase shows up in the Bible in several other places and carries a very specific meaning. The first time it appears is in the book of Isaiah:

> *How beautiful upon the mountains are the feet of him who brings good news, who proclaims peace, who brings glad tidings of good things...*
> *(Isa. 52:7 NKJV)*

Isaiah's words are alluding to when a messenger would bring news of a military victory over an enemy nation. In order to grasp the power behind this analogy, think through the following scenario. Imagine that you are a woman in ancient Israel during a period of time when one of the surrounding nations is sending an army into your land. Their plan is to completely take over your country and dispossess you and your people from your homes and families. You know that if they defeat your military they are eventually going to march right into your neighborhood and remove you from your home. Your children will either be killed or sold into slavery, which would involve heavy labor or sexual slavery, or both. You will most likely be raped and sold into slavery yourself. Either way, you are getting exiled from your land and your family.

The Awake Tree

So the time comes for Israel to forge a resistance and your husband goes out to war with thousands of other men in order to meet this threat. For weeks and weeks, you are forced to wait for news of the war effort. There are no 24/7 news networks, no cell phones, and no other forms of communication to find out how the war is progressing. In all likelihood, you will simply have to wait until one side has won before you find anything out. So throughout this time, your mind begins to spin together nightmare scenarios of the worst possibilities. Day by day you look out into the mountains to see whether or not the black banners of the enemy's army will slowly rise over the hills bringing the march of doom and death.

With all that in mind, let's then imagine that on one of those mornings of torturous waiting and wondering, you look out into the mountainside and you see a dancing speck cresting the top of a hill. You immediately realize that it is a singular person moving swiftly and quickly over the hills and toward your village. Before long, his shape and image is clearer and you find that he is a messenger sent from the general of Israel's army. As he gets closer and closer you realize that he is skipping and shouting. You and others from the village run toward him in order to make out what he's saying as you're not sure if his intense shouts are communicating pain or celebration.

But then you finally get close enough to hear him as he runs into the edge of the village and his words catch your ears: *The battle is over! The war is done!* He goes on to declare that the enemy nation has been utterly defeated and will not be crossing your borders. Israel is safe and all is well. He then comes to you personally and tells you that your husband is alive and he is coming home soon.

In one moment, all of the paralyzing fears and nightmare scenarios that have plagued your mind for weeks on end would be obliterated into ashes, making way for a surge of bliss. An unspeakable joy would fill your heart, which would lead to tears and laughter and song. Dancing would soon commence as well. Deep peace would return to your wearied soul as you slowly take in the fact that your family is safe and your nation is at peace. There would be no words to communicate the depth of relief that you would experience upon hearing and *trusting* in that messenger's news.

Now depending on the depth of your imagination, you may have caught a glimpse in your own heart of how truly *beautiful* the feet of that messenger would be. Hopefully you can see at least some of the beauty in his steps as he dances along the mountainside toward your fearful and burdened village. This is the imagery Isaiah chose to use to communicate the good news of God's coming salvation. It was likened to a messenger eliminating all worry of exile, slavery, separation, and death. This should also help you understand why Jesus and the apostles carried this imagery forward when they chose to use the word "gospel" to describe their own message. The word "gospel" was a Roman term that signified a military victory over an enemy nation. Roman messengers would come into the land proclaiming the gospel, or good news, of Rome's victory over a particular army. Such an announcement would always lead to celebration and joy throughout the whole territory. It went hand in hand with Isaiah's prophetic words.

For this reason, the apostle Paul directly quotes this passage from Isaiah when he speaks about the preaching of the Gospel in his letter to the Romans (see Rom. 10:15). Later in the New Testament, Paul alludes to this verse a second time when he calls for all believers to have their "feet fitted with the readiness that comes from the Gospel of peace" (Eph. 6:15). Paul wanted people to continually plant their feet in the message of grace that brings unspeakable relief to the soul. He wanted the church to be carriers of that message, spreading this same elation and reprieve to the world around them.

So we can see how appropriate and fitting the maidens' response is when they describe the beauty of the Shulammite's feet. They have seen the splendor of her life's message and now understand more of its meaning. Having crossed through the realm of fear (and *Mahanaim*), the Shulammite brings news from the other side. She bears the message of the eternal smile of a happy Father, which washes away all fear of exile and retribution. She also declares the message of Jacob's true name—which is also *our* true name.

In all of this, we find that the Shulammite has become a true ambassador for Christ. When Jesus spoke through her in the previous verse of the Song, He was making an appeal to the seeking world:

> *Therefore, we are ambassadors for Christ, as though God were making an appeal **through us**; we beg you on behalf of Christ, be reconciled to God.*
> *(2 Cor. 5:20)*

The people are now responding to the good news of this message. The Gospel in its full articulation is always attractive and lovely to the weary soul. Yet it is often hated by the soul who wants to cling to religious idols and fear. So before we move on with the Song, let's notice that Isaiah did not say, "How beautiful on the mountain are the feet of those bring news of judgment and religious obligation!" The Gospel is not an announcement of judgment with exacting conditions and parameters for someone to narrowly escape a fate of exile and death. The Gospel is a joyful announcement for all people no matter where they are. It is a royal and authoritative message that conveys a complete victory over sin and death. *It reveals that the enemy wasn't just badly wounded at the cross. He was defeated, plain and simple.*

Jesus took on the sin of the whole world. He became sin itself and gave us His righteousness. God is not counting people's sins against them! *This* is the message of reconciliation that a true ambassador carries (see 2 Cor. 5:18-21). The words "be reconciled to God" mean that people can run right into the arms of a loving Father, arms that were spread out once and for all on the cross, forever revealing His heart of tender mercy. Like Jacob's surprise encounter with Esau, people can run into the embrace of a God who will fall on their neck with tears and kisses and tell them that they never needed to do anything to earn His love. All they need to do is open up and receive it.

The Shulammite has personally received this news for herself. Now the world is seeing the joy and peace on her life and is finally taking notice of the appeal of Christ within her. This will help them understand another facet of her journey as they continue in their adoration and praise.

The Jewel in our Hip

"The curves of your hips are like jewels," they go on to say. "The work of the hands of an artist."

Having seen the triumphant message that her feet carry, they now move their gaze up to her hip. Their focus shifts to the *way* she walks since the "curves" of the hips speak not only of shape but of movement. This is describing how she walks out the message that her feet are carrying. To take in the full weight of this metaphor, we'll have to return to the story of Jacob and his infamous wrestling match. There, we find this same Hebrew word for "hip."

We explained earlier that when Jacob wrestled God it was a picture of all Israel (and thus all of mankind) wrestling with their Creator. Eventually God told Jacob to let go, for the "dawn" was breaking. This spoke to the resurrection of Christ. The rising of Jesus from the grave was the dawning of new day when we would no longer have to strive and wrestle for the blessing of heaven. As the true and final representative for humankind, Christ would bring heaven's blessing and favor back to us.

To demonstrate this point even further, God dislodged a bone in Jacob's hip, leaving him with a life-long limp. Jacob would no longer be able to walk in his own strength. Several translations point out that God actually "shrank" the muscle around his hip (Gen. 32:32 NKJV). Jacob's personal strength was minimized and from there on out he would have to use a staff to support his walk. We did not look at this element of the story before, but it is one more facet in the Scriptural diamond that declares the work of Christ on our behalf.

Jacob needed to learn to let go of personal effort in order to rest in something, or Someone, outside of himself. This rest would lead him back to Canaan, the place that represents our original friendship with God. Jacob was also named Israel, meaning "one who strives with God." God declared that Jacob had wrestled with both God and man and had "prevailed" (Gen. 32:28). Of course, Jesus is the One who has prevailed as both God and man. He is the true Israel, the true Prince of God who came *as Jacob*—as each one of us. This is part of what it means when the Scriptures say that He *became sin* for us (again, this is the "appeal" of His message and the dance in the Shulammite's sandaled steps). Ultimately, it would be Jesus who would not "let go." He would hold fast to faith and obedience *for us*. His resurrected life would then become our everlasting goodness before God.

287

Thus in the story of Jacob's wrestling match, the broken hip and the breaking of the dawn are two edges of the same revelatory sword. The dawning of His resurrection would become the everlasting Staff upon which we would lean. Jesus would become our true walk of righteousness. This is the essence of the Gospel's message. Hence, the description of the feet leads to a natural understanding of the hips. The observing world sees that the Shulammite is not walking in her own strength anymore. As she walks, the curves of her hips are revealed and the people see the "jewel" within her walk. That jewel is the revelation of Christ within. He is the precious treasure within the field of humanity. The Shulammite has simply discovered that treasure and is now walking it out.

The Power of "Aman"

The onlookers then say that this is all "the work of the hands of an artist." Here is where this revelation becomes abundantly clear and all questions will be settled as to whether or not the Gospel is being communicating in parable form. Solomon's use of the word "artist" in this portion of the Song is quite an interesting word choice. In the Hebrew, it's a very famous and recognizable word. It's the word *aman*. That should look familiar to you. This is the word that is usually translated as "amen." It is being used here in a slightly different form, but the root meaning remains completely the same. It is the well-known Hebrew word that essentially means agreement. *Aman* is another word for *yes* or *so be it*.

So let's think about what the ladies are saying in light of this word choice. Replace the word "artist" with the word "amen" or "so be it." The "work" of her moving hips (her righteous walk) is the result of *aman*. It is "the work of the hands of amen." In other words, her walk is the result of having simply said yes and amen to the Good News! Hidden within the Hebrew wording of Solomon's text we continue to find a treasury of Gospel truth.

This becomes even more clear when we consider the word "hands" in this statement. In the Hebrew, the word for "hands" is often translated as "power." This is because the hand was a symbol of one's strength (thus the "hand" of God was associated with His power throughout the Scriptures). So let's utilize all the meanings of these Hebrew words and restate the verse:

The curves of your hips are like jewels (your walk is the very walk of Christ within). All of this is **the result of the power of** *"***amen.***"*

In other words: *You are walking this out because of your heart's agreement with the Gospel!*

The Shulammite truly believes in the happy message her "feet" are carrying! This is the power behind her jeweled and radiant walk. We find then that a deeper understanding is dawning upon the minds of the seeking queens, concubines, and maidens. Earlier, they were more interested in gazing upon her in a general way, and from a distance. Now, through Christ, they have greater insight as to where her peaceful light comes from. They see that it all comes down to a wonderfully joyful message of union—and simply saying "yes" to its intoxicating truth.

A Belly of Wine

They move further up. After seeing the staff and foundation that she is leaning upon, they take notice of the "wine" flowing from her innermost being. The Song puts it this way: "Your navel is like a rounded goblet which *never* lacks mixed wine."

Take a good look at the word "never." Let it sit and swirl on the pallet of your mind as though you were tasting the Scriptures like wine. Swish it around in your heart and swallow it down slowly.

Think carefully of the implications behind this statement. *Within us is a never-ending supply of the wine of the Spirit of God.*

The navel is the bully button and we know very well by now that these are spiritual metaphors. This is referring to her "innermost being," the place where Jesus said rivers of living water would flow (Jn. 7:38). The wine and living water are both metaphors of the same reality and Person—the Holy Spirit of God. And so we find that this is speaking of an unending fountain of living wine flowing from within the church.

It is apparent that as the Shulammite walks out the Gospel before the people's eyes she is becoming an intoxicating and refreshing drink to the nations. This is not just a woman standing still and radiating an otherworldly glow. She is out in the world bringing relief to human suffering through acts of healing, mercy, and justice. She is releasing tangible power and renewal to the people around her. Furthermore, she is bringing people into an awareness and encounter with the presence of God, which always brings the utmost peace and joy.

But also take note that she is releasing *mixed* wine to the seeking world. In ancient times, mixed wine was when alcohol was enhanced with psychotropic elements. This is not a joke. In Solomon's day, wine was often mixed with things like wormwood, myrrh, and narcotics in order to give it a more inebriating effect. Oftentimes, these types of wine were given to criminals before an execution in order to completely knock them out. This is a strong metaphor in the Song with an intense purpose behind its wording. The Holy Spirit is such a powerful drink that He will knock us off our feet and inebriate us from *all* the cares and worries of life. He will anesthetize us from fear and give us a true sense of carefreeness. What people seek in drugs and alcohol is actually the pure bliss of God's presence. That is what the Bride is embodying and releasing to the world.

God's people are called to be drunk on this wine of grace, which is a drunkenness without a hangover and without the destruction of the life and body. It is an intoxication that lifts the soul up to a place of pure rest. In fact, this is how the church was kick-started on the day of Pentecost. In the second chapter of Acts we find that Peter and the gang were filled with the wine of God's presence, which had descended upon their hearts like tongues of fire. Like the Shulammite, this encounter then drew in the observing and questioning world. We'll find that the story of Pentecost actually ties in significantly with this portion of the Song, especially as we look at the next poetic symbol spoken over the Shulammite...

A Harvest Within

"Your belly is a heap of wheat fenced about with lilies," they say.

There is a natural advance from the wine to wheat. Wine is the symbol of the Spirit and wheat is a symbol of the harvest. Both these elements are intimately connected.

In the story of Pentecost (which is also called the Feast of the Harvest and the Feast of First-fruits), many people from the "queen" of humanity and many young "maidens" of Jerusalem were assembled together for the celebration (see Acts 2:1-41). People came from all over the world to visit Jerusalem during this time. The biblical account lists a multitude of nations that were represented at this feast. It was there that these nations first saw the Shulammite Bride beginning to arise and shine as 120 believers stumbled into the light of day after their encounter with God in the upper room. They were filled with the mixed wine of heaven and were praising God loud enough for a crowd in a Jewish festival to take notice of them. That means they were being seriously disruptive.

At first the people did not understand what was happening and accused them of being drunk on literal wine. But this is when Peter boldly stood up and preached to the crowd (or you could say that His Beloved within him rose up from the inside and addressed the questioning "maidens"). His feet carried the glorious message of the Gospel to the nations that were assembled in Jerusalem. At that moment, people were drawn in and began to truly drink of this message flowing from Peter's innermost being. The wine convicted their hearts and they asked what they should do. Peter answered with the Gospel's simple call of repentance (to change the mind) and urged them to believe in the work of Christ. He admonished the people to be fully immersed—*baptized*—into this glorious work. Out of this moment came the first harvest of souls into the Kingdom of light and truth.

It is no coincidence that during his sermon Peter quoted from the book of Joel. Though Peter doesn't quote this part of the prophecy, Joel's words included a day when "the threshing floors shall be full of *wheat*, and the vats shall overflow with new *wine*" (Joe. 2:24 NKJV). These two symbols connect with Solomon's Song as well as the first revealing of the early Shulammite church in the book of Acts. The wine within the awakened Bride always leads to a harvest of wheat. This is why the Song shows the wine in the center of her belly while the wheat surrounds it. The wine of the Spirit draws in the harvest. Additionally, the harvest is kept—*fenced in*—by a revelation of love and identity, which is what "lilies" have always represented.

Discipleship After the Harvest

From the beauty of her feet, to the movement of her hips, to the wine of the Spirit and the resulting harvest, the Song continues as the people look further up her glorious and shining frame. At first all they could see were the feet, the message of the Gospel itself. This led them to understand the power of her walk and then the life-giving wine being offered to them. As they drank, they were harvested into the Kingdom themselves. Because of this, they now behold the imagery of her breasts, which is a symbol of nourishment and discipleship. "Your two breasts are like two fawns, twins of a gazelle," they say. The progression of the poetry could not be more perfect.

Our last study of the Song covered this metaphor of nourishment to the spiritually young. This also includes the additional imagery of multiplication as seen in the "twins of a gazelle." Earlier, the Lord was speaking of her potential and prophetically declaring her identity as a nurturer to the nations, one who is like a mother nurturing her child. Now she is walking this out and the world is seeing and experiencing it for themselves. They are now awakening to the life of Christ for themselves. But their encounter does not stop there. The people of the world are also offered milk with their wine (see Isa. 55:1). They now need to be discipled and built up in this message of grace just like babies need the milk of their mothers to grow strong.

Behind the chest of the Shulammite is a heart of compassionate love with a desire to tenderly care for others and help them navigate through the same difficulties and doubts that she experienced in her own journey. The church is called to be a helper of people's faith, an encourager, and one who builds up others in their true identity in Christ. We are called to do this through intimate relationship, which includes spiritual mothering and fathering. All of this happens alongside an unwavering stance on the Gospel as we continually remind people of the full truth of what Christ accomplished.

So once again we see that the church is the vehicle whereby the milk of the Gospel is fed to the world so that all can grow into maturity in Christ. Deep within us is all that we need to release this edifying milk to the world. That is our great calling and this work of discipleship is promised to happen until we *all* come into the unity of the faith and stand up in the full stature of Christ. In other words, it will happen until we see a full harvest of wheat that completely resembles the original Grain of Christ.

The Church as the First-Fruits

All of this brings us back to something we also saw in our previous study. The church is the full manifestation of what Eve represented. She is the true "mother of all the living," which is the meaning of Eve's name. The Shulammite is finally stepping into this mantle and destiny. She has left the land of deception and is embodying the great truth of her Beloved's Song. She has become the *first-fruits* of salvation that calls the rest of the world into the same harvest of spiritual awakening.

The apostle James is the one who called the church a "first-fruits of all He created" (Jam. 1:18 NIV). James is essentially teaching that the church is the first-fruits of a greater harvest—for the term "first-fruits" implies that there is more to come. This is not to minimize the significance of the first-fruits. A farmer absolutely delights in the first crops of the season. He offers it to God, celebrates over it, eats of it, and shares it with family and friends. But in the coming of first-fruits there is an implication of a greater and fuller harvest. So if the church is called the first-fruits then that surely means there is something more to come. Something involving the great "queen" of humanity.

This concept is not just something we're pulling out of one verse from the book of James or some subtle implication in the Song of Songs. This first-fruits identity of the church is actually implied throughout the entire Bible, being fully unveiled in the book of Revelation. It is there that Jesus compares the church to a *lampstand* (Rev. 1:20). With a little bit of digging, we'll find that is a vibrant picture of this first-fruits calling.

The Lampstand and the Almond Tree

To understand the lampstand and why Jesus compares it to the church, we have to go back to the tabernacle of Moses. The lampstand was one of the holy objects located in the inner room of the tabernacle. It had six branches connected to a center pipe and was made of one hammered work of gold. The purpose of this lampstand was obviously to give light to the inner room; however, its light was specifically directed at a special table in front of it. Upon this table, the priests would set out a piece of bread called the "showbread" or the "bread of the presence" (see Ex. 25:30). So the lampstand would primarily illuminate this sacred bread.

What's very important to understand is that the lampstand was fashioned after the image of an almond tree (see Ex. 25:31-40 for the full details). Its six branches are meant to be tree branches and the cups that hold the oil lamps were meant to represent the beautiful white blossoms of the almond tree. The fire on the cup is like the bearing of its fruit. Now in the Hebrew, the almond tree is called the "awake tree." This is because the word for "almond" can be literally translated as "awake." The almond tree was given this particular name because it was the first tree to blossom in Israel as the spring approached. This is still true of the almond tree today. Even before winter is officially over, this tree comes to life while the rest of the trees are still "asleep."

Therefore, we find that the almond tree is a type of "first-fruits" tree. It bears its fruit while the rest of the trees still lay closed and hidden in the midst of winter. The almond tree gives hope of a great springtime when the other trees and plants will open up with the glorious flowers and fruits lying dormant within them. This is what the lampstand is fashioned after. And again, its purpose in the tabernacle was to give light to the sacred bread. Now hopefully you're not getting lost in all this imagery and symbolism. We'll attempt to tie this together now and look at the beautiful message being communicated through the Scriptures. All of it brings us right back to this great vision of the Shulammite church.

Jesus compared the church to the lampstand, which was fashioned after the almond tree—the "awake" tree. Thus, the church is truly the first-fruits of a springtime awakening that calls the entire world into the hope that we presently bear. We announce the springtime of hope and resurrection even before it fully appears, just like the almond tree announces springtime before the world can see it.

While the winter of sin appears to persist, the church shines with the fire and fruit of grace. They are the "awakened" ones. They have awoken to love, to the Song of the Ages, and have broken through the winter's lies. They have realized that in the death and resurrection of Christ, the winter is already over. The rain of judgment is gone. The dawn has broken and there is a new identity and a new hope right in this present age.

Furthermore, the church reveals Christ just like the golden lampstand illuminated and revealed the sacred bread. The sacred bread in Moses's tabernacle was always pointing to Jesus, since He is called "the Bread of Life" (Jn. 6:35). Consequently, we are commissioned to reveal the Bread of life to the nations. Like Joseph's storehouse of grain, we invite the nations to partake of this life-giving Bread. We have been called and chosen to be a tree of awakening that yields the hope of an even greater awakening throughout the entire world. The church has truly been chosen by the Lord for this glorious and global purpose.

But it is here that we must recognize that our *chosenness* is not about us. One of the great tragedies of church history over the centuries is the teaching that our "election" means we are saved from hell while others are chosen for damnation. This couldn't be further from the truth! Like any other election, *we are elected on behalf of others.* We are chosen to serve and awaken the maidens and queens around us, just like Israel was chosen to be a nation that would teach the world about God (Ex. 19:5-6).

We live in a world that is lost in an orphan mindset and a false identity, still fearful of the Father and held captive to guilt and shame. Their hearts are closed tight like petals in the winter; like a hardened nut that has yet to be cracked. The church is like the almond nut that has cracked open by faith—by simply "waking up" and seeing the love of God and trusting in the springtime of His resurrection. The Shulammite is the one who went down to the garden of union and said *aman* to the Gospel of grace. She left the realm of "two companies" and entered into the sweet love of the Trinity. Now she gives hope to the rest of the "nuts" that are out there, those who are still closed behind their own rigid walls of fear.

While the world sleeps, the Bride manifests the awakened life. She is a lampstand for the world, shining upon the Bread of life within the tabernacle of humanity. She bears this Gospel of peace to everyone, calling each person to open their heart's eyes and break through the shell of unbelief. From there, she nurtures and disciples them to rise up and blossom, until the whole world is filled with the fragrance of heaven.

20

Brick and Gem

———— •◆• ————

Your neck is like a tower of ivory,
Your eyes like the pools in Heshbon
By the gate of Bath-rabbim;
Your nose is like the tower of Lebanon,
Which faces toward Damascus.
(7:4)

When Christ Himself was describing the Bride's features He started with her head and moved down (Sgs. 4:1-5). Now the observing world praises her by starting at her feet and moving up. The contrast between these two starting points marks a difference in perspective. It also marks the joining of earth's song with heaven's. Christ was beholding His church from a heavenly viewpoint, the view that already sees us as perfect. However, the world's perspective was much different. They did not start with a perfect picture. Instead, they first took notice of the message being carried through the feet of her life as she trod the dust of this broken world. But understanding this message helped them to look up and see the full glory within her. They began to see what was already true from the eyes of heaven.

The Song of the Ages: Part II

From there, the world began to join with the Song of the Ages, which is a declaration of a finished reality that is slowly invading time and space. The perfection of heaven is now touching down on the earth like a beautiful sandaled foot touching the soil; like an eternal wave crashing on earthly shores.

In receiving a more complete vision of the Bride, the world will now acknowledge that she represents something much bigger than they'd ever imagined. They are seeing that she is far greater than an organization, and even larger and more important than an entity that meets needs or shows compassion or releases signs and wonders. More than all of this, the church reveals the very culmination of human existence. The Shulammite ultimately gives a living picture of how humanity is supposed to live together and function.

We will find here that this Song holds a key that unlocks not only the door to spiritual freedom, but the doors to every other area of life and culture, whether anthropology, economics, government, or beyond. Mankind has long desired what the church truly is. In fact, we've been trying to create it ourselves since the very beginnings of civilization...

Babel's Building Material

As they look up from the feet toward the full stature of her identity, the world compares her neck to an "ivory tower." The first time this word "tower" shows up in the Hebrew Scriptures is extremely important. It is from the time when mankind came together to create a structure that would reach the heavens. This of course is the notorious Tower of Babel. Humanity had a desire to re-attain heavenly perfection and decided early on that they would accomplish this themselves—brick by brick.

Brick and Gem

We will take a good look at the account of this story for it will bring more understanding into the swelling poetry that is encompassing the Bride.

> *Now the whole earth used the same language and the same words. It came about as they journeyed east, that they found a plain in the land of Shinar and settled there. They said to one another, "Come, let us make bricks and burn them thoroughly." And they used brick for stone, and they used tar for mortar. They said, "Come, let us build for ourselves a city, and a tower whose top will reach into heaven, and let us make for ourselves a name, otherwise we will be scattered abroad over the face of the whole earth."*
> *(Gen. 11:1-4)*

Mankind's departure from Eden was a journey further and further east, which was actually a journey further away from the original source of intimacy and identity—the essential things that the Shulammite has been recovering since she began to follow the Great Shepherd. She has been moving "west," so to speak, back into the Promised Land of grace and truth. In Genesis, however, we find the opposite happening. Mankind was moving further away from Eden, and was falling further away from grace. Yet all throughout that time, their hearts continued to hunger after the heavenly glory of Eden.

This is obviously a good and God-given desire. The problem comes when people try to attain it the wrong way. Outside the realm of grace and friendship, the only way the world saw to reach this perfection was through their own self-works. Therefore, they envisioned a plan to construct a tower that would reach into the heavens. The building of this tower is another metaphoric picture of how mankind was still feeding off the Tree of Knowledge of

Good and Evil. It is the way of self-effort and religion coupled with a mindset of division and separation. Babel was indeed a real place with a real structure that was partly erected, but the story speaks to this deeper and recurring issue within the heart of humanity.

The Tower of Babel was built with bricks that were smothered in a tar used for mortaring glue. These are the same types of bricks and mortar that we find later on in the biblical narrative during the story of the Exodus. Pharaoh had forced the Israelites into slavery and their primary task was to make these specific kinds of bricks in order to build up his own empire (see Ex. 1:14). Such bricks were used amongst all the ancient kingdoms. Spiritually speaking, they represent the slavery of human works. It also relates to the systems of control where leaders create empires by their own sweat and effort (or better yet, the sweat and effort of the slaves underneath them).

Of course, even in these debilitating systems, mankind can accomplish a lot together. God acknowledged this and declared that the unity of man could achieve what their hearts desired (Gen. 11:6). But being "east of Eden," their accomplishments would only lead to more slavery and control. Indeed, the first dictators and kings arose during this season and we know from both biblical and non-biblical records that humanity was filled with unprecedented levels of human trafficking and genocide. Consolidating together at this self-made tower would have been an even greater manifestation of darkness. It also might have hindered the great Messianic promise of restoration. So God came and disrupted their plans by confusing their language (Gen. 11:7). This particular project was dismantled, but man has continued to build new forms of this tower all throughout history, all in the same effort to reach the heavens. They have continued to rely upon the bricks of human strength and slavery.

Besides these elements, there is another important aspect to the bricks of Babel and Egypt. Each brick was made the same. There was no diversity or distinctiveness amongst them. They were all created by the same process and filed away into the same reserves to be used in the predetermined and rigid plans of kings and their architects. The deeper meaning of this is quite simple. These manmade bricks not only speak of man's efforts, but they also speak of the way that we see and use people. Each person is just another brick to be used for the agenda of the empire. There is no inherent uniqueness or value to the individual. These systems of control thus carry a sense of suffocating uniformity amongst mankind. Like the square shape of a brick, each person is supposed to fit into a box with little freedom for creativity and spontaneity.

Thankfully, the Scriptures give us a much different vision of the true structure that needed to be built. This structure comes with completely different material than bricks. The vision for this building shows up in several places in the Bible, the clearest of which is the book of Revelation. There we find the creation of a structure that is built not by the hands of man but by God (see Rev. 21:2 & Heb. 11:10). We also find that the Lord does not use square bricks of baked clay to create this entity. Instead, He uses beautiful and precious stones. Let's explore this further as it will help us gain even more insight into the poetry at hand.

The Revelation and the Song

A quick word about the book of Revelation as we move forward. This may come as a surprise to some, but Revelation is like a sister book to the Song of Solomon. This is because both books build up toward a poetic and metaphoric description of the Bride of Christ. Obviously, the books use different imagery, but both of them are apocalyptic in their style (the word "apocalyptic" simply means "the uncovering of something hidden"). Revelation uses a building metaphor to uncover this hidden truth while the Song uses the imagery of a woman. But both are pointing to the same higher reality.

In Revelation, the apostle John is given an invitation to see something that we have been catching glimpses of throughout the Song. An angel appears to him and says, "Come here, I will show you the bride, the wife of the Lamb" (Rev. 21:9). Next, John is carried away in the Spirit to "a great and high mountain" and is shown the church in all of her glory. This is perhaps the same Summit of *Amana* where the Spirit enabled us to behold our full identity from a heavenly perspective. In the case of John's Revelation, we do not see a beautiful and radiant woman from this height. Instead, his vision consists of the "holy city, Jerusalem, coming down out of heaven from God" (Rev. 21:10).

As he looks at this city, John sees an array of precious gems. Each gem is unique, varying in shape and color. From jasper to amethyst, there is a wide scope of beauty and diversity to the materials that make up this grand metropolis. These are far from the bricks and tar of Babel, which hold no intrinsic value. This is now the true "empire" that God always had in mind—a Kingdom built not on the backs of slaves through fear and control, but on the shed blood of the King's own back. And this Kingdom is where each member can enjoy true Edenic glory.

As we said before, mankind has continued eating from the proverbial Tree of Knowledge in his efforts to attain godliness and perfection. That was the original lie that we discussed at the beginning of our journey. Adam and Eve were told that if they ate from that tree then they would become "like God" (see Gen. 3:5). Instead of resting in the fact that they were already made in His likeness, Adam and Eve pursued this by the work of their own hands. They and their children then continued this pursuit even as they moved eastward. Meanwhile, God continued to call all of us back to the place of rest. A place where He Himself builds His Kingdom—or we could say that He *reveals* the Kingdom that was already there from the start.

Let's bring all of this back to the story of the Shulammite. She represents those out of the queens, concubines, and maidens of humanity (both the religious and non-religious people of the world) who have laid down the bricks of self-effort and rigid conformity. She has left Egypt in search of the way of trust and intimacy. She has moved from Babel to Eden, Egypt to Canaan, Babylon to Zion, law to grace, and fear to love. In doing this, she has become the true "tower" that mankind has always sought after. But this tower is not made from the burnt bricks and mortar of man's organizing labors. This tower is made of "ivory," which is a strong white substance that speaks of the pure righteousness of God. She is built up by His righteousness, not her own. And because of this, she is emerging as the heavenly Jerusalem that we see at the end of the Bible.

The Building of the Bride

The construction of this righteous city began when Jesus Christ resurrected from the grave as the first-fruits of a new humanity. At that moment, Jesus became the "cornerstone" of a new heavenly structure (1 Pet. 2:6). Traditionally, the cornerstone is the most important stone in a building. When laid, it becomes the reference point for all other stones, determining their positions within the entire structure. The life of Christ is our true reference point. As we come together to form the "building" of the church, Jesus is the alignment and mirror of our own identity. He gives direction and specification for how we are to connect and bind our hearts to one another.

After the resurrection and the placing of the Cornerstone, the "foundation stones" were laid next (Rev. 21:19-21). This happened at Pentecost, the Feast of First-Fruits that we discussed earlier. During this feast, the Spirit manifested as fire and became the true mortar that would glue people together in love. The Holy Spirit appeared upon the twelve apostles and the early believers, all of whom became the first living stones within this new city of righteousness. This moment was coupled with a strange and fascinating sign. Suddenly, this small group of believers were able to speak the different languages of the nations who had gathered at Jerusalem for the feast. This was the first release of the gift of tongues.

This momentous event signified that the dividing curse of Babel was broken and reversed. Instead of division and separation, a new language of the Spirit was ignited, which brought people together to hear the glorious announcement of the Gospel. This was a sign that the true "tower" was now being built. This would be done by the hands of the Spirit and not by the work of human flesh. Pentecost became the first-fruits of a harvest that would free the planet from its addiction to division as well as its slavery to the controlling systems of man. The Shulammite was birthed here and became a sparkling tower that was covered with the ivory righteousness of God.

Now it's important to recall how the symbol of ivory showed up earlier in the Song. We discussed King Solomon's literal throne and how it was made of ivory (Sgs. 5:14). We found that the imagery of ivory speaks to the authority of the true King, Jesus Christ. It is fitting then to use ivory to describe the neck, since the head is *enthroned* upon the neck. This paints a beautiful picture of how the church is the living throne of God. We are the citadel where His authority and rule is decreed; a spiritual city that manifests His righteous reign.

Obviously, the city is a metaphor just as the beautiful woman from Shulam is a metaphor. All of this is about people—living stones—being united with the Father in the Holy Spirit through the work of Jesus Christ. These people may meet together in buildings, but the building is very far from the point. The church is meant to be a colorful and global incarnation of the God who is Love. This obviously looks much different than the beige images formed by Babel's bricks. This is a Kingdom of freedom, diversity, righteousness, generosity, forgiveness, and peace. And these things come not by the force of a government or a priest or by a moral code, but by the pure love of a renewed heart that has found its rest in the Cornerstone—Jesus Christ.

Eyes Like Pools

Let's move to the next description of the Bride for it will bring together an even more unified picture of Revelation's city and Solomon's bride. The world continues to look up and they glimpse the very top of the ivory tower. They proclaim that her eyes resemble the "pools in Heshbon by the gate of Bath-rabbim."

In our last study we saw how the eyes can symbolize the Spirit. Earlier, Jesus had compared her eyes to doves, just as His own eyes were compared to doves (Sgs. 1:15 & 5:12). The dove is a direct symbol of the Holy Spirit, and so in both the eyes of the church and the eyes of Christ we can see the Spirit of God. Interestingly, in Revelation, the sister book of the Song, Jesus's eyes are explicitly called "the seven Spirits of God" (Rev. 5:6). We've also looked at how the eyes truly are a window to the soul. When we open our eyelids, the inner *us* is seeing out into the physical realm. When you look into the eyes of another human being, you are peering into the depths of their own inner self. This is why there is a certain pressure you feel when you make deep eye contact with another human being. In that moment, you get a sense of the weight of that person's spirit peering back at you.

This time around, the Shulammite's eyes are compared to the beautiful blue pools of water found outside a certain gate in the city of Heshbon. Already, the comparison to pools of water is making another connection to the Spirit. The observers are giving a different analogy for the same thing. However, this passage about her eyes is sometimes translated as the "fishpools of Heshbon" (Sgs. 7:4 KJV) This is because these particular pools of water are believed to have been used for keeping beautiful and exotic fish. As people came to "the gate of Bath-rabbim," they would pass by these artificial pools filled with different kinds of fish. So it's clear that this is another reference to the Spirit in her eyes. Yet there is something more that the maidens are adding into this feature of her face when they allude to fish.

The mention of fish-pools calls to mind Jesus's words to His disciples, that they would be "fishers of men" (see Matt. 4:19). Fish are very often a symbol for the nations of the world, all of which are called into the Kingdom of light and truth. So what's beautiful about this metaphor of "eyes like fish-pools" is that the Bride sees all people *through the perspective of the Spirit*. She truly does have eyes like Jesus, for she sees people from His heavenly perspective!

Just as Jesus saw the finished product in her before she believed it or saw it for herself, this is how she views the people of the world. She sees the finished work of Christ throughout all humanity. In other words, she sees the "fish" of the world already in the water of the Spirit! The nations are looking into the eyes of the church and they are seeing themselves covered and embraced by the presence of God. Like Paul, the Bride has chosen to see "no man according to the flesh" (2 Cor. 5:16). And so we come back to this all-encompassing truth once again. The Bride sees people through the Spirit's eyes and thus sees their true and original identity—even if they haven't yet accepted it for themselves.

It is this kind of love and confidence that draws in the nations. She does not treat people like dirty heathen. Instead, she sees them as lost brothers and sisters who are just as loved by the Father as she (for how we treat others begins with how we see them). Just like she was drawn closer to Jesus because of His constant love and encouragement (calling her lovely and perfect even in her stumbling), the Shulammite is now doing the same to the world around her. She does not see prostitutes or orphans or tax collectors or prisoners. Rather she sees sleeping kings and queens, disciples and disciple-makers. She sees all as heirs to the eternal life of the Spirit.

The world feels genuinely safe and protected under the shade of this nurturing mother, the Bride of the King. Because of the love that is exuding from the church, the people of the world are being drawn into the *gates* of the Kingdom. This insight gets even more powerful when we consider the name of the gate in Heshbon. The gate of Bath-rabbim is a Hebrew word for "daughter of a multitude." It most likely got this name because of the large crowds of people who would pass through these gates as they walked by the pools filled with fish.

So let's stop for a moment and get the full visual of this in our heads. Day in and day out, multitudes of people are heading through this gate called Bath-rabbim as they go into the city. As the moving crowd approaches this gate they pass by two round pools of water on either side, each of which is sparkling with light and filled with exotic fish. Now imagine the aerial view of this scene. Those two pools of water might resemble two blue eyes, which probably gave the inspiration to Solomon as he wrote the Song.

Back to Revelation

This metaphor is the work of a divine Artist, the very Spirit of the Creator who has been gently flowing through the ink in Solomon's pen. The Spirit is giving us a portrait of the nations being brought into the Kingdom—the original Promised Land for which they have always longed. All of this imagery brings us right back to the book of Revelation. In its glorious description of the Bride, we see the city gates of the New Jerusalem and find that the multitudes are being called to enter through them. Let's look at the account of it again. This is soon after John arrives on the great mountain and sees the heavenly city with its precious stones...

> *And the city has no need of the sun or of the moon to shine on it, for the glory of God has illumined it, and its lamp is the Lamb. The nations will walk by its light, and the kings of the earth will bring their glory into it. In the daytime (for there will be no night there) its gates will never be closed; and they will bring the glory and the honor of the nations into it...*
>
> *Then he showed me a river of the water of life, clear as crystal, coming from the throne of God and of the Lamb, in the middle of its street. On either side of the river was the tree of life, bearing twelve kinds of fruit, yielding its fruit every month; and the leaves of the tree were for the healing of the nations.*
> *(Rev. 21:23-26, 22:1-2)*

The vision says that the kings of the earth will bring their glory into this city and that the nations will walk by its light. It also says that there will be healing for these nations. Right now, we need to be clear that this is not just a vision of the church after Christ has returned and everything is perfect. The book of Revelation is often taught that way because people have read it more academically than metaphorically and apocalyptically. (They have also read it more as a "revelation of the end-times" instead of the proper title of the book—"The Revelation of Jesus Christ.")

John's vision of the Bride was actually an encouragement to the persecuted church to know their true identity and calling. Though it will have its ultimate fulfillment in Christ's return, the vision still carried strong implications for this present age as it gives prophetic direction for the church's place in an unhealed world. For in this vision there are still those outside the gates who are in need of light and healing. If someone does not want to wash their robes in Christ's blood by trusting in His grace, then they are more than welcome to stay outside. They can stay stuck in a false identity of sin and shame and exist outside the realm of love (Rev. 22:14-15). Yet for those who want to lay down the bricks of Babylon and receive the grace of God, they can "enter in" and experience this heavenly city at any time. As we said before, all queens can become a bride in a moment. Paradise is already at hand.

In John's vision we also see a river that exits the city and goes out into the world. This means it goes past the open gates to water the earth. Here again is the imagery of water right by the city gates, like the fish-pools by Bath-rabbim. But there are even more connections between this vision in Revelation and the poetry of Solomon's Song. In Revelation, this water of life has its source at the throne of God (see Rev. 22:1). In the Song, the fish-pools lie above the "ivory" neck. As we explained before, ivory speaks to the throne of God. And as we know, this throne of authority is resident within His church. It is because of this inner authority that His people are equipped to be a pool of refreshing water, which heals the world of its lies and divisions. Through the Spirit, the "fish" of the nations are caught and brought into the city of

God. The multitudes of lost sons and daughters are brought home to their true Father.

A Collision of Prophecy and Song

Each of these images collide beautifully when we see the full portrait of the Bride and Bridegroom being painted throughout the Scriptures. There is Adam and Eve in the Garden, Solomon and the Shulammite in the Song of Songs, and the heavenly city in Revelation. Moses, Solomon, and John were not the true authors of these concepts. All along it was the Holy Spirit, and He inspired many more people to tell the story of the Bride and her promised impact on the earth.

The prophet Ezekiel was another person who participated in this discovery. In one of his visions, Ezekiel was shown the temple of God, which of course represents the church. He saw that out of the gates of this temple went forth a river of life-giving water. This river moved "east" and brought healing to the land around it (see Ez. 47:1-12). What's incredible is that Ezekiel's life-giving river also had fish in it! Here we find yet another connection within the Scriptures.

In Ezekiel's vision, we see that on either side of the river were fishermen (Ez. 47:10). These fishermen were extending their rods and catching fish that were *already* in the water. When we go back to Revelation, we find a different symbol on both sides of the water. Instead of fishermen, we see a tree of life that extends out its branches over the water, having leaves that heal the nations (Rev. 22:2)

All of this is communicating the same essential thing. We are indeed the fishermen that help bring the nations home to the Father. Furthermore, we are branches on the great tree of Christ. The beautiful leaves of our lives—leaves of mercy, compassion, and truth—bring change to the world and draw in the fish who are swimming unaware in the glory of God. *In Him they live and move and have their being.* But we are the shining ones who are called to awaken them to this reality. We are the true tower of righteousness, built on the Cornerstone of Christ, calling all people to look up from the ground and listen to the Song of the Ages.

Heavenly Discernment

The culmination of everything we've seen comes when the queens of humanity turn their attention to the Shulammite's nose and compare it to a famous military tower in Lebanon. "Your nose is like the tower of Lebanon, which faces toward Damascus," they say. This is now the second time the word *tower* shows up in this final description of the Bride. It is yet another hint at the contrast between the tower of Babel and the city of the Bride.

The nose is commonly interpreted as a symbol of discernment. It is with the nose that one discerns the differences in scents. A good nose can smell if something is off or even poisonous and it can equally distinguish if something is sweet and pleasant. So this is speaking of the Bride's ability to discern, and in this context it is speaking of a heavenly discernment that comes from a high and towering vantage point. She discerns people and things through the perception of heaven. Thus, this metaphor builds upon the previous image of her fish-pool eyes. Everything is building toward this glorious perception and the tower overlooking Lebanon further establishes this truth.

We previously studied how the northern lands of Lebanon were filled with the cedar and fir trees that would be used to build Solomon's temple. As the tower of Lebanon looked out upon Damascus, these are the trees that would fill its view. And as we've seen before, all these trees pointed to one Tree—the Tree of

Calvary, which would be used by God to build His ultimate temple and the true tower to heaven.

Accordingly, it is the aroma of this Tree that has filled the nostrils of the Bride, like the scent of cedar filling the military tower of Lebanon. Everything is now filtered through this heavenly scent, including the world around her. In fact, this is the same aroma that fills the very nostrils of God as He surveys the world from His glorious throne.

A throne that sits at the top of the tower of His Bride...

21

The Space Between

Your head crowns you like Carmel,
And the flowing locks of your head are like purple threads;
The king is captivated by your tresses!
(7:5)

W e ascend now to the pinnacle of the tower. It holds a
crowning surface that causes us to see and smell with
the same eyes and nose as the Shulammite. This has
been our destination all along, but in order to fully reach it we will
have to make one more excursion into the Old Testament. This
will serve as a specially marked trail that leads straight to the full
view at the top. It is a trail that was pioneered by three prophets.

The queens of the world exclaim and shout, "Your head crowns
you like Carmel!" They are referring to Mount Carmel, which was
a tall and sacred mountain in the northern region of Israel, which
also had exquisite views at its crest. In particular, Carmel had a
beautiful view of the sea.

It is there that our trail begins.

Incarnation and Evaporation

The key story in the Bible about Mount Carmel involves Elijah, who is the first prophet in our current journey. The story centers around a dark period in Israel's history when the land lay under the rule of a weak and evil king named Ahab. Because of the wickedness of his kingdom, the nation fell under a drought that lasted for three and a half years, which was a natural sign of a spiritual reality. The lack of rain signified a lack of God's glory and righteousness reigning amongst His people.

Elijah received word that the drought was going to break. But in order to see the manifestation of this, Elijah and his assistant needed to ascend the mountain of Carmel and look out toward the sea.

> *Elijah climbed to the top of Mount Carmel and bowed low to the ground and prayed with his face between his knees. Then he said to his servant, "Go and look out toward the sea." The servant went and looked, then returned to Elijah and said, "I didn't see anything."*

> *Seven times Elijah told him to go and look. Finally the seventh time, his servant told him, "I saw a little cloud about the size of a man's hand rising from the sea."*
> *(1 Kgs. 18:42-44 NLT)*

Six times Elijah prayed for rain and each time his assistant went to look and see if rainclouds were forming over the water. Each time there was not a cloud in sight. As you probably know, rain comes from large bodies of water through the process of evaporation. Water rises from the ocean and forms into a floating cloud that will drop its moisture back upon the land. The process is quite beautiful. It's like an intimate dance between earth and heaven where the waters of the sea become the waters of the sky and return once again to earth. It is a merging of the heavens above and the earth below.

Unfortunately, Elijah's servant did not see any evaporation happening. The waters surrounding the earthly shores of Israel appeared to be separate and isolated from the heavens above. It was a pretty candid parallel of their present circumstances. The intimate dance between the people and their God had ceased and the result was a spiritual drought. But this would all change after one more time of prayer. Elijah prayed again, a seventh time, and his assistant finally saw a small cloud rising from the water "about the size of a man's hand." This lead to a great downpour and the breaking of the drought.

Many people read this story and think that it's a lesson on persistent prayer. I understand and appreciate this connection, but there is something much deeper going on here. In reality, Elijah is another type and shadow of Christ, who is the ultimate Intercessor. This is the reason that the *seventh* instance of prayer brought about the rain. Being the number of completion, the sevenfold prayer speaks of Christ's finished work of intercession on our behalf.

Intercession is simply the act of intervening on behalf of another. That's why praying for another person can be referred to as "intercession." Clearly, Jesus came to intervene on our behalf in order to restore the broken relationship between earth and heaven. His whole life was a type of prayer, which reached a fulfilling answer in His resurrection and ascension. In becoming flesh, Jesus had literally united Himself with the dust of creation. At the cross, He took the corruption of this whole creation down to the grave with Him, and when He rose, a new creation was rising as well. He was like a cloud the size of a man's hand rising from the sea of humanity to restore the dance of union between earth and heaven.

It is fascinating that the Gospel accounts give strong evidence that the time of Jesus's earthly ministry leading up to His ascension was three and a half years long—the same length of time as Israel's drought. But the parallel continues. Once Jesus died and resurrected after three and a half years of ministry, only a small group of people actually witnessed it. So like Elijah's cloud, this event appeared somewhat small, like a cloud "the size of a man's hand." But from heaven's perspective, this was the beginning of a great downpour. Jesus rose so that He might fill all things with His glory and restore creation to that intimate dance. And indeed, this is what the Scriptures declare. Jesus ascended like water from the sea so that He could pour out His life and fill *all things*:

> *He who descended is Himself also He who ascended far*
> *above all the heavens, so that He might fill all things.*
> *(Eph. 4:10)*

Amana, Lebanon, Carmel. Each of these high places speak to the same reality we keep coming back to. From the perspective of Christ's finished work, we are able to see the restored union between earth and heaven. But in this present age, we do not yet see the full manifestation of it. All of it is contained in the Person and work of Christ, and that is where our focus needs to be. We have to rise up in faith and look beyond the natural realm. We have to ascend in our vision instead of seeing according to the flesh. Hence, the first *six* times of prayer did not work, for that represented man's insufficient works and our fallen perspectives (six, again, being the number of man). We have to keep looking until we enter into that realm of the "seventh prayer"—the place of agreement with Christ's work.

This is the vision that crowns the head of the Shulammite.

A Prophecy of Worldwide Awakening

Another prophet who illuminated this truth for us was a man named Habakkuk. He had been told by God to ascend a guard post, which was perhaps similar to the tower of Lebanon. This man lived during another time of darkness and rebellion in Israel. Justice had become a mockery and the wicked seemed to triumph in every scheme they devised. Habakkuk had grown very weary of it all and issued his complaints to God. His grumbling included one of the biblical images of men being compared to fish. He described the people around him as "fish in the sea" who were being baited and captured by the evil forces around them (Hab. 1:14-15). One force in particular was the nation of Babylon, which alongside the Tower of Babel, has always represented man's broken and oppressive ways.

Habakkuk's vision was filled with violence, corruption, and defeat. He *discerned* nothing but wickedness in the people around him and poured out his protest to God accordingly. It was out of these sorrowful prayers that Habakkuk was called to ascend the guard post and wait for a vision from the Lord. He obeyed this call and waited as a prophetic promise was imparted to him. The Lord spoke to Habakkuk and declared that one day *"the earth will be filled with the knowledge of the glory of the Lord, as the waters cover the sea"* (Hab. 2:14). Though God said the manifestation of this promise would tarry, the prophet needed to live by faith and learn to see from this higher perspective (see Hab. 2:3-4). One day, righteousness would shine forth and the *knowledge of the glory* would fill the entire world.

The Hebrew word for "knowledge" is of vital significance. We've unpacked the meaning of a lot of Hebrew words and phrases, but this one needs our undivided attention. The word for "knowledge" is one that can simply be translated as *awareness*. In fact, some translations render the prophecy as "the earth will be

filled with an awareness of the glory of the Lord" (Hab. 2:14 NLT).
The word for knowledge or awareness has to do with perception.
It involves perceiving something and becoming acquainted with
its true nature. This is not just head knowledge, but an intimate
knowing of the heart and soul.

The implications of this cannot be minimized. Today there are
untold numbers of Christians who misquote this prophecy and
speak of a day coming when the glory of God will fill the earth.
But they miss the key word that Habakkuk wrote down.

It is not the glory of the Lord that is going to fill the earth.

It is the *knowledge* of that glory.

In reality, the glory of the Lord *already* fills all things. However,
not all have been made aware of it. Not all have been "intimately
acquainted" with this glory. Some fish are still swimming unaware in
the sea of His all-encompassing grace. Many of them are growing
weak and tired as they swim against the currents of love. This can
happen through ignorance or rebellion (or both), but either way
people are stuck behind their own walls of blindness while the
glory of God calls them to let go and stop paddling upstream—to
simply turn around and find rest.

Another way to say all of this is that not all people have *woken
up* to the glory. We have been utilizing this metaphor of sleep
throughout the whole Song for this very reason. The idea of sleep
paints a clear and simple picture of someone being *unconscious*
of something. When you are asleep, you are not aware of your
surroundings. You're not even aware of yourself. Your eyes are
closed and your mind is darkened to the things around you. Yet
when you wake up, you come into awareness. Nothing has changed
expect your perception.

Such has been the journey of the Bride. The Shulammite has been growing into a *consciousness* of union. She has been coming into a trusting awareness of the great love and glory that was always present. Her embrace of this led her to be the first-fruits of this great prophecy of awakening. And it turns out that Jesus wanted to partner with His Bride to release this awakening, or awareness, amongst *the whole earth*. This is why her life so parallels the two symbols of the lampstand and the almond tree. The first gives light in the dark while the latter bears fruit before other sleeping trees. And so the hope remains that one day the lights will come on globally and all will wake up to the glory of the Lord. This awakening will fill the earth "like the waters cover the sea."

The Union of Water and Sea

When you think about it, the phrase "like the waters cover the sea" seems silly and redundant... The water *is* the sea. Why would the prophet talk about this awareness filling the earth like the waters "cover" the sea? We'll find that at its core this statement conveys a stunning truth that coincides with everything we have been discovering.

The word for "cover" means to overlay or conceal. The verse could be translated, "like the waters *conceal* the sea." Again, this seems to be a weak and unfitting metaphor, but it ties together quite impressively when we realize something: *Just like the "water" and the "sea" are actually one entity, so is the "earth" and the "glory"...*

The Bride's heavenly perspective sees and discerns that God's glory is *already* united with the earth. His glory *is* the earth. And not just the earth, but the people in it. The Father's glory *is* mankind, which are His offspring—whether lost or found. Mankind "is the image and *glory* of God," Paul declared (see 1 Cor. 11:7). In the end, the problem is that the knowledge of this union between God and creation is lacking. And this is the problem that leads many astray, propelling them to swim upstream in the sweat of religion and in the knowledge of good and evil as they attempt to build their own broken towers to heaven, trying to accomplish something that is already finished.

Instead of beholding the work of Christ, which has re-united creation with the glory of God, people's eyes are filled with the darkness of shame and a resulting sense of separation and distance. This was Habakkuk's problem as his own eyes were focused only on the darkness around him. He was beholding the "sea," but was still stuck in Elijah's first "six" times of prayer, which represents the natural perspective.

Yet God called him to a watchtower so that he might receive a vision of hope—the hope of glory. And at that moment, the Lord gave Habakkuk the promise of this same vision coming to the entire earth!

The Third Prophet

The last prophet in our journey was given this same word of promise as well. With identical words, the prophet Isaiah declared that the whole earth would be filled with the awareness of God's glory (see Isa. 11:9). Interestingly enough, before he spoke this prophecy, Isaiah was also shown that the earth was already *full* of this glory. He learned this truth from the mouths of angels during a heavenly encounter.

> *And one called out to another and said,*
> *"Holy, Holy, Holy, is the Lord of hosts,*
> *The whole earth is **full** of His glory."*
> *(Isa. 6:3)*

322

The Space Between

The literal Hebrew translation of that last statement is this: "The fullness of the whole earth *is His glory.*" Translations like the King James and the New American Standard actually put a footnote in the text to point this out. The Hebrew makes it very clear that the earth and the glory are one—just as the sea and its water are one.

Isaiah was given this amazing revelation during the year King Uzziah died, which was not exactly a shining moment in the history of the earth (Isa. 6:1). Like Elijah and Habakkuk, Isaiah lived during a rebellious time. But it was then that he was taken up to heaven and given a higher perspective. And yet even with this new vantage point, the prophet was still consumed with an earthly mindset. In this place of unparalleled holiness, Isaiah became consumed with a consciousness of sin. He suddenly believed that he would die and be "ruined." He probably wanted nothing more than to hide from the holiness of God, just like all his forefathers had done and were continuing to do. The prophet confessed darkness in himself and then expanded this confession to the darkness in the people around him. Look at his words:

> *"Woe is me, for I am ruined! Because I am a man of*
> *unclean lips, and I live among a people of unclean lips. For*
> *my eyes have seen the King, the Lord of hosts."*
> *(Isa. 6:5)*

This is the age-old reaction of fear and shame dating all the way back to Adam. But just as He clothed the shameful Adam, God brings a similar response of comfort to Isaiah...

> *Then one of the seraphim flew to me with a burning coal*
> *in his hand, which he had taken from the altar with tongs.*
> *He touched my mouth with it and said, "Behold, this has*

touched your lips; and your iniquity is taken away and
your sin is forgiven."
(Isa. 6:6-7)

In response to Isaiah's confession, one of the angels goes to the altar with some tongs and picks up a burning piece of coal and touches his lips with it. All of a sudden it is declared that Isaiah's iniquity is taken away and his sin is forgiven. Now let's think about this honestly for a moment. Do you think that a piece of coal could actually remove someone's iniquity?

Of course not. We know there is only one thing that truly removes sin, and that is the blood of Jesus. How then was Isaiah's iniquity removed, especially considering this encounter happened before Christ came to the earth?

The Eternal Reality

The first thing to recognize is that Isaiah was having this encounter in the realm of eternity. Even though this event transpired during the Old Testament, the actual experience did not occur within the confines of time. This piece of coal rested upon a heavenly altar that mirrored the earthly altar of incense in Solomon's temple. As we've noted before, incense was a symbol of intercession. This piece of coal is actually pointing us to the eternal intercession of the Lamb.

Christ's work stands outside of time itself. In the book of Revelation, the apostle John declared that Jesus is the Lamb slain from before the foundation of the world (Rev. 13:8). With that in mind, we find that the angel was essentially ministering the *eternal Gospel* to Isaiah (see Rev. 13:8 & 14:6). From before time existed, the heart of God had already provided His covering of mercy and forgiveness to every member of humanity. The mercy in His Lamb-like heart rose like sweet incense toward His nose. This is because the Father has always reigned from a position of mercy. His throne is the very Mercy Seat of heaven and His nostrils were always filled with the aroma of the cross, even before Calvary occurred in time and space.

High above the earth, Isaiah experienced a verse right out of the Song of the Lamb. It is the same song the apostle John mentions in Revelation after he writes about the slain Lamb and the eternal Gospel (Rev. 15:3). The angels Isaiah saw were seeing from outside of time, in the realm of eternity where God had already made peace with *all things* through the blood of Christ. This revelation was hidden in ages and generations past, but was finally unveiled in Jesus's incarnation and death. There are few places that make this mystery clearer than the book of Colossians:

> *For it was the Father's good pleasure for all the fullness to dwell in Him, and through Him to reconcile all things to Himself,* **having made peace** *through the blood of His cross; through Him, I say,* **whether things on earth or things in heaven.**
> *(Col. 1:19-20)*

This is the revelation that kissed Isaiah's lips. He had confessed darkness both in himself and his people. However, the touch of God's grace cleansed his defiled speech and allowed him to understand the beautiful Song that was being sung by the flying seraphim. It turned out to be the Song of the Ages!

You may have thought we had drifted away from the story of the Shulammite when in fact we have come right back into harbor. Isaiah's encounter with heaven parallels the Shulammite's encounter with the Beloved. In the very beginning of the Song, the Shulammite had confessed darkness in herself. Yet the Lord responded by saying that she was "lovely." He then deepened the truth of her loveliness by bringing her to the table of the Lamb, which was like an altar burning with the same coals of grace that touched Isaiah's lips.

The Purpose of the Blood

Whether Elijah, Habakkuk, Isaiah, or the Shulammite, all of these people engaged in a similar discourse with the Divine. All along, God desired that we join the chorus of heaven, beholding the truth that the whole earth is full of His glory. There is in fact no separation between heaven and earth, for the Lamb has eternally triumphed over sin and judgment. In reality, there was never a separation between the two, except in the heart of man. It was therefore man's heart that needed to be cleansed—not God's. *The blood of Jesus was for us—not for an absent and angry father in the sky.*

The writer of Hebrews states this emphatically. After describing Jesus's ascension into the heavenly throne-room (the same that Isaiah saw), he builds up toward the call to have *our hearts* sprinkled clean from the consciousness of evil (see Heb. 9:1-10:23)! An evil conscience involves "discerning" ourselves through a corrupted lens. At Calvary, this lens was shattered as the eternal realities of grace broke through the veil of our blindness and guilt. The great mystery hidden during previous ages and generations was unveiled in that moment as the love of God was fully exposed.

While many continue to see through an old lens of sin, the Bride beholds something else. Her heart has been pierced by the cross of Christ and now she stands at the Summit of Amana (or the "tower of Lebanon," or the crest of Carmel). There she beholds the full glory of God, not only in herself, *but now in the entire earth.* No longer is she partaking of the Tree of Knowledge of Good and Evil. Her eyes and nose now discern only God's life and glory, which fills and surrounds all things, even the lost fish of the nations.

Looking Back

We have just about reached the full vista of the Bride's gaze. It would probably be good then to take a pause. A water break, so to speak, to reflect on what we've discovered so far.

The burning coals of God's heart and the eternal kisses of His Word have truly met the shoreline of the Shulammite's soul. She longed for this kiss from the beginning, but did not understand what it fully entailed. Nonetheless, the kiss came to her as it did to so many other figures in the Bible. It came with wave after wave of truth and grace, pounding their doused light upon the veiling walls of her heart. Over and over again, God released his Trojan horse of poetry and riddles in order to awaken His sleeping Bride.

We have found that this kiss was actually uncovering something startling within the sands of her being. From the start, the waters of His glory were calling out to the waters within her. The Promised One was calling out to a hidden Promised Land within. Deep was calling unto deep. All along, the shore of her heart was covering an infinite treasure of beauty, the very treasure she was searching for out in the sea!

Of course, this did not come as too strong a surprise, for the Beloved had already said she was like a sealed rock garden with hidden fountains (Sgs. 4:12). The "streams flowing from Lebanon" had been there all along—all around and all inside. Her eyes, like ours, were simply closed to it. And so the Song of the Beloved proceeded from the lips of her Creator, calling her to see it—and trust it.

And trust she finally did. But it did not stop there. As the melody of the Song continued, as God "took it from the top" and continued to shatter any semblance of religious thinking, the Shulammite began to see that this same glory was residing in the entire sea of creation. Seeing herself through the eyes of the Beloved, she could now do the same with the world around her.

How Heaven Flows to Earth

And so it is out of this glorious vision that the final praises toward the Shulammite begin to reach their climax as the queens, concubines, and maidens sing about the locks of her hair. Earlier, we found that hair is a symbol for wisdom. Christ, who is our Wisdom, is the crown of the Shulammite's life (1 Cor. 1:30). The people proclaim that this crowning wisdom resembles "purple threads," which is a regal color of authority and power. This reveals a wisdom that is rooted in the complete triumph of Christ. This statement is then followed by one of the most important parts of the entire Song. The people finally shift their focus away from the Bride and look at her adoring Bridegroom. Their jubilant praise finishes up by declaring how the King is captivated by the "tresses" of the Bride's hair.

The Hebrew word behind "tresses" is another storehouse of intense revelation. It is the sweet cherry on top of the cake of the unveiled Shulammite. The word has two different meanings. It is like an English word with multiple definitions even though it's spelled the same way. (An example of this would be the word "wave." A wave could refer to the gesture of someone's hand, but it can also refer to the waves of the sea.) The word for tresses is *rahat*. This can refer to flowing locks of hair, yet the same word can also refer to a "watering trough." *Rahat* is hollowed out wood that forms a channel or trough for watering or feeding animals (see Ex. 2:16).

There are many other words that Solomon could have used to describe the different facets of the Shulammite's hair. The fact that he picked this particular word is striking. With spiritual eyes, we can see how this verse is describing the King's delight over one who has become a trough or *channel* for His Spirit! The realities of heaven run like a river through the channel of her life. It then flows out to nourish the people of the world.

It's astonishing when you connect this revelation with the previous words about her head. The onlookers had compared her head to Carmel. We didn't mention this before, but the Hebrew word for "Carmel" literally means *Garden Land.* So the description of tresses or "channels" give us the image of water running down the "garden" of her head. This all contains a subtle but powerful reference to the book of Genesis. There we find a group of rivers that "flowed out of Eden" (Gen. 2:10). Through the Song of Solomon, we discover even more that the Garden of Eden was always pointing to the Bride! She is indeed a Garden of awakened love. Out of this love, rivers of glory flow from the "tresses" of her life to water the earth.

Water Carts at the Sea

On this final note of watering troughs, there is one last trail through the Old Testament we need to take before we enter into a much needed *selah.* You will need to bear with a few more symbolic details along the way. These are metaphors and pictures which are only meant to bring us to an even clearer vista of all that was in God's heart when He composed this eternal Song. This final trail through the Scriptures will begin back at Solomon's temple...

Within the temple was the Holy Place, which contained the golden lampstands that gave light to the room and were fashioned after the image of an almond tree (2 Chr. 4:7). As we saw earlier, these lampstands clearly represent the church. Now Solomon's temple specifically had ten lampstands in the inner room. Some commentators believe this number represents the nations of the world and thus the church's ministry to those nations. In Genesis, we find ten generations populating the whole earth from Adam to Noah. Then we find another ten generations repopulating the earth from Noah to Abraham. Furthermore, the beast in Revelation had ten horns on its head (Rev. 13:1). While this might speak to ten specific rulers or nations, it also highlights how all the nations of the world have been influenced by the power of darkness. And so Solomon's temple gives us an opposing image of comfort and hope. It reveals a new government of light that will ultimately reign over the nations—the Lampstand of the church. This is the heavenly government of Jesus and His Bride.

These lampstands were stationed on the north and south side of the inner room—five in the north and five in the south. What's important to note is that directly outside this room were ten other items that were also stationed to the north and south. In the outer court, there were "ten watering carts" positioned just like the lampstands (1 Kgs. 7:37-39). These carts had wheels that allowed priests to transport water throughout the outer court, which would be used for washing the sacrifices and other acts of cleansing.

We can easily assume that the God of mystery and riddle is speaking the same message through these ten watering carts as He did through the ten lampstands. These carts also represent the church, but in a different way. Not only does the church give light to the nations—she also gives *water*. She is a moveable "cart" that carries the waters of His grace to those in the outer court of unbelief. In other words, she is a channel or "tress" for His Spirit to flow to all people.

Now here's where we start to round the bend and get a more complete view of the message being communicated. These ten watering carts in Solomon's temple were directly associated with an item called the "Molten Sea" (1 Kgs. 7:23-26). This was a basin of water that was also located in the outer court. The Molten Sea earned its title because of its enormity. The basin held thousands of gallons of water. It's assumed that the ten watering carts were used to fill this giant basin, and also to take water from it.

Underneath this great Sea was something spectacular. Solomon had commissioned a master craftsman to sculpt twelve bronze oxen, three of which faced the north, three that faced the south, and the same with the east and the west. The Molten Sea was placed upon the shoulders of these twelve oxen. Hopefully you can get a visual of all this in your head.

This image speaks to us of the mystery of the Bride. The oxen holding up this basin are a symbol of apostolic ministry, which treads the earth and plows the harvest fields so that Christ can bring awakening to people's hearts. The Molten Sea thus connects back to the heavenly city in Revelation. There we find twelve open gates that surround the city—three on the north, three on the south, and so forth (Rev. 21:13). All of these images are showing how the church is a gateway for the nations to enter into the cleansing waters of grace.

The Sea of Humanity

So this Molten Sea certainly equates to the waters of God's grace and glory. But it is also an image of something else. Throughout the Bible, the sea is a clear symbol of the masses of humanity (see Rev. 17:15). We saw earlier how the Scriptures spoke of the "abundance of the sea" coming into the house of God. This was primarily talking about the peoples of the earth coming to the Lord (see Isa. 60:5). Then, in Revelation 13, the beast with ten horns arose *out of the sea.* The beast rises from the *nations* of the world.

In the Old Covenant period, Solomon's Molten Sea with its twelve supporting oxen was a picture of the twelve tribes of Israel ministering to the entire sea of humanity. It was a symbol of their calling and thus it was placed in the outer courts to show Israel's priestly ministry to the Gentile nations. But in the New Covenant, we find that this was really pointing to the church. It is the church that holds up and establishes the entire world through her union with Christ. Indeed, the prophet Isaiah declared that the "government" would be on the shoulders of the Messiah (Isa. 9:6). If the Bride is the Messiah's body, then that means He works through His Bride to uphold the earth!

This great basin of water in Solomon's temple also had another interesting feature. It was made to resemble the shape of a large blossoming lily (1 Kgs. 7:26). So think about the spiritual implications of that. The water of the Sea (as in all humanity) is surrounded and fenced in by a giant lily. This brings to mind the image of the Shulammite's belly. Do you remember how it was described?

A heap of wheat, fenced in by lilies.

The wheat and the sea are images of the same thing. They are both pictures of the nations, which are contained within a lily— for that is how God sees them. They are His beloved creation whom He would give His life for. All nations are called to arise and blossom into their full identity as God's treasured lilies. The church has a "belly of wheat" because she is called to help birth the harvest of humanity into this reality. She is also like the twelve oxen carrying the basin of water, for she carries this cleansing revelation to the people of the world.

A Resolved Conflict

So at this point it may appear like there's a conflict in the spiritual meaning of the water. On one side, the water clearly represents the cleansing waters of God's glory. On the other side, the "sea" represents the masses of humanity. But this conflict is resolved when we remember the great prophecy uttered by Habakkuk and

The Space Between

Isaiah. And that brings us back to where we started. God's glory already "covers the earth as the waters cover the sea." The glory of His grace covers and fills the entire globe. The fullness of the earth *is His glory.* Every fish of the sea—every tribe, tongue, and nation—is already swimming in the sea of His love. For the glory of God and the dust of the earth have been united in Christ.

Back in Genesis, at the very beginning of creation, we find a separation between the "waters" of the earth and the "waters" of the heavens. Look at it closely:

> *Then God said, "Let there be a space between the waters,*
> *to separate the waters of the heavens from the waters of*
> *the earth." And that is what happened. God made this*
> *space to separate the waters of the earth from the waters*
> *of the heavens.*
> *(Gen. 1:6-7 NLT)*

We find that this separation was on the *second day,* well before God said, "it was very good." There is yet another parable here, another message representing the greater Song and story of creation. It is revealing a time of separation that would lead up to the "seventh" day, when God would complete His work through Christ. In reality, the Lord never intended there to be a separation between the sea of His grace and the sea of humanity. The Genesis account spiritually acknowledged this separation would happen, but it also gives the promise of redemption. Through Christ, the eternal seventh day would come. The separation would be removed. The walls on the shoreline would be broken down and life would re-emerge. And like the rainbow, God would give us evaporation and rainfall as another "sign" of this amazing truth.

Through Christ's incarnation, earth and heaven are truly reconciled. The "space between" is filled and now there is an eternal marriage between the two. This is because Christ has filled the gap for us. He represented each one of us and fulfilled the wedding vows on our behalf. This is all a completed work of grace that the world is simply invited to believe. This is the message that the awakened church carries.

In Christ, all of creation has said "I do" to the love of the Father. And after saying "I do" came a kiss. The kiss between the waters of earth and the waters of heaven. Right then, it was finished. And now nothing can tear the two asunder.

Again, from the Beginning

God is an artist and a poet. He chose not to lay all of this out in a line-by-line textbook fashion. Instead, He opened His heart and sung out a melodic tune of poetic grace. As a result, we have been bathed and inundated by an assortment of mysterious lyrics. We have walked the bending trails of Eden and scoured the courts of Ezekiel's visionary temple. We've seen the building plans of Solomon's temple and surveyed the body of the Shulammite from head to foot (and back to the head again). We've also looked with the apostle John at a great city descending from the sky. In the end, we found that God has been trying to make the same point over and over and over again. His waves of truth have not stopped— and they will not stop until we all see the fullness of the eternal Gospel. The Gospel of a completed union.

And this is what has "captivated" the King as seen in the last verse of our study. God Himself is utterly ravished by the beauty of the Son and the redeemed Bride, the one who has become a channel for Christ's glory to manifest. This word "captivate" is scandalous. It is literally the same thing as saying "the King is held captive." The verse is stating that God is *imprisoned* by the beauty of His Bride and the tresses of her life.

The Space Between

There is no describing the offensive weight and wonder of this statement. God's heart is actually moved and undone by this great union. The impact on God's heart is so intense that He allows words to be written by Solomon that appear blasphemous. They are words that declare how His breath is taken away and His knees are weak. His emotions are overrun by love and ecstasy. Elohim, the Lord God, has been held hostage.

Of course, God is not bound to anything. He is the freest Being there is. Yet somehow, He has allowed Himself to be imprisoned by love. And perhaps this is because true freedom exists in such a place—the place of giving your heart away to another. Such love is the source of all that we discovered and unpacked throughout this journey.

Right now, we end in the same way we did last time—with a ravished and captivated God. Hopefully this time around we can see a little bit more of *why* He's so ravished. We are glimpsing more of what God has seen all along. This is the great seascape at the top of Carmel. It is the redeemed landscape seen from Lebanon's tower. It is the highest vision—the Summit of Truth, now expanded to include *all creation*.

The Song has given us a wider perspective as the queens, concubines, and maidens were also caught up into its mesmerizing lyrics. They saw how the King completes His Bride, and how the Bride is a perfect fit for her King. Each one of these queens are now invited into this same glorious picture—a picture that has been painted and promised for thousands upon thousands of years.

The marriage is sealed. The work is finished. All are queens of a glad and victorious King. Now they must only awaken to love.

Amen.

Sixth Selah

As the weight of these things hits our hearts, it will be good to come away once more and rest under the shade of God's love. We need to be still and know that He is God. He will be exalted in the nations. He will build His church and fulfill all of His plans and purposes. There is a sovereignty, a good and glorious sovereignty, that we can rest under, even as we realize that we play a part in all of this. These things have been etched into stone and written upon ancient ballads of love. But more than that, they have been written into His heart. And in His heart, true reality abides. That's why in the realm of eternity these things are already established. They are simply breaking forth into time and space. We only get to be the "tresses" of the King, from which the realities of His heart flow into the earth.

And this flow is such a simple thing—so simple that it may seem impossible to our backbreaking, brick-laying ways. So let me make one last attempt at showing you the utter simplicity and ease of our part in this...

In the last chapter, we saw how the Hebrew word for "tresses" was the same word used for the wooden troughs that fed and watered flocks. It pointed to the image of the Bride being like a "trough" to nourish the nations. It was a word that showed up several times in the Old Testament. But later, in the New Testament, there is another wooden trough that shows up. It is perhaps the most famous feeding trough in all of human history.

It is the manger.

Yes, the Christ was born and laid into a simple feeding trough, just like the ones found in the Hebrew Scriptures that use the same word for "tresses." As we already noted, Hebrew words can mean several different things. English translators chose to interpret Solomon's use of the word *rahat* as "tresses," because they figured it was a love poem and a man wouldn't compare his wife's hair to an animal trough. But it turns out that this Hebrew poem could be translated into something like this:

The King is captivated by the manger of the Bride!

The church is simply a manger for the glory of Christ to be born into. And this is really what God is ravished by. Even in the mess of our brokenness, even in the midst of pig slop and hay, we are still custom-designed for glory. And we are surely containers of glory, no matter how unattractive the manger of our life appears.

Christ is in us, and that is enough. Period.

So this is the sixth *selah*. As we've seen a few times now, six is the number of man. Let this then be another reminder that man is like a manger, custom-made to host the presence of the King. We are not the presence itself. Yet, because of our union with Jesus, we are! And, mysteriously, we can take no credit for it. Nor do we need to muster it up or re-create it. Like a manger in a stable, we can learn to just *be*. To be open, available and present, so that heaven's purposes can rest upon us.

To be continued…

About the Author

Nick Padovani is a husband, a father, a social worker, and a friend of Jesus. He is also the pastor of a beautiful and flourishing church in northern New Jersey. It is his joy and passion to see God's children awaken to the full inheritance in the love of Christ.

For more books, updates, and scheduling, please visit:

www.NickPadovani.com

Nick Padovani is also the senior editor of the online publication *Elisha's Riddle*. The publication celebrates and declares the mystery of Christ that is hidden throughout all creation. It produces weekly articles, newsletters, and different forms of media that center around the finished work of the cross. It also chronicles hope-filled and prophetic news from around the world:

www.ElishasRiddle.com

CPSIA information can be obtained
at www.ICGtesting.com
Printed in the USA
FFOW03n1250151017